Partnership Governance in Public Management

The ability to create and sustain partnerships is a skill and a strategic capacity that utilizes the strengths and offsets the weaknesses of each actor. Partnerships between the public and private sectors allow each to enjoy the benefits of the other: the public sector benefits from increased entrepreneurship, and the private sector utilizes public authority and processes to achieve economic and community revitalization. *Partnership Governance in Public Management* describes what partnership is in the public sector, as well as how it is managed, measured, and evaluated. Both a theoretical and practical text, this book is a what, why, and how examination of a key function of public management.

Examining governing capacity, community building, downtown revitalization, and partnership governance through the lens of formalized public–private partnerships—specifically, how these partnerships are understood and sustained in our society—this book is essential reading for students and practitioners with an interest in partnership governance and public administration, and management more broadly. Chapters explore partnering technologies as a way to bridge sectors, to produce results and a new sense of public purpose, and to form a stable foundation for governance to flourish.

Seth A. Grossman is the Executive Director of the Ironbound Business Improvement District (IBID) in Newark, New Jersey, and President of Cooperative Professional Services, a consultancy that provides research, planning, and management services to Business Improvement Districts (BIDs). He designed and directs the Rutgers University National Center of Public Performance Online Business Improvement District Management Certification Program.

Marc Holzer is Dean of the School of Public Affairs and Administration, and Board of Governors Professor of Public Affairs and Administration at Rutgers University, Newark, New Jersey. He is a Fellow of the National Academy of Public Administration and of the World Academy of Productivity Science. Since 1975 he has directed the National Center for Public Performance, and he is the founder and Editor-in-Chief of the journals *Public Performance and Management Review* and *Public Voices*.

MARC HOLZER, SERIES EDITOR

MUNICIPAL SHARED SERVICES
A Public Solutions Handbook
Alexander C. Henderson, Editor

E-GOVERNMENT AND WEBSITES
A Public Solutions Handbook
Aroon Manoharan, Editor

PARTNERSHIP GOVERNANCE IN PUBLIC MANAGEMENT
A Public Solutions Handbook
Seth A. Grossman and Marc Holzer

MANAGING THE NEXT GENERATION OF PUBLIC WORKERS
A Public Solutions Handbook
Madinah F. Hamidullah

MARC HOLZER, SERIES EDITOR

Partnership Governance in Public Management

A PUBLIC SOLUTIONS HANDBOOK

Seth A. Grossman and Marc Holzer

Routledge
Taylor & Francis Group

NEW YORK AND LONDON

First published 2016
by Routledge
2 Park Square, Milton Park, Abingdon, Oxon OX14 4RN

and by Routledge
711 Third Avenue, New York, NY 10017

Routledge is an imprint of the Taylor & Francis Group, an informa business

Library of Congress Cataloging-in-Publication Data
Grossman, Seth A.
  Partnership governance in public management: a public solutions handbook / Seth A. Grossman
and Marc Holzer.
    pages cm. — (The public solutions handbook series)
  Includes bibliographical references and index.
  1. Public-private sector cooperation.   2. Public-private sector cooperation—
Evaluation.   3. Public administration.   4. Public administration—Evaluation.   I. Holzer,
Marc.   II. Title.
  HD3871.G76 2015
  351—dc23
  2015015012

ISBN: 978-1-138-92051-4 (hbk)
ISBN: 978-0-7656-4405-3 (pbk)
ISBN: 978-1-315-68688-2 (ebk)

Typeset in Times
by Apex CoVantage, LLC

Printed and bound in the United States of America by Publishers Graphics,
LLC on sustainably sourced paper.

Contents

List of Illustrations

FIGURES

TABLES

Preface

The capacities of partnership represent a movement past traditional adversarial relationships often experienced as political and management differences between governments and business. The ability to create and sustain partnerships is a skill and a strategic capacity that utilizes the strengths and offsets the weaknesses of each actor. Such partnerships allow the public sector to enjoy more vigorous entrepreneurship, while allowing the private sector to utilize public authority and its necessary processes to achieve economic and community revitalization. The public sector takes on private aspects and the private sector takes on a measure of public responsibility.

In this book we examine governing capacity, community building, downtown revitalization, and Partnership Governance through the lens of formalized public–private partnerships—specifically, how these partnerships are understood and sustained in our society, and the management technology that moves from theory to practice. The arrival of *Partnership Governance* is discussed as an evolution of democracy through partnerships and the need for partnership capability in modern public management beyond the progressive era. Both a theoretical and practical text—this book is a what, why, and how examination of a key function of public management: partnering.

For public administration, this phenomenon indicates that government and governance processes are shifting. Centralized hierarchical government is not the progressive element in society that it once was. The acceleration of public–private partnerships is an example of informal government that is more horizontally networked and less vertically controlled. Formal government will not go away, yet evidence points to an enhancement of civic responsibility, local management capacity, and sustainable planning by these partnerships. Also, private sector technologies (business administration) were and still are necessary in public realms. Today, however, the technologies of public administration are more and more the skills required for successful private sector operations.

As markets are sustained by civil society, local and global companies must effectively participate in public processes, perceive social impacts, and generate aspects of civil society. The skill set required to do this successfully is derived from public administration and is well defined by the term "Partnership Governance." It integrates and

ix

reinterprets necessary activities of society in the management of public concerns. Consequently, we may also find that the skills of public administration are applied in the private sector, as private companies require public solutions to real-life situations. This is not a new phenomenon, but it helps to define public administration in the 21st century. Public managers must be trained in the capacities of partnership desired by civil society, governing entities, and private companies.

Acknowledgments

We acknowledge the support of Rutgers, The State University of New Jersey and The School of Public Affairs & Administration, the numerous Business Improvement District managers throughout the United States, Australia, and Canada for their participation in necessary research, and the City of Newark and Flemington, New Jersey.

Series Editor's Introduction

The impetus for this series of public management handbooks is simply that public managers must have ready acccss to the best practices and lessons learned. That knowledge base is surprisingly extensive and rich, including insights from rigorous academic studies, internal government reports and publications, and foundation-supported research. Access to that knowledge, however, is limited by substantial barriers: expensive books and academic journals, "thick" academic language and hard to decipher jargon, and just the sheer volume of information available. Our objectives in initiating this series are to identify insight based in practice, to build competencies from that knowledge base, to deliver them at an affordable price point, and to communicate that guidance in clear terms.

GROUNDED INSIGHTS

Each volume in the series incorporates case-based research. Each will draw helpful insights and guidelines from academe, government, and foundation sources, focusing on an emerging opportunity or issue in the field. The initial volume, for example, addresses shared services for municipalities and counties, e-government and websites, managing generational differences, government counter-corruption strategies, public sector innovation, and performance measurement and improvement.

COMPETENCIES

We initiated this *Public Solutions Handbook* series to help build the necessary competencies, empowering dedicated, busy public servants—many of whom have no formal training in the management process of the public offices and agencies they have been selected to lead—to respond to emerging issues, to deliver services that policymakers have promised to the public, to carry out their missions efficiently and effectively, and to work in partnership with their stakeholders. Enabling practitioners to access and apply evidence-based insights will begin to restore trust in governments through high-performing public, nonprofit, and contracting organizations.

Just as important, students in graduate-degree programs, many of whom are already working in public and nonprofit organizations, are seeking succinct, pragmatic, grounded guidance that will help them succeed far into the future as they rise to positions of greater responsibility and leadership. This includes students in master of public administration (MPA), master of public policy (MPP), master of nonprofit management (MNPM), and even some master of business administration (MBA) and doctor of law (LLD) programs.

AFFORDABILITY

Handbook prices are often unrealistically high. The marketplace is not serving the full range of public managers who need guidance on practices. When faced with the need for creative solutions to cut budgets, educate for ethics, tap the problem-solving expertise of managers and employees, or report progress clearly and transparently, a grasp of such practices is essential. Many handbooks are priced in the hundreds of dollars, beyond the purchasing power of an individual or an agency. Journals are similarly priced out of reach of practitioners. In contrast, each volume in the *Public Solutions Handbook* series is modestly priced.

CLEAR WRITING

Although the practice of public administration and public management should be informed by published research, the books that are now marketed to practitioners and students in the field are often overly abstract and theoretical, failing to distill published research into clear and necessary applications. There is substantial valuable literature in the academic journals, but necessarily, it is written to standards that do not easily connect with practitioner audiences. Even in instances where practitioners receive peer-reviewed journals as a benefit association membership, they clearly prefer magazines or newsletters that present information in a straightforward journalistic style. Too often, readers set the academic journals aside.

I am proud to announce the third volume in the *Public Solutions Handbook* series: *Partnership Governance*, edited by Seth A. Grossman. This volume addresses the fundamental issue of our need to work together in a productive manner, and provide the capability to get things done. Governance is this process. It engages us in how we address and manage empowerment. As Seth Grossman points out, one of the key aspects of trust is the ability to empower and be empowered. That is, we trust people who empower us and allow us to empower them. This tells us that governance intrinsically involves trust. Successful governance, and the partnerships that arise within the processes of governance, requires trust. In this process, each partner, and the partnership as a whole, must perceive the sense of being empowered; empowered to get things done and make things work. Partnerships, or the lack of them, determine how we allow or deny, achieve or disrupt empowerment. In practice, partnerships are foundational to governance, a necessary collaborative process. The cornerstone of society hinges on this need expressed through a variety of partnerships. This book is for practitioners who seek an understanding of the nature of partnerships and the application of public–private partnerships. It is also a call to look at our professional responsibilities as public administrators to facilitate the empowerment processes of democratic government.

Partnership Governance Introduction

If we look, partnerships are found in almost every aspect of government. They are pragmatic particularly when engaging the private sector. Partnership Governance, which
describes the process of multisectoral partnering, can be appropriately associated with
the evolution of democracy as a form of citizen action and expanded public management capacity. And it is here that we find expressions of concern when we could find
curiosity. Democratic behavior by its nature is an ever-evolving prescription to citizen
participation. Not unlike the organic nature of democratic processes, Partnership Governance is dynamic. Our opinions of these processes often depend on which side of
the public–private spectrum we are associated with—some see it as detraction, others
as an enhancement. On one hand, we can perceive the concept of partnering as challenging democratic accountability when the partnership moves toward privatization. On
the other hand, governmental partnerships are equally challenging to the free market
when the partnership moves toward publicization and expanded forms of governance
and community development. As precursors of democratic capability, it is observable
that partnerships are dynamic building blocks of communities. Some succeed better than
others, but again it depends on which end of the spectrum we are making our evaluation,
and the strength and purpose of the partnership.

The Partnership and Collaborative Governance Movement is well illustrated and
practiced by Business Improvement Districts (BIDs). This book examines BIDs as
public–private partnerships (PPPs), emblematic of Partnership Governance, from policy, planning, management, and implementation perspectives. Business Improvement
Districts are distinctive, formalized partnerships between the public and private sectors
operating at the local subgovernmental level; PPPs that focus on downtown revitalization and business development in zoned business corridors. (Although emerging, indications are that the BID model is being used in purely residential areas as Neighborhood
Improvement Districts [NIDs].) There were more than 1,001 BIDs in the U.S. in 2011,
and an estimated 2,500 worldwide (Becker, Grossman, & Dos Santos 2011). BIDs are
special districts established at the local level of government to bring together public,
private, and civic actors to address necessary revitalization, economic development, and
quality of life improvements in a designated business area. BIDs are unique because
they are established by local ordinance, usually managed and overseen by private as
well as public agents, and funded through a special assessment. They offer an avenue
of public impact, participation, and organization for invested private actors. The BID

partnership represents a movement past a traditional adversarial relationship often experienced between government and business, and the beginning of a legal partnership that utilizes the strengths and offsets the weaknesses of each sector. Such partnerships allow the public sector to enjoy more vigorous entrepreneurship while allowing the private sector to utilize public authority and processes to achieve economic and community revitalization. The public sector takes on private aspects and the private sector takes on a measure of public responsibility. BIDs represent a worldwide evolution in the capacities of government to develop and transform local communities and their cooperative economies. BIDs represent a relatively new form of governance, Partnership Governance that relies on a functioning partnership between the public and private sectors at the neighborhood level. BIDs appear to extend functional aspects of democracy that invite and permit traditionally business and private citizens into the formal processes of community development and governance.

REFERENCE

Becker, Carol, Seth A. Grossman, & Brenda Dos Santos (2011). *Business Improvement Districts: Census and National Survey*, Washington DC: International Downtown Association.

1

Origins of Partnership Governance

> It is the long history of humankind (and animal kind, too) that those who learned to
> collaborate and improvise most effectively have prevailed.
>
> *(Darwin 1859, paraphrase)*

In modern times, it is generally understood that 'governance' is the process by which
public needs and services are identified, agreed upon, and pursued and that "the context
of governance" is "[a] system for the legitimate direction of society" (Uveges & Keller
1998, p. 30). This is different from 'government,' which relates to the specific jurisdiction in which political authority is exercised. Governance points to a deep human agency
and informs us of "a change in the meaning of government, referring to a new process
of governing; or a changed condition of ordered rule; or the new method by which society is governed" (Rhodes 1996, pp. 652–3). It points to collaboration and partnerships,
the need to organize and work together with others, participate in government, plan
jointly, to learn from others, build trust and agreements, identify sustainable resources,
and manage change and outcomes by social/political processes (Golembiewski 1977;
Holzer & Gabrielian 1998; Saranson 1972; Uveges & Keller 1998). This is both a challenge and a demand for public managers (William 1994). Holzer and Gabrielian point
out the challenge of governance, echoed in partnership and collaboration theories, that
"the problem of theoretical reconciliation of conflicting paradigms is not an easy one"
(Holzer & Gabrielian 1998, p. 52), chiefly due to the "complexity of human nature"
(Holzer & Gabrielian 1998, p. 72). This is what Partnership Governance claims to do. In
the context of public administration (and equally applicable to private sector administration), "governance is a broader term and encompasses both formal and informal systems
of relationships and networks for decision making and problem solving" (Policy Consensus Initiative 2005). Partnership Governance is a term that organizes this process and
its disputes and offers an avenue of solving and supporting the potential of democratic
government in partnership with its citizenry; it is a collaborative process.

This book addresses the subject of Partnership Governance and management in public
administration. "Modern network society is characterized, among other things, by interdependencies between actors. . . . It is not surprising that in public administration, many
writers see a trend from government to governance" (Edelenbos & Klijn 2007, p. 25).
Continuing along these lines, Partnership Governance refers to the evolution of government (Holzer & Gabrielian 1998) and, we believe, the organizing principle of "the new
governance"—New Public Governance (NPG) (Salamon 2002, p. vii). If you are an
observer of government, it is apparent that there is an ongoing and fluctuating force—a

recurring, ebbing, and flowing "tide" of governmental reforms (Light 1997)—between command/control and collaboration/flexibility (dominance/actualization, conflict/cooperation) methodologies of public management. These nodes, (both) necessary to provide for and manage public interests, address social order in our civilization and require different methods of examination. These fluctuations are also at the heart of many debates regarding the purpose and performance of public administration in the context of governance. Even a casual glance at the history of government indicates that it has always been this way. So it is with 'Partnership Governance.'

Examinations of the fluctuations, mentioned above, reveal that one node eventually calls forth the other. As soon as one node is fully articulated, the other eventually demands attention in an ever-evolving manner. This is the circle of the life of governance. In practice, the nodes do not deny each other but, building upon each other, mingle and adapt to social evolution. Today, due chiefly to global boundary spanning, the relentless advance of information and communication technologies, and the democratization of markets, the tide is swinging toward collaboration/facilitation. This is the journey we will take and the following are the questions that launch this expedition. In relation to public organization and management, why is there a clear and present human need for collaboration and partnership in our thoughts and actions, and why is it so often neglected in just those ways? How are collaborations/partnerships working in public processes and government?

PARTNERSHIPS IN GOVERNANCE

Partnerships in governance may have been around since the beginning of civilization, and they act on specific multisectoral opportunities in modern public management. Partnerships have a functional aspect, but also a policy aspect. When we look at partnerships through the lens of policy, government looks different (Lowndes & Skelcher 1998). First, we see partnerships everywhere, they decentralize government, and they create multilevel production networks. Partnerships are found in almost every aspect of government, and they involve nonpublic actors beyond "iron triangles" (Vernon, Spar, & Tobin 1991) to public planning, management, and service delivery. Secondly, whether these partnerships are building a bridge, providing safe and clean environments, strengthening communities, or developing an economy, they tend to be pragmatic and results oriented. This alters or augments our understanding of governance. "Governance is ultimately concerned with order and collective action" (Stoker 1998, p. 17). As Blessett, Alkadry, and Rubaii (2013) state, "governance . . . speaks to the interactions and engagement of administrators with multiple constituents within varied environments" (p. 302). This tells us that governance often challenges the divisions and separations of government, and the same is true of public (and public–private) partnerships.

> [T]he rise of "governance" as a theoretical perspective and empirical reality brought
> into play a competing organizational dynamic rooted in the private sector . . . in

which government is one among many actors and in which government officials enjoy no presumption of primacy, even though they are democratically elected representatives of the people within governance networks.

(Kincaid & Stenberg 2011, p. 197)

Today, the rise of Partnership Governance describes the process of multisectoral engagement and can be appropriately associated with the evolution of democracy as a form of citizen action as well as the corresponding public management capacity. And yet, it is here, at these points of evolution, that we often find concern based on ideological aspirations when we might expect to find curiosity. Command and Control Governance and Partnership Governance are different strategies and perspectives. Fluctuations between the methodologies may appear to be reactionary but may be better understood as organic trends to meet evolving social expressions.

Charles Darwin may have seen collaborative phenomena in nature over 100 years ago, but the subject of governance can be aptly attributed, as it pertains to the study of present-day public administration, to H. George Fredrickson, as early as 1971, as a balancing weight to scientific management and, two decades later, the New Public Management (NPM) movement. His ideas continue to guide us today on public governance, decentralization, equitable partnerships, and cooperation within the changing arena and adaptive responses of modern society (Fredrickson 1971, 1999, 2012). In our society, this discussion takes us immediately to the reasons, purposes, and politics of our bifurcated social-economic system particularly between, of, and in the public and private sectors. Partnership Governance and collaborative government concepts are mutual "cross-sector concepts spanning the public, private, nonprofit, and citizen domains" (Purdy 2012, p. 410, summarizing the Policy Consensus Initiative in 2005) Fredrickson (1971) and later Bozeman (1987) make an important observation of this unifying system: designed as a public benefit. "The governance perspective also draws attention to the increased involvement of the private and voluntary sectors in service delivery and strategic decision making" (Stoker 1998, p. 19) This has not always been the way societies were intended to operate, and it remains a challenge, both at heart and at a distance, in the understanding and management of government in modern times.

FROM NPM TO NPG: THE SIGNIFICANCE OF GOVERNANCE AND THE EMERGENCE OF PUBLIC PARTNERING

"The first message of governance is to challenge constitution/formal understandings of systems government" (Stoker 1998, p. 19). At the end of the 20th century, at the height of NPM and a growing disillusionment with government, arrived a call for better approaches to governance. The Fredrickson view of the 21st century includes the primacy of collaboration at the core of a new approach to governance. This is not only to further necessary equitable considerations for public management, citizen participation, and politics as essentially governance (Fredrickson 1971), but also to solve public problems peculiar to an advancing technological society. NPG emerges in defense of the strengths of communities and our citizenry in active democratic engagement but, again, also refers to the profession of public management that is less centralized, as prescribed by NPM privatization precepts (Osborne & Gaebler 1992; Savas 2000). It is also in reaction to public agency dissociated from everyday public processes (Agranoff & McGuire 2003; Salamon 2002).

For the NPG, the process of collaboration, i.e., the management of collaborations, is partnership regardless of the level or scope of collaboration (Gulick 1937). This is the theme we will build on in this paper. Jan Kooiman's (1993) view is that governance is fundamental to public management. Governance identifies the organizational nature of public processes, its partnering tendencies and evolution to higher levels of organization as institutional socioeconomic and political relationships in society. Myungsuk Lee points out that governance "also denotes government management capacities" (Lee 2003, p. 6), which is key to understanding the role of partnerships.

Lester Salamon refers to "the new governance" as a "framework" that "emphasizes the collaborative nature of modern efforts to meet human needs" (Salamon 2002, vii). If we can accept that there is a "collaborative nature," the primacy of partnership, rather than only the nature of disaffiliated competition, then we can see not only another view of policy development (planning), which requires partnerships, but also their implementation, which is an associated need to manage policy to achieve desired results (Pressman & Wildavsky 1973). Salamon uses the word "emphasizes," indicating that we are not inventing collaboration, but unconcealing it or further actualizing it, thereby recognizing that it is part of our nature and, even if minimized, is undeniable. From this point of view, it is reasonable to conclude that at every level of government, governance operates in a collaborative manner. At any time, government reaches across and participates with all sectors of society and economics (Fry & Nigro 1998), and this exposes the actions of governance. These sectors are fundamentally described as public, which is understood as government, and private, which is understood as business and citizenry. All elements and segments of society can be said to originate in one of these sectors, even as sectors continuously evolve, merge, collaborate, mingle, and operate at various levels of impact hierarchy. The management of these collaborations, formally and informally, consists of acts of governance. This idea goes back to the beginnings of modern public administration (Gulick 1937), because "public administration is a composite of many disciplines and fields" (Chandler 1998, p. 743).

Governance is derived from collaboration and is not the same as cooperation or competition, as it is defined by its "mutuality and organizational identity" (Brinkerhoff & Brinkerhoff 2011; Velotti, Botti, & Vesci 2012). Creating and managing mutuality and organizational identity defines partnerships as well. In public administration, the work of collaboration links partnering with governance. Governance and partnership are terms that can be used in both public and private realms but are distinct in public administration because they address interdependent public goods, values, and purpose rather than only independent individual agendas. Herbert Simon (1997) recognized the limitations of individual action, as did Dwight Waldo (1948) when he cited a need for "post-bureaucratic" modes of organization. These other modes are collaborative and partnering. Bozeman (1987) later talked about evaluating all organizations, both public and private, as to their "publicness." This publicness was not only a sense of transparency and accountability, but also the process whereby private citizens and businesses merged and blended their actions in creating societal values and defining and implementing public solutions that prevented the erosion of these values (Denhardt 1993). Governance implies partnerships. Partnerships, not only on a principal-agent basis, but also a collaborative basis, redefine the role of government and public management. Partnerships redefine how government and public structures operate intrinsically and extrinsically. Government stability, in a partnership system, relies on the success of each partner within the partnership as a whole.

A partnership operates as a complete phenomenon with a minimum of two partners as well as the (whole) partnership itself (partnerships, of course, can have more than two partners). Collaboration and network theory describe the processes of social interaction fundamental to partnership. If you witness and/or participate in a collaborative function, you will find a partnership at one or another stage of development. At the same time, governance is an organizing principle of collaboration. Partnerships are the resulting organizational function of collaboration and governance. The new governance movement speaks not only to the function of collaborations in the building of successful societies and the "tools" necessary to accomplish these endeavors, but also to the management of the resulting partnerships (Agranoff & McGuire 2003; Fry & Nigro 1998; Grossman 2012; Salamon 2002; Velotti, Botti, & Vesci 2012).

Often governance and management are collapsed as being the same thing. They represent another functional dichotomy. But it must be noted that there are more similarities than differences between public management and governance, as their outcomes are similarly evaluated by outcomes. In general, management refers to performance technologies, and governance refers to organizing principles/policy of social action. Both intend to produce results that further share values and agreements. At every level of public action, we address effective governance and management from a variety of policy positions. Again, these policy positions reflect the important dichotomies in public administration theory: politics/administration (Wilson 1887), efficiency/effectiveness (Taylor 1911), facts/values (Simon 1997), science/morals (Waldo 1964), public/private (Allison 2004), as well as law/performance (Moe 1984), control/choice (Ostrom & Ostrom 1971), service/citizenship (Fredrickson 2012), and control/collaboration (Agranoff 2003). Upon examining Partnership Governance, we add another public administration dichotomy: governance/management. In practice, these dichotomies represent binding matrixes, one relying upon and fulfilling the other. It is the dichotomies of public administration that make the profession of public management relevant. And, this remains so in the realm of Partnership Governance.

Discussions on the disputes between the merits of government and private sectors in furthering collaborative solutions to public needs are well advanced by Lester M. Salamon. He reminded us, in his introduction to "Tools of Government" (2002) that "[l]argely overlooked in this dispute, however, has been the extent to which actual public problem solving has come to embrace collaborative actions of governments at multiple levels and both government and private institutions" (Salamon 2002, p. vii). He goes on further to define the actions called the new public governance. "This framework emphasizes the collaborative nature of modern efforts to meet human needs" (ibid.). NPG undoubtedly began as a response to the NPM of the 1990s, and rather than only a counterpoint to NPM it absorbs NPM into the NPG movement much the same way that partnerships absorb collaboration. These two movements set the stage for Partnership Governance.

Partnership Governance is the pragmatism of the new public governance. When describing the "art of leading across boundaries," Ricardo S. Morse (2010), referencing Jeffery Luke's "strategies for an interconnected world" (1998), echoes Salamon and further states that "the big problems that the public sector is concerned with today are almost without exception the kinds of wicked, boundary-crossing problems that require collaborative work" (Morse 2010, p. 434). In 2012, Rosemary O'Leary and Nidhi Vij, summarizing the work of C. Huxham (2000, p. 341), wrote "relationships between individual participants in collaborations are often fundamental to getting things done" (O'Leary & Vij 2012, p. 514). Consequently, our collaborative nature acts as the *genetic material* of partnerships, and partnerships are what collaborations look like when they are formalized, organized, and managed. Collaboration theories inform the practice of partnering. It is the nature, management, and organization of partnerships that provide resolution to the challenge of collaboration and inform public management professionals in public and multisectoral arenas. "If governance is going to make an impression as a societal practice and as a scholarly activity it has to be multifaceted" (Kooiman 2003, p. 6) Public-public partnerships between governments and governmental institutions are challenging due to jurisdictional issues. Intriguing and impactful types of partnerships that challenge and inform public management currently seem to be public–private partnerships. Public–private partnership is emblematic of partnerships in general and is both straightforward and complex. The nature of a relationship between public and private parties working together, collaboratively, in a partnership is well understood and defined, providing us with an infrastructure of partnerships (Becker & Patterson 2005; Carroll & Steane 2000; Grossman 2008; Hodge & Greve 2007; Mauldin 2012; Velotti, Botti, & Vesci 2012). They appear complex because each entity, private or public, has distinct interests and objectives, expertise and resources, and they work together in a cooperative-interdependent manner with the overall goal of improving the public domain (Linder 1999). Public-public partnerships are often more elusive, due chiefly to political interests.

When we review the literature, the descriptions of collaboration look like partnerships (Agranoff & McGuire 2003; Bryson, Crosby, & Stone 2006; Getha-Taylor 2012; Huxham & Vangen 2005; MacDonald, Stokes, & Blumenthal 2010; Mendel & Brudney 2012; Morse 2010; O'Leary & Vij 2012; Pressman & Wildavsky 1973; Silvestre & de Araújo 2012; Sirianni 2009). Clearly, the terms are not only correlated, but also descriptive of each other. Collaboration is at the heart of partnerships. However, often what is missing is a thorough discussion of the management and organizational structure of collaborations. Collaborators will frequently talk about partnering and partnerships in relation to collaboration but not address the practical (how to) and management structure of partnerships. There is extensive discourse when "collaboration occurs in the context of public management" (Purdy 2012). This includes discussions about cross-sector collaboration (Bryson, Crosby, & Stone 2006), new governance (Salamon 2002), collaborative governance (Agranoff & McGuire 2003), and collaborative management (Huxham & Vangen 2005). Partnership is not just another form of collaboration; it is the formal organization of collaboration. Partnerships are more than a method of collaboration; they are the functional operations and management of collaboration. *Partnership Governance, therefore, refers to the pragmatic organizational application of collaborative governance.* Consequently, we can examine governance in terms of the organizing principles of partnerships.

Understanding partnerships has its pitfalls if we address partnerships only as dichotomies (a descriptive discussion) and not as complete conditions (a prescriptive application). Jos Raadschelders and Mark Rutgers (1999) arrived at a similar conclusion about public administration dichotomies that provides us with some insight into partnerships. They observed that "public administration couldn't be understood" without examining three dyads: public/private, policy/administration, and state/society (p. 30). Pitfalls arise when partnerships are analyzed by looking at only the parts rather than the partnership as a whole and its impact on the parts. This is largely due to dichotomization theories of public administration that on the surface seem to present adversity and the importance of parts (e.g., politics vs. administration), but taking a step back reveals a whole system, a partnership—*two sides of the same coin* (e.g., politics/administration as one unified discourse). Today, public administration cannot be understood without examining these (and other) dyads not only as dichotomies, but also as partnerships (Svara 1985). As we observe dichotomies, we must also understand the partnerships that fulfil their purposes. Of course, there are certainly more than three dyads that impact public administration. Raadschelders and Rutgers didn't refer to the dyads as partnerships, but it is not difficult to see a dyad as a binary partnership: as the integral relationship of dichotomies. In this way Salamon (2002), again, appears to be correct; collaboration is overlooked as the glue that forges the dyadic field, not always as an argument, but a dyadic partnership.

Often collaborations, because they are synergistic, are conceptually collapsed as the same thing as partnerships. They aren't. What is the difference between collaboration and partnerships? Collaboration is a social behavior. It is not a product of partnership. If collaboration is "working in association with others for some form of mutual benefit" (Huxham 1996, p. 1) and to "increase public value" (Bardach 1998, p. 8), then we are informed of a possible organizational structure of collaboration, i.e., partnerships. Huxham and Vangen (further summarize collaborations as being "about drawing synergy from . . . differences . . . different resources . . . different expertise . . . different purposes . . . different benefits" (2005, p. 82). Collaboration empowers partnerships (Himmelman 1996). Collaboration isn't an organizational structure, but behavior. Partnership on the other hand is not behavior; it's the organizational structure of collaboration. Collaboration and partnership are thereby intertwined, and in the public realm they form the purposes of governance. The organizing principle of governance employs collaborative functions that make partnerships possible. Partnerships are predicated on the need to share the process of collaboration: shared risk, resources, efficiency, coordination, learning, values, energy, resources, and leadership.

Partnerships also have a pragmatic synergy with management. When management is mentioned in the discussions of collaboration, we can observe a partnership emerging. One definition of a partnership is a collaboration that divides its outcomes equally and its outputs equitably. This implies that partnerships are managed, or at the least elicit management. Partnerships and how they are managed in government, both public–private and public-public as cross-sector collaborations (Agranoff 2006; Bryson, Crosby, & Stone 2006), are evolving to complement command-and-control policies due to the increased requirements of public management. Robert Agranoff, reviewing the Federalist Papers about intergovernmental relations and referring to government partners, observed "[c]ollaboration as a means to an end, not an absolute requirement" (2011, p. 68). That end is a partnership. This is important because collaboration and resultant partnerships are not the only, or always the best, way to conduct government. But, more and more, this perspective has become a necessary component of our understanding of governance and public management. Nonetheless, collaboration does not always end in partnership, which further identifies the difference between collaboration and partnership.

Even though the term 'Partnership Governance' would not have been considered, the rumblings of Partnership Governance began even before NPM. Terry Moe was prescient on the pending issue of collaboration in his 1984 book *The New Economics of Organization*, when he wrote, "the principal-agent model will likely give way to a more eclectic methodology within which that model plays a less pronounced but integral role" (1984, p. 758). Moe was clear that this was an organizational model that with a very short leap takes us to a partnership model. The end point of eclectic methodologies, while retaining the promise of democratic principles, may look quite different from the beginning. In the case of 'Partnership Governance,' which involves the governance of all sectors of society, governance assumes a different end than a principal-agent model. Moe's idea of an "eclectic" methodology seems more of a warning of changes to come than a promise. By 2011, and in terms of the NPG movement, Brinkerhoff and Brinkerhoff (2011), issuing less of a warning, interpreted eclectic to be transforming, and furthered the idea that collaboration could (would, should) replace traditional principal-agent relationships. This is an honest reaction to the public/private dispute championed by NPM and its changing role to meet society's needs to absorb innovation and new conditions of economic normalcy. To correctly delve into this concept, we should describe not only governance but go further and look at the nature of partnerships. Today, this appears less eclectic and quite normal. But a look back can tell us how we got here.

THE NATURE OF PARTNERSHIPS—AN EXPLORATION

After we have examined the meaning and practices of collaboration and governance as they relate to Partnership Governance, we must further examine the term "partnership."

In this section we will look at key epistemological explanations of partnership. This is an attempt to get to the fundamental, essential elements of the phenomena of partnerships. What are partnerships? What is their purpose? And how do they change our understanding of human behavior applicable to governance? It is a term that is interpretable in a variety of disciplines. In public administration, the term denotes the foundation and management of social/political processes. We begin our description of partnerships by discussing context/content and use a strange but helpful term, "holon," invented by Arthur Koestler (1967, p. 48). Holons, as described by Koestler and Ken Wilber, are wholes and complete entities that are both wholes and parts. They are essentially partnerships. This is helpful to our understanding of partnerships because it describes not only the parts of a partnership, but the partnership as a whole, and the nature of partnerships in understanding functional realities. The explanation of partnerships begins with a look at models of the partnerships depicting Individuals and Organizations. The premise is that partnerships not only are everywhere, but also are functional aspects of reality. That means they can be managed and measured.

We have concluded that collaboration is a behavior that elicits learning, growth, and development and is a key process of partnerships. Governance, the ordering and organization of social partnership systems, is the social function of Nature—seeking more complete forms of organization; what we can refer to as agreement making. Partnerships are organizations that act as the synergistic aspect of both collaboration and governance and essentially all social phenomena. Partnerships allow us to understand social functionality—organization building, development, and management at all levels of organization.

We can experience, therefore, reality partnership at three levels:

1. What it is—its 'Being'
2. How it communicates what it is—its Language
3. How it is experienced in the 'World'—its essential reality (Figures 1.1 and 1.2). As a complete entity, partnerships manage both the network of conversations (individual communiqués, i.e., monologues) and agreements (social communiqués, i.e., dialogues) that tell us what the partnership is.

This correlates to three fundamental concerns of philosophy (a tripart model) in terms of the human experience described in the 1854 lectures by Victor Cousin (1854) as Truth, Goodness, and Beauty (correlate to Being, Language, and World). We can apply this model to our understanding of Individuals (I) in Figure 1.1 and Partnerships (We) in Figure 1.2. We begin with the 'being' of something, its truth—what we are referring to. Then the 'language' of it; its goodness; how we communicate about it. Then, how it is experienced in the 'world'; how we participate with/in it—its reality to us. Together, Figure 1.1 portrays the individual (a normative reality) and Figure 1.2 portrays the partnership phenomena (an evolving reality). In this case, the phenomenon of the individual is in the language of representation or an "I"/"It" or me relationship. The phenomenon of partnership is the language of collaboration, or what the phenomenologist Alfred Schutz describes as the fundamental "we-relationship" (Schutz 1966, p. 82). Collaboration, which formulates partnerships, is a well-known trust building process (Agranoff & McGuire 2003; Edelenbos & Klijn 2007; Getha-Taylor 2012; Golembiewski & McConkie 1975; Putnam 1993). Due to the importance of trust in regard to collaboration and partnerships as a concept, experience and practice are well documented.

Partnerships are differentiated from other relationships by the management of a collaborative process much in the manner that Barbara Gray (1989) describes: "a process through which parties who see different aspects of a problem can constructively explore their differences and search for solutions that go beyond their own limited vision of what is possible" (Gray 1989, p. 5). We are hard pressed to separate the process of partnership from the management of the process. Much is the same for all collaborations. Partnership Governance does not deny that hierarchies are developmental as well as value ranking (Wilber 2000), but also addresses the collaborative functions of heterarchies: organization within a hierarchical level (Figure 1.3). Partnership Governance can also be called "heterarchic governance" (Kooiman 2000), and there is a hierarchy to partnerships as there is to everything. We are not describing hierarchies as levels of superior

Figure 1.1   **An Epistemological Model of the Individual**

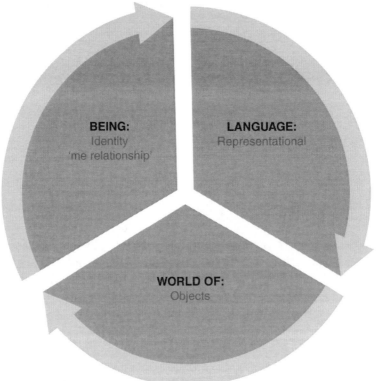

(Derived from Heidegger [1927/1992]. Note: This is a model of how the meaning of something becomes known in an epistemological partnership.)

Figure 1.2   **An Epistemological Model of Partnerships**

Being, Language, World of Partnership

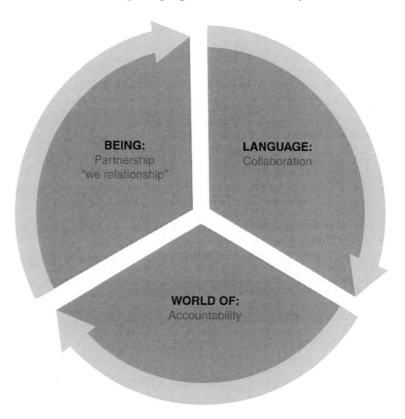

Being– Partnership
Language– Collaboration
World– Accountability

value, but complete levels of capability, with each level having its essential value. Each level is of importance unto itself and to the levels below and above it. "Partnerships are a result of a policy to collaborate—to be multilateral rather than unilateral" (Grossman 2012). Ken Wilber (2000) in describing the nature of reality and evolution grasped an integrative truth that also describes the function of partnerships. This concept is that all things are both wholes and parts of other wholes in a hierarchy of integrating and disintegrating capacities. "A hierarchy is . . . a ranking of orders of events *according to their holistic capacity*" (Wilber 2000, p. 25). Upon examination, Wilber's argument tells us that there is nothing (in Nature) that isn't a partnership (a WholePart) and nothing that is *only* a whole thing or only a part (subwhole) of a thing; all things are partnerships all the time and occur that way throughout evolution's developmental hierarchy. (Note: Dyads can be understood as complete partnerships rather than parts vs. parts. For example, politics/administration as two parts can also be understood as a unified whole partnership, as *PoliticsAdministration*.)

The Greek philosopher Plotinus observed 2,000 years ago that "all development is envelopment" (Plotinus, 205–207 BC). He conceived of a universe as a living chain of being that looked a lot like a partnership; unbroken series of ascending and descending partnership systems: partnerships within partnerships. This exists not just in the external world as it functions but internally as we perceive things. This is exactly what Wilber is describing. We can see that *development* is rational and envelopment is *transrational*. Transrational means it is rational-plus, not beyond or across rationality; more than rational, which would be more than the rationality of an individual and that of an organized group of individuals; i.e., a partnership. Rational refers to the individual. Transrational refers to partnership. We understand that rationality utilizes deductive reasoning and introspection and grasps multiple perspectives, which leads us to its transrational equivalent: partnerships. However, rationality is ego centered and describes the responsibility of the individual: our autonomy rather than the responsibility of the whole community. Rationality has us see ourselves as chiefly individuals in a relationship (positive or negative) with others. Transrationality has us consider ourselves as the whole community, *not separate or independent* from that community. Rationality has us consider ourselves as an independent identity, a part of a community. Rationality is idealistic, futuristic, strategic, and content oriented—all qualities that society builds on. Transrationality builds on those attributes and is realistic, in the present, transformative, and contextual. It transcends and includes the individual. For example, trust is one of "the pluses" in a rational system that is able to convert that system to a transrational system. Plotinus and Wilber tell us that healthy/successful systems develop and envelop, therefore they are both rational and transrational (*RationalTransrational—wholeparts*) at the same time. Much has been said about our rationality. Little is understood about our transrationality even as we are in it every day.

According to Figure 1.3, evolution is understood as the vertical emergence of new partnerships embracing preceding partnerships. Partnerships evolve by creating a new context, framework, or morphogenetic field that embraces other such phenomena, thereby becoming a part of a new context but retaining the preceding partnerships, which comprise other partnerships (Figures 1.4 and 1.5) (Wilber, 2000). "And thus, the forms of life throughout the universe become divided into groups subordinate to groups" (Darwin 1859). De-evolution is the erasing of a partnership to its constituent parts, which are wholes unto themselves, e.g., atoms are whole and complete as atoms but are parts of molecules. However, molecules are not parts of atoms. Evolution is hierarchical—upward and downward forever. That is, we see the possibility of partnerships embracing smaller partnerships 'all the way up' the chain of Nature, from the smallest particle to the largest universes: a nesting effect, with smaller partnerships resolved within larger partnerships going the other way 'all the way down' the chain of Nature from largest to smallest ad infinitum. The concept provides a unique analysis of the role of partnerships: *The role of partnering is to create new contextual partnerships to resolve concerns that lower level partnerships cannot solve.* Partnerships allow us to answer the question, why

Figure 1.3   **Hierarchy/Heterarchy**

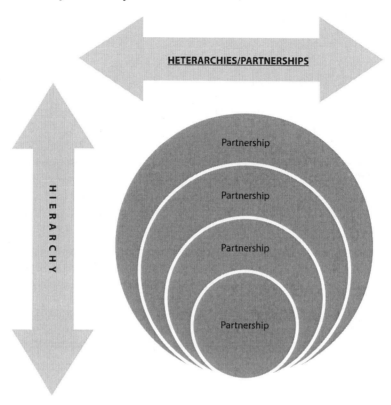

partnerships? Each partnership is at its level of development (hierarchy) and is a horizontal heterarchy that embraces and transcends its partners in order to solve problems that its constituent parts cannot solve alone.

Heterarchy is the organizational function of a partnership, is equivalent to functionality, and describes a partnership's internal differences or parts within the partnership. The purpose of a partnership is to address how pragmatic relationships change over time, creating new and embracing contextual partnerships, a new context for action, and a new transformative agency of causal actors in order to accomplish something the constituent parts cannot accomplish alone. "Each emergent holon transcends but includes its predecessor(s)" (Wilber, p. 59). The new partnership infuses each partner with new perspectives and capabilities that were not available by each partner acting alone. The system is more than the sum of its parts. Partnerships not only share capabilities and risks, but also create a new paradigm to understand, manage, and incorporate change necessary to produce results. The other function of a partnership is then to master the possibilities and capacity within the partnership: its heterarchy. For example, a public–private partnership has each part/sector master the goals and challenges of the partnership and allow for technology transfers between parts/sectors.

"The way to determine the hierarchy, or significance, of a holon is to remove a whole/ part of the holon. Significance refers to the depth, agreement, or capacity of the holon; i.e. the amount of the universe within it. Fundamental means the amount of other holons that depend on it for their existence" (Wilber 2000, pp. 70–1). Here again, we can substitute partnership for 'holon.' What will happen is that everything "above" it (more significant) will disappear. But all things less significant and more fundamental will remain. For example, if we remove one of the partners, the partnership and everything the partnership can achieve disappear even as the partners continue to exist (and everything that is part of them). Another example, if we remove molecules from the universe, all living and occurring things above molecules, from cells to galaxies, will disappear, but all things below will remain and be dissolved into atoms and the parts of atoms. Therefore, atoms are more fundamental to the universe than molecules or galaxies, but galaxies are more significant because more of the universe is within them. The partnership is more significant because it embraces and signifies more, but it is less fundamental, and depends on the partners. There are always less of things that are of significance even as they encompass more, and more things that are fundamental even as they encompass less (e.g., there is one nation called Canada, but many provinces. Nations are more significant than provinces but less fundamental than states. Also, there may be many partners in a partnership, but only one partnership).

COLLABORATIVE/PARTNERSHIP ACTION: COMING TO TERMS WITH THE RESULTING TRANSFORMATION

The partitioning of a public realm and a private realm represents one organic partnership system that has always been in flux as economies and cultures develop, taking on more interdependent relationships in the 21st century and utilizing effective technologies and the strengths of each sector. The need to build and maintain infrastructure and institutions of the system to sustain society is a primary directive of government. The building of functional, management, and service capacity for growth is a continuing process and transverses these sectors. Dividing our socioeconomic system into a private and public sector is useful chiefly because the whole socioeconomic system (culture) functions as a partnership weaving a tapestry of communal competence and prowess.

Partnerships are developed human capacities that are learned, developed, and applied. The nature of these partnerships, in terms of traditional governance, is changing from vertically oriented forms of coordination to more horizontally oriented forms of cooperation and collaboration (Kort & Klijn 2011) (from two-dimensional–top/bottom to multidimensional–whole-partnerships/parts [Figure 1.4]). The risks of noncooperation, sectoral miscues, and misunderstandings of our interdependent socioeconomic systems can cause not only mismanagement, loss of public trust, and substantive fiscal miscalculations, but the erosion of a functioning society (Figure 1.5).

A distinction and blending of private to public, and equally public to private, technologies is fundamentally democratic, as is information sharing and entrepreneurship, which are the foundations of modern economies. Additionally, the technological age, its costs and assumptions, seem to require partnerships and networks more than ever before as it

Figure 1.4 **Two Dimensional–Top to Bottom (Vertical) to Multidimensional–Whole-Partnerships/Parts (Horizontal)**

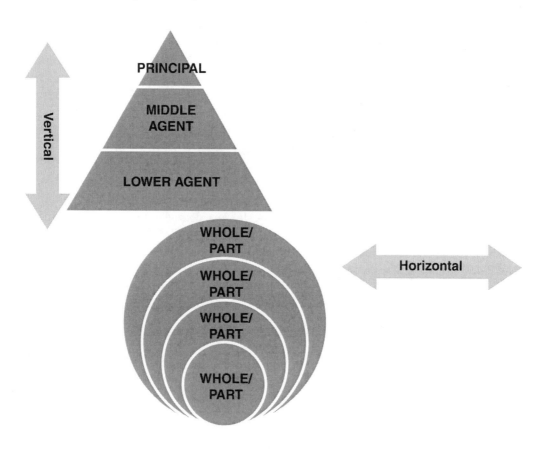

Figure 1.5 **Noncooperation, Control, Miscues, Adversity, Misunderstanding, and Performance Loss**

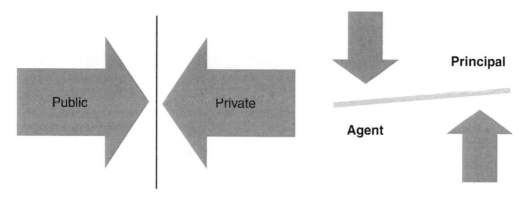

creates new economies and social values. Consequently, as partnerships succeed in managing conflict, assets, and diversity, the need for partnering skills across sectors and jurisdictions is emerging as a professional field within public management. While discussing public–private partnerships in urban regeneration projects, Michael Kort and Erik-Hans Klijn emphasize the importance of management, noting that the "organizational form may be less a factor than managerial capability" (2011, p. 618). This tells us that management is primary in any partnership even as partnerships take many different forms along the continuum of public to private. At the heart of a partnership is the ability to mitigate the weaknesses while sharing the strengths of each party (sectors) to achieve stakeholder buy-in and apply results-oriented management technologies. Figure 1.6a shows us one type of partnership that we call situational, transactional, or convergence partnerships well suited for project-oriented endeavors such as transportation and other infrastructure improvements.

Because the partnership does not embrace the entirety of the partners, some feel it is not a true partnership. These are transactional partnerships generally with shorter-term, project-oriented goals (such as transportation projects) (Figure 1.6a). Other partnerships, such as business improvement districts or the 1960s Model Cities programs, are capacity, immersion, or transformation partnerships that expand, improve, or create whole new potentials for a community (Figure 1.6b). Transactional partnerships reside often within transformational partnerships and are a result of the needs of that partnership. Transformational partnerships create new contextual and community capacities that manage transactional partnerships (Figure 1.7).

Figure 1.6a **Transactional Partnerships: A View of Partnership Convergence as Overlap—** *Normative* **View of Partnerships**

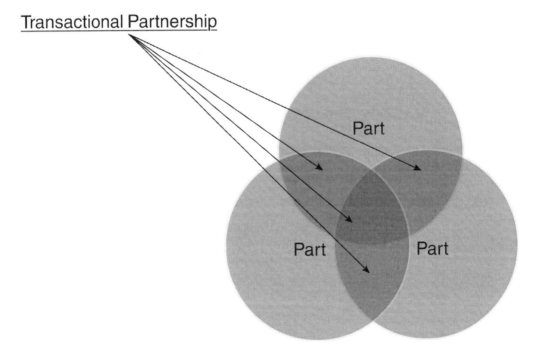

Figure 1.6b **Transactional Partnerships: A View of Partnership as Immersion—*New* Capacity/ Field of Partnerships**

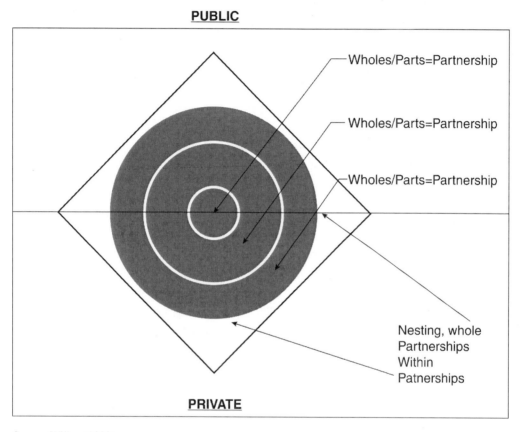

PUBLIC

Wholes/Parts=Partnership

Wholes/Parts=Partnership

Wholes/Parts=Partnership

Nesting, whole
Partnerships
Within
Patnerships

PRIVATE

Source: Wilbur (2000)

Controversies surrounding governmental partnerships tend to travel along the partnership continuum from concerns regarding privatization and exclusion to publicization and government intrusion. There are those who are unsure (or, on the other hand, overly sure) of the privatized conveniences of profit seekers at the private end and the partisan and special-interest power politics of government at the public end. It is clear that PPPs are not strict forms of privatization, nor should they be. They are also more appropriately understood as forms of the democratic process that call for the citizens and the private sector to become involved and accountable to the public and be creative in harnessing resources and solving immediate social and economic problems. Partnerships are poorly evaluated when the aim is to diminish either aspect of the partnership. An expectation of diminishing attributes contributes to diminishing results, and the practice of mutually expanding and synthesizing attributes in these partnerships functions to reduce risk and produce results.

Often overlooked in evaluating governmental partnerships is the level of partnership competence from conception to implementation. Partnership management and planning are skills well suited to the public manager, but often poorly identified. This may be the

Figure 1.7   **Transformational Partnerships Embracing Transactional Partnerships**

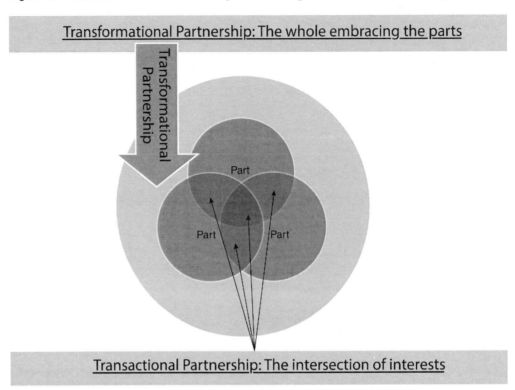

single reversible liability for a governmental partnership. As we move toward a variety of Partnership Governance forms to solve social and technical problems and reduce investment risk in public projects, the field of public administration must identify and provide a variety of partnership management skills. Democratic behavior by its nature by most accounts is an ever-revolving prescription to citizen participation. It continuously redefines citizenship and participation as culture and technology develop. Not unlike the organic nature of democratic processes, Partnership Governance is dynamic. Our opinions of these processes often depend on what side of the public–private spectrum we are associated with. Some see it as detraction from the norm, others as an enhancement.

On one hand, we can perceive the concept of partnering as challenging democratic accountability when the partnership moves toward the private sector, as *privatization* (Figure 1.8a). On the other hand, governmental partnerships are equally challenging to free market thinkers when the partnership moves toward the public sector, as *publicization* (Figure 1.8b) and expanded forms of governance and community development (Grossman 2010). The dynamics of independence and interdependence, distinction and commonality, are important variables in the partnership process. Nonetheless, as precursors of democratic capability, it is observable that partnerships are fundamental building blocks of communities. Communities begin with partnerships, and may end with the success or failure of the partnerships as an institution. Some succeed better than others, or last longer than others, but it depends on which end of the spectrum we are making our evaluation, and the strength and purpose of the partnership.

- *Privatization:* Where the private sector is contracted to provide public services (Savas 1997) (vendor—does not extend government) (Figure 1.8a)
- *Publicization:* Where private citizens/corporations assume public accountabilities and services (agent—extends governance) (Grossman 2008) (Figure 1.8b)
- *Partnership:* Where public and private actors develop common agreements and manage those agreements; commit equitable resources that reduce inherent sectoral risks that change normative paradigms of governance; and where there is a promise/performance process that examines the reality of the partnership (Partnership extends capacity of all partners.) (Grossman 2008) (Figure 1.7)

Figure 1.8a   **Privatization**

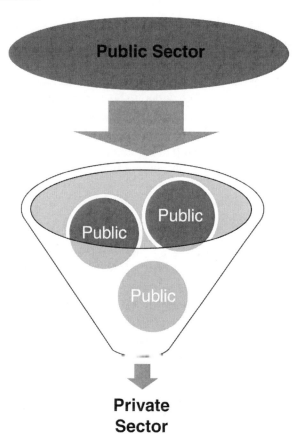

Figure 1.8b **Publicization**

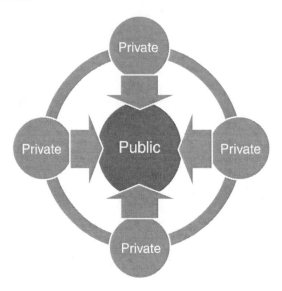

When we address the strength and purpose of a partnership, ethical problems seem to emerge when trust devolves by private agendas. To many it appears as if public processes are tainted by distrust and greed, and usurped by private agendas. Partnerships in government, particularly PPPs, experience this dilemma as much as any public activity. The trust we wish to have in public process seems often to be by the individuals who are also disinclined to attribute success to partnerships. These actors may explain evolving individualism but cannot explain the concept, implication, and practice of the skills of trust involved in partnerships in which the partnership is paramount. Without distorting its explanation toward distrust and its inherent limitations, purely rational models tend to be less satisfying in explaining why anyone partners. Consequently, the purpose of partnerships is to reduce the risks of distrust, and trust is its greatest strength. Efforts in explaining these most pressing concerns of governance, trust, and the reduction of the risk of distrust appear unclear and virtually unanswered unless a transrational/partnership model is applied up front.

We can't fully understand collaborations, therefore partnerships, if we do not understand the nature of trust (Bardach 1998). This is a primary theme in any discussion on collaboration and Partnership Governance. In the article "Cross-Sector Understanding and Trust," Heather Getha-Taylor drives this home, stating that "managing trust begins with understanding the concept of trust in the context of partnerships" (Getha-Taylor 2012, p. 218). Trust seems to refer to the integrity of a partnership built upon how well it manages its agreements to deliver on its promises. We can call this performance or accountability. Trust is complex because it is a social aspect of being human, often identified as being the most important social aspect (Fukuyama 1995). It has internal and external components as well as both an emotional and an intuitive aspect, and a cognitive aspect that can be considered a skill. Trust and the process of agreement making are synergistic, they are experienced as collaboration and work toward and sustain partnerships. We need to look at collaboration as a functional aspect of social capability. Since it is functional rather than behavioral, collaboration is a process of agreement making it the context of capacity building. Agreement is also at minimum a skill, and at maximum a level of cognitive development. Agreements are organizational communications and exist in dialogue rather than monologue (i.e., agreeing with our self is absurd because it's unnecessary; disagreeing with our self is potentially pathological). Agreements have a direct relationship to partnering (Huxham & Vangen 2005). Like governance, agreement causes more and more capable partnerships. This is because it utilizes higher levels of collaboration, therefore higher levels of trust. As stated above, partnerships are the resulting phenomena of Nature's direction to build more and more complex organizations; everything comes into existence by virtue of agreement.

Figure 1.9 (the left side of the figure) provides us with a view of disagreement.

Disagreement is not a separate or opposite phenomenon to agreement, but an aspect of agreement—a lesser aspect. The opposite of agreement is more like misunderstanding. Trust exists in the same way. Distrust can be understood as not a separate or opposite phenomenon of trust, but an aspect of trust—a lesser aspect, an erosion of trust. The opposite of trust is more akin to fear. Trust and distrust are correlated to agreement and disagreement often based on the maintenance or destruction of an agreement (e.g., we trust people who maintain their agreements, and we distrust people who break their agreements). Agreements foster commitments, while disagreements foster complaints. A complaint is based on

Figure 1.9   **Trust, Cooperation/Collaboration Matrix**

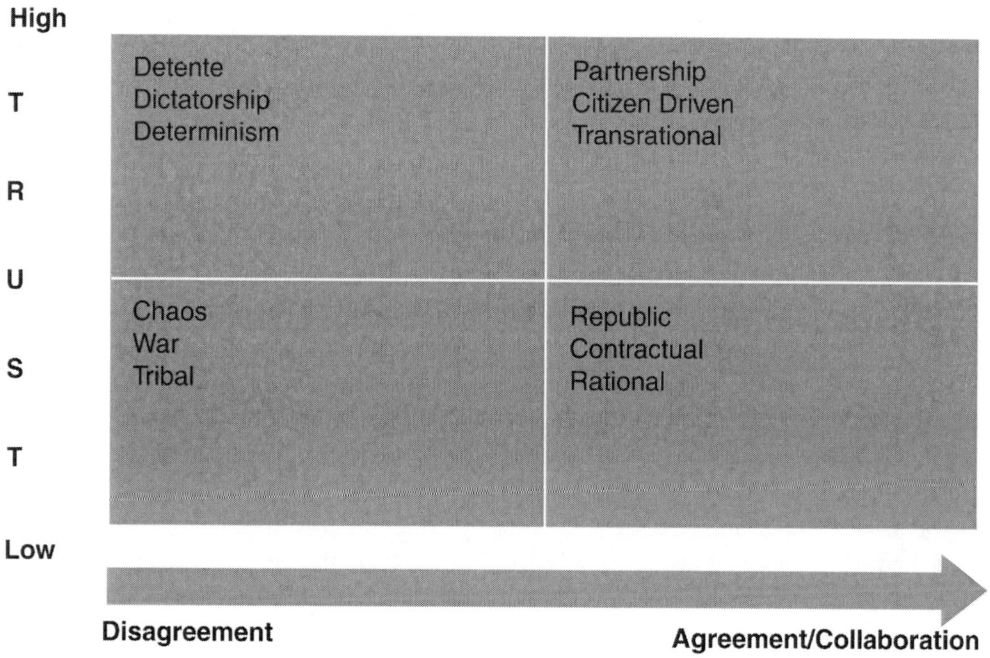

High

T

	Detente		Partnership
	Dictatorship		Citizen Driven
	Determinism		Transrational

R

U

S

	Chaos		Republic
	War		Contractual
	Tribal		Rational

T

Low

Disagreement   **Agreement/Collaboration**

expecting something to happen with no evidence that it will happen, and/or trying to pretend we know something we don't know. It is built on an upset, which is a thwarted expectation—the expectation that something should happen a certain way, we should know something we don't know, and/or we should be committed to something, but we are not. Complaints are a result of a poorly articulated or unspoken promise and result in either meaningless performance or confused performance. A partnership is a structure to manage agreements and commitments about future possibilities, legally and effectively. It requires a highly institutionalized level of management, commitment, responsibility, and accountability.

Disagreement is often the starting point of the collaboration process. One thing that is common in all partnerships that don't work is a managed disagreement/distrust based on broken agreements; i.e., a disagreement/distrust. Similar to Holzer and Gabrielian's remedy for pathological bureaucracies (1998, p. 85), when we address broken agreements, we have the availability of a new agreement, therefore, a partnership and the opportunity for progress. We know we are in a distrust relationship—a disagreement—when what we experience is an undelivered, thwarted, and/or undeveloped array of agreements: a broken agreement. We remedy this by identifying and communicating the broken agreement, and then by identifying something to agree on and managing the agreement. Disagreement becomes agreement when trust is more fully actualized, and is sufficiently able to create a new context with another; new partnerships, which can contain the meaning and purpose of the agreement. Again, trust plays a key role; a certain capacity for trust must be reached before we can actualize an agreement. This emphasizes the need, stated above, to address broken agreements if we are to entertain the possibility of a partnership. Lastly, trust and power are correlated in agreements (Huxham & Vangen 2005). Trust empowers each partner and the partnership as a whole. Trust grants and sustains the value of the other. Power is the ability to create, communicate, and maintain synergetic value that allows for growth and development; it is an ability to discern, communicate, and act decisively on these synergies.

The importance of agreement creation and management in Partnership Governance is a central concept regarding the Agreement-Management-Commitment-Accountability Collaboration Model (Figure 1.11). This model describes key capacity domains/dialectic fields of public collaboration/partnership management. Effective professionals master a skill set that generates, maintains, and forges agreements, management, and commitments, as a result of collaborative processes, that form and sustain partnerships. Consequently, mastery in public management is identifying, creating, and sustaining public partnerships.

A UNIVERSAL STRUCTURE OF PARTNERSHIPS: AGREEMENTS-MANAGEMENT-COMMITMENT-ACCOUNTABILITY DOMAINS

As stated above, partnerships are based on an Agreement Model (Figure 1.12). They are whole partnerships, uniting 'wholeparts' into new capacities. An agreement is the heart of a partnership, and certainly the foundational step (Grossman 2008; Huxham & Vangen 2005). Agreements are the basic outcomes of successful collaboration. The management of agreement determines the depth and significance of the partnership, and commitment determines its longevity. Agreements, like partnerships, disintegrate into their constituent parts when they are not managed and have poorly articulated commitments. Furthermore, the dialectic of agreements is trust and power as described above.

There is something formal about partnerships; something contractual that supports the need for well-articulated purpose, agreements, and expectations. For example, a PPP is a *formal agreement* between a public agency (federal, state, or local) and a private (sector) entity (Forrer et al. 2010). However, public–private discussions, relationships, or planning processes, as important as these activities are, are not partnerships (they are relationships) unless an agreement, like a contract, is explicitly articulated and managed. As stated above, partnership agreements are not only transactional but also transformational simultaneously. Accountability extends not just to outputs, but also to outcomes that must be managed over long periods of time. The partnership agreement is based on a promise between two or more actors with a distinct "What by when formula"; i.e., exactly what will be done and by exactly when. The formula requires management. All contracts may not be partnerships, but all partnerships are contracts based on this promise-performance formula.

Within each partnership variation there are two consistent, complementary themes: 1) enhanced capability through collaboration (Axelrod 1984; MacDonald, Stokes, & Blumenthal 2010; Navarro-Espigares & Martín-Segura 2011; Silvestre & de Araújo 2012) and 2) an imperative of trust as it reduces the risk of uncertainty (Edelenbos & Klijn 2007; Getha-Taylor 2012; Linden 2010). There is a need for those involved in management, as in almost all forms of Partnership Governance, to approach cooperation (Alchian & Demsetz 1972) and trust as necessary skills and to become bridges between government (the public sector) and the private sector. Not just bridges, but also partnerships, managed partnerships—formal collaborations. This requires the managers of partnerships, especially PPPs, to walk a tightrope between the public accountabilities associated with the public sector and the entrepreneurship associated with the private sector. Fundamentally, partnerships are created to implement what either part/sector cannot do on its own, thus lowering the risk of societal investments. In general, this describes the purpose of Partnership Governance.

Partnership administration is a **multisectoral expertise that bridges business, government, planning, and community development knowledge and skills to solve public problems.** Governance in a public/private structure raises critical opportunities regarding management that form a hybrid of both public and private technologies, democratic representation, accountability, transparency, and responsiveness. The attributes of entrepreneurship (innovation, leadership, and the management of community/collective assets) also characterize the purpose of public–private partnerships. These partnerships tend to have direct social and economic impacts at the local and sublocal government levels. Whether the PPP is legally formed as a contract, municipal commission, quasi-governmental public authority, nonprofit, or other entity, its management oversees the day-to-day operation of specially designated entities, formulates their budgets, and determines strategies for success.

It is intuitive that partnerships by their nature are formed by, and require, not only cooperation, but also collaboration. They are dialogue and participation driven. The process of arriving at consensus-oriented agreements, as well as the mutual qualitative imperative, requires skillful collaboration from management of the partnership. Cooperation establishes new modes of interaction and mutuality but retains independence, recognizing that multiple inputs can produce more together than each alone. Collaboration causes new partnerships through fusion or communion and the functional networks of society as a new interdependent policy. Partnerships are a result of a policy to collaborate, to be multilateral rather than unilateral. For example: In successful PPPs, we see this process implemented either of a new organization that integrates existing organizations or stakeholders under one umbrella organization or in the creation of a new umbrella organization. Partnerships create new whole capacities and organizations. We see new leadership emerge and existing leadership evolve to embrace all parts of the partnership. Hickman and Sorenson allude to this embrace in their book *The Power of Invisible Leadership*. A partnership, as a whole, creates an "invisible leadership . . . in which common purpose, rather than any particular individual . . . inspires leaders and followers to take action on its behalf" (Hickman & Sorenson 2013, p. 1). A partnership changes the behavior of its constituent parts completely. It embraces disparate rational elements under a transrational umbrella (Schlechty & Whitford 1988). Partnerships, because they develop and envelop, change the meaning of things: our thoughts, behaviors, and actions. Difficulty arises when the new organization erodes the partnership and is not inclusive, collaborative, and synthesizing. It develops but does not envelop or vice versa. If that happens, either it takes on the unintended role of a subdepartment of the primary actor or it acts as a single-issue advocate competing with other self-identified agencies, thereby violating the premise of the collaboration. Essentially, the partnership ends.

The Agreement-Management-Commitment-Accountability Partnership Model describes the collaboration process that causes partnerships (see Figure 1.10a). It is a model of the key domains and dialectics of collaboration that engender partnering and are necessary for the emergence and success of a partnership. Domains are fields of competency evolving from Agreement to Management to Commitment to Accountability. They are the dialectic skill areas that must be mastered. The model depicts the attributes of collaboration, not the partners of a partnership. The result of the collaboration process (Figures 1.10a and 1.10b) is an organizational partnership (Figure 1.10c). It is the fully articulated collaboration process that allows for a partnership. The domains/dialectics in the model (Figure 1.11) tell us a partnership is present or emerging.

Ken Wilber (2000) points out those partnerships (i.e., holons) can become pathological and dissemble when they, arrogantly, determine they are not a WholePart, but only a whole or only a part. They become 'arrogant' when they determine they are the *only* whole thing or the *only* part of importance in existence, or the most superior whole or part that exists. It is pathological because there is no such thing as a whole that is also not a part, or a part that is also not a whole. There are only *WholeParts*. As to pathological partnerships, everything else then is not a whole partnership, but only a part to be dominated by the pathological partnership. David Booher (2004), describing inauthentic collaborations, which are basically pathological partnerships based on disagreement models, warns us of the telltale sign of pathological partnerships. Holzer and Gabrielian (1998), commenting on the pathology of public bureaucracies, warn us about the nature of partnership pathology, noting that "bureaucracies can be run by fear, but at a very low level of production" (p. 85). Fear-based pathology is recognizable in all inauthentic partnerships. They further state: "One means

Figure 1.10a   **Domains of Agreement-Management-Commitment Partnership Model: Fields and Field Attributes of the Partnership Model**

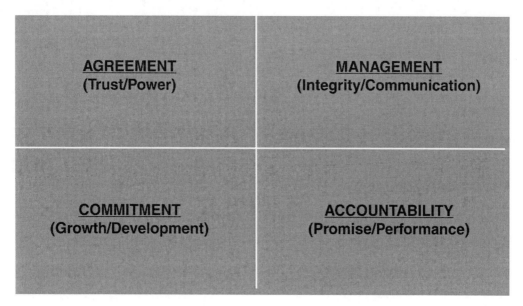

of overcoming such pathologies is joint management—workforce cooperation" (ibid.), which forms partnerships but indicates that management must acquire appropriate skills. "To be authentic requires the appropriate organization, methods, and tools; facilitative leadership; and deliberative space free of coercion" (Booher 2004, p. 44). Pathological partnerships are *domination partnerships* based on force. Healthy partnerships are *actualization partnerships* based on maximizing the partnerships' potentials (Wilber 2000, pp. 30–1), as described in Figure 1.10c—the partnership as a whole and all it constituent parts. This is true on a hierarchical basis ("the one dominating the many" [Wilber 2000, p. 32]) and on a heterarchical basis ("the many dominating the one" [ibid.]). The cure for pathological partnerships is actualization partnerships. In practice, this is accomplished by using the Agreement-Management-Commitment-Accountability Partnership Model described in Figure 1.10a, which resembles a complete actualizing partnership, in which collaboration is an outcome or product.

This model indicates that partnerships tend to have a beginning, a middle, and an end and are built on an Agreement rather than a Disagreement Model. When the agreements erode into disagreement, or simply are completed, the partnership is no longer relevant. The traditional way of addressing community and economic development needs has been by either providing money for a project or identifying some singular need or problem and organizing an effort to meet it or resolve it. This is a fix-it model, well suited when something is actually broken but poorly suited when the problems in a community have to do with enhancing the systemic organizational aspects of the community. Partnerships have arisen as another way to strengthen and broaden unity and possibility within a community. Partnerships develop out of the recognition that there is greater

Figure 1.10b **Collaboration Emerges out of the Model**

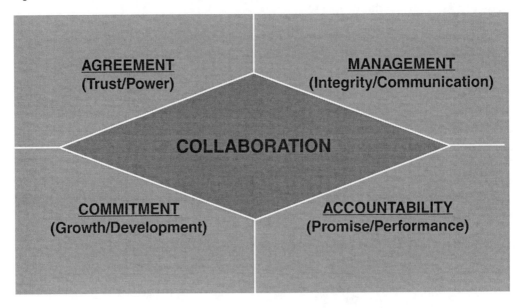

Figure 1.10c **Partnership Develops and Embraces Collaboration**

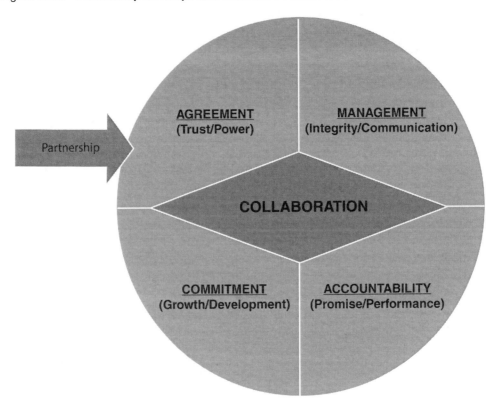

power available in communities through their neighborhoods, towns, business organizations, and corporations than the people involved often realize. This collective power resides in the relational purpose expressed and acted on as a functioning and real dialogue between community stakeholders that works to invent and implement a positive future rather than attempting solely to fix something from the past. When we see this model, we know a partnership is in action.

PARTNERSHIP: AGREEMENT–MANAGEMENT–COMMITMENT–ACCOUNTABILITY MATRIX

1. *Agreement*—on identification, goals, values, and assets common to all
2. *Management*—having professional and specified management capability for the agreement
3. *Commitment*—reliable and sufficient source of funds/resources
4. *Accountability*—based on a promise-performance axiom: what by when. (i.e., *what* will be accomplished and *when* it will be accomplished in the future). Both should be as articulate and exact as possible.

1. *Agreement*—Successful collaborations work on agreements, not disagreements. (These agreements are the values and assets of the partnership.)
2. *Management*—Agreements are maintained through professional management; therefore, management is the key to successful collaboration.
3. *Commitment*—Success is achieved when collaborations, as partnerships, are committed to accomplishing their agreements. Commitment is an absolute and equitable contribution of resources by stakeholders in an ongoing manner; that is, over time. This enables accountability.
4. *Accountability*—Accountability is always a public phenomenon. As collaboration generates partnerships, accountability organizes the results of the partnership. Partnerships provide a big enough accountability for transformation. The promise-performance axiom that is the dialectic of Accountability, literally what the partnership can be counted on to do, states that it requires a promise to accurately perform, i.e., there is no truly meaningful performance without a promise. A promise states *what* will be done (agreement) and *by when* (management). A promise, therefore, has an articulate *what by when* formula. It's a statement of integrity that provides agreed-upon and measurable standards for performance and unites individuals to accomplish goals. The promise does not fix past problems but is designed to envision a clear and real future for the partnership to act and measure success. Without it, we are dealing in fantasy and magic rather than reality and understanding.

A Disagreement Model (the left side of Table 1.1) is: Disagreement-Management-Compromise-Ad hoc. This indicates that disagreements are also deliberate and managed systems. This model may have its uses, but it has different purposes and outcomes than an Agreement Model. We can expect to find little evidence of innovation or entrepreneurship because disagreements imply that a direction for the community has not been

Table 1.1

Agreement–Management–Commitment–Accountability Trust Matrix

	LOW	(*TRUST*)	HIGH
AGREEMENT	Instant Gratification Output-only orientation Adversarial. Dichotomous		Real Change Outcome Orientation Partnership
MANAGEMENT	Ad hoc/ Proxy Manipulative Exclusive Miscommunication		Professionalism Transparent Inclusive Communication
COMMITMENT	Deception Compromise Incompletion Short-lived		Commitment Collaboration Action Longevity
ACCOUNTABLITY	Disagreement Confusion Low-performance No measurement		Promises Clarity High-performance Balanced measurement

obtained or desired. On the other hand, communities that put their plans into action and achieve results have discovered something important about partnering. They discovered agreements and how to manage them with a sustainable commitment to reach a well-defined objective. A commitment is credible not because people are motivated to keep it, but because institutional or structural arrangements compel their compliance.

Where we put our attention has a lot to do with perceptions and attitudes but also extends to an ability to get something accomplished. When attention is on disagreement, exclusionary experiences occur that, at best, result in a compromised effort rather than cooperative progress toward identified and needed goals. The *attention* of disagreements is on the individual. The attention of agreements is on the community or partnership. Disagreements are distinguished by the presence of competing monologues; agreements by dialogue.

Agreements are different. In discussing how social reality is constructed, Searle (1995) pointed out, "[T]here are portions of the real world, objective facts in the world that are only facts by human agreement" (pp. 1–2). If our attention were focused on community agreements, the community in which all the individuals or subgroups participate, an inclusionary experience would occur. Disagreements are concerned with an individual's, or a single group's, idea of self. Miller and Illiash (2002) observed that "the more humans agree, the more institutional facts they accept, and, therefore, the more reality humans perceive" (p. 95). Agreements, like partnerships, broker a broader concern about how the entire community envisions itself, consequently, what it is willing to support. This vision is not arrived at by compromise because compromise implies giving something up. The vision is arrived at through creativity, dialogue, and the building of consensus, which implies expanding, embracing, and growing capabilities aligned with transformation and entrepreneurship.

Disagreements and agreements are not accidental. They are managed. To endure over time, each has to be maintained by a partnership structure. Sometimes, the structures are apparent and institutionalized and sometimes they are less visible. Nonetheless, it is not just a matter of agreeing or disagreeing or only the focus of our attitudes or attention that makes things happen or not happen. What matters is the structure that manages what we experience.

This still does not completely explain why something progresses or why something is accomplished or effective over time. There can be agreement and management, but there is one additional ingredient necessary to obtain positive results. That ingredient is commitment; i.e., the commitment of funds or other capital resources. Money and commitment are inseparable concepts in our culture. Where we put our money and other resources is directly linked to the commitment we have to make things happen. This is something widely observed in public administration. This correctly implies that commitment is a public attribute, not a private matter, furthering the public intention of partnerships as the foundational building blocks of society. Partnerships occur in a partnership hierarchy. Deeper, more encompassing, organizational levels are reached when whole/parts (partnerships) collaborate with other whole/parts (partnerships) and become new emergent partnerships.

PARTNERSHIPS, PRAGMATISM, AND PUBLIC MANAGEMENT: THE PUBLIC–PRIVATE PARTNERSHIP CHALLENGE

When Edelenbos and Klijn state that "[a] PPP . . . is based on the idea of mutual added value" (2007, p. 27), this is true of all partnerships and defines their purpose: to add value to each part, which value is conveyed by the partnership, not by the parts. Due to costs, implementation, and maintenance, providing for societal needs and protecting individual and community investments can be a risky business. A proven method of reducing risk is to unite disparate forces, put the best partners together, utilize the strength of diversity to reduce the weakness of specialization, and build a new and more effective entity through partnerships (Holzer & Gabrielian 1996). This is the challenge of our time. This is the challenge of government. Partnership Governance is the field of this endeavor. It describes collaborative action rather than only regulatory activities of government. Both are needed and "an active partnership and active regulatory agency may well complement each other" (Lubell et al. 2002, p. 158). Collaboration, which is a fundamental operation of partnership, has almost as many definitions as partnership. Both, in pragmatic terms, can be described as systems of agreement management. Collaboration describes the process or construction of the system, and partnership defines the organization or boundary of the system. Often not addressed is that in each case neither succeeds when management is not central; both imply deliberate management. Partnership Governance tells us that a system of agreement management "emphasizes the collaborative nature of modern efforts to meet human needs, the widespread use of tools of action that engage complex networks of public and private actors, and the resulting need for a different style of public management, and a different type of public sector emphasizing collaboration and enablement rather than hierarchy and control" (Salamon 2002, p. vii). When partnerships are employed, it tells us that a society is assessing its needs from an innovative position, its points of reference have shifted, resources and assets have been redefined or newly discovered, and authority has been decentralized to identify suitable partners.

In their 2002 article on watershed partnerships, Lubell et al. underscore the innovative aspects of Partnership Governance and consequently the different style of change and asset administration that occurs when partnerships are employed by concluding that "partnerships emerge because of their comparative advantage over command-and-control institutions in responding to the increasingly acute, unresolved problems of . . . management," and reinforce the bond of management to Partnership Governance in resolving collective issues and conflicts associated with communal assets (2002, p. 159). Often the intention to partner may exist but is not sustainable as a result of poor management. Poor management often appears counterintuitive to common sense. Common sense indicates that one might expect partnering to occur in order to share and exploit commonalities if for no other reason than to promote cost savings and avoid "a tragedy of the commons" (Hardin 1968). However, tendencies to protect turf and authority often conflict with logical collaboration at all levels of government. That is, until a problem veers close to a real or perceived tragedy, the complete partnership model is often in place (Figure 1.11). Further, the separation of federal and local governments, although politically derived, may have the tendency to restrict logical collaboration and common purpose. This is because the uncommonness of common purpose is, frankly, not that uncommon, and the purposes of divisiveness over unification are more persuasive if perceived to be politically advantageous. In such settings, collaboration and partnership would be expected to be less available.

As stated above, an issue at hand that is not severe enough to compel a partnership is less favorable to the success of the partnership. Problem severity, problems not solved well by command-and-control policies, support partnerships because partnerships create new avenues of power and authority as well as an expanded nontraditional resource base. Partnerships are established when agreements about commonalities are clear and the cost of maintaining the partnership is not greater than the cost of maintaining the conflict (Hartley, Serensen, & Torfing 2013; Ostrom 1990). Despite politics, the reality is that in the field of management, partnerships occur quite regularly, and are a required management capacity. Let's be clear, due to the challenge of managing collective assets, the primary purpose of government, there is almost no action a government takes, all the way up and all the way down, that does not involve some type of explicit or implicit partnership. We can conclude that PPPs are the modern system of government. However, the term 'partnership' is not common, and in its place we have political or legalistic terminology. But it all looks like partnerships, and lately more so.

Partnerships between public-public agencies appear to be trending upward, particularly concerning shared service provision. This is due to an expanding sense of the middle class, whose interests, needs, and desires are changing not only the global/local economy, but also our sense of society. The cutting edge of Partnership Governance is not within government, but on its edges when public and private entities collaborate as PPPs. "Public–private partnerships have enjoyed a global resurgence and have become icons of modern public administration" (Hodge & Greve 2009, p. 33). This is propelling, more *and more,* a postmodern form of governance to the extent that a large segment of governmental public sector activity, from planning to policy and building to management, is conducted by PPPs. The nature of PPPs is also changing public-public partnerships because it is changing government. Much of the discussion in this book, therefore, is about PPPs, how they are managed, and how these partnerships are redefining our society.

By combining private and public resources and expertise with governmental powers, Partnership Governance provides an essential institutional framework for government to compete in a variety of markets and public arenas. Competition is, of course, not solely finance oriented, but also includes asset building, value enhancement processes, management technology transfer, and organizational development. It is noted that government partnerships, due to their variety, are referred to in a number of appropriate descriptive ways that retain the integrity of this complexity. Governmental partnerships, from a management rather than a process point of view, can be viewed as four basic types, although in practice, types may overlap and exhibit more than one of these attributes:

1. Politically (network-quasi-governmental)
2. Organizationally (PPP management corporation)
3. As a legal contract (project) between government and a private entity
4. Institutionally having governance status (subunit of government) (Figure 1.11)

Again, it is the PPPs that reveal the complexities of governmental partnerships. This is because partnerships by their nature are innovative devices, require flexibility, and as governmental actions would be considered *of but not in* government. Partnerships that are *of but not in* government are usually PPPs. Partnerships that are in and within government are usually public-public partnerships.

Planners and engineers tend to work in contractual, project-oriented PPPs in infrastructure and transportation. Public managers tend to concentrate on institutional, organizational, and network PPPs (Hodge & Greve 2009, p. 36). These types do overlap, such as Business Improvement Districts that have aspects of all four types (Figure 1.11). As a creature of the legislative process, they have political ramifications; as nonprofit or commission management corporations, they are functioning organizations; as agencies receiving public funds and dispensing public services, they are contractual; and as special district subunits of government, they have institutional status. This is why BIDs are a key focus in the study of PPPs and, consequently, Partnership Governance.

As stated earlier, we can find a number of descriptions of PPPs along the continuum of public–private partnering (Figure 1.12). Although this will be discussed further on, there is no one description, nor should there be, that fits all, due not only to the nature of partnership, but to the nature of the partners. Yet, there are four themes that tend to guide PPP descriptions:

- PPPs are managed along a continuum of public to private according to need.
- PPPs represent a hybrid, not a dichotomy.
- Hybrids, like PPPs, will contain some aspect of both parts in their operations.
- PPPs are designed to reduce financial, social, political, and technological risks.

"PPPs refer to a wide array of relationships between government entities and nonpublic actors." They "involve collaboration between at least one government entity and one or more nonpublic actors for the pursuit of public objectives" (Erie, Kogan, & MacKenzie 2010, p. 646). E. S. Savas defines PPPs "as any arrangement between government and the private sector in which partially or traditionally public activities are performed by the private sector" (2000, p. 4). But this broad statement instantly becomes limiting, as it seems only transactional and not intended to produce significant changes in the nature of governance or public management that true partnerships tend to produce, and it speaks chiefly, possibly only, to privatization aspects of PPPs. Barbara Gray, while discussing collaboration and dispute mediation, defined partnership as a new context for solving collective problems within which "parties who see different aspects of a

Figure 1.11   **Typology of Governmental Partnerships**

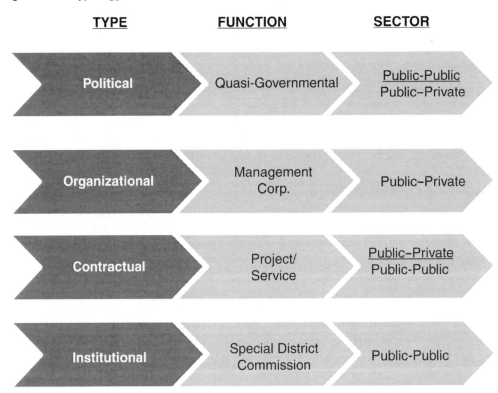

Figure 1.12   **Continuum of Public–Private Partnerships—Public + Private = 100%**

NOTE: Total partnership is always 100%. Public and private mix may be in any combination of percentages that equal 100%. Ex: 50/50; 60/40; 70/30; 80/20; 90/10. In each case, the combination equals the complete partnership.

problem can constructively explore their differences and search for solutions that go beyond their own limited vision of what is possible" (1989, p. 5). Edelenbos and Klijn describe PPPs in a more contractual way: "as cooperation between public and private actors with a durable character in which actors develop mutual products and/or services and in which risk, costs and benefits are shared" (2007, p. 27).

CONCLUSION

In the 21st century, Partnership Governance provides a unique perspective on the collaborative and network aspects of public management. The advancement of this field, as a concept and a practice, is a consequence of the New Public Management of the late 20th century, globalization pressures, the current New Public Governance (NPG) movement, and the advent of a more strategic rather than bureaucratic state. Today, partnering is the new governance and it continues to evolve particularly to address new trust environments due to social/economic changes. The term 'Partnership Governance' is applicable to these phenomena but is prey to thinking in parts rather than the whole of the partnership. And this devaluation, as the field maneuvers across sectors, is hermeneutically abstract, but we have attempted to pin down a universally accepted definition. If we do not embrace the whole partnership, rather than only the parts, as a new and complete phenomenon, then our assessment of partnering in the evolution of democracies is less substantial. Consequently, we experience a loss of trust. Throughout the world, PPPs have emerged at the local level of government and uniquely as Business Improvement Districts challenging many of our ideas about Partnership Governance. They have received some careful scrutiny in the past twelve years because they provide insights about the challenges of modern government, which in large part drill down to trust and partnership building. They also reveal the complexities of partnering and, therefore, effective methods of performance measurement. An effective approach to addressing the gap in performance criteria in the field of Partnership Governance is to use an integrated balanced approach. In essence, it's about the partnership.

KEY POINTS

- New Public Management (NPM), an inner examination of government, has ignited an outward examination of governance: New Public Governance (NPG). This governance is concerned with skills and technology of collaboration and partnerships.
- Partnerships are reexamined as pragmatic functional aspects of collaboration, and are both manageable and measurable. They require new approaches and new skill sets for public managers.
- Partnerships are WholeParts, or 'holons': more a transrational than simply rational approach to problem solving.
- Partnerships are not only an accumulation of parts, but whole synergistic entities. This is important because partnerships solve problems, are entrepreneurial and innovative, and are designed to reduce risk by providing encompassing new contextual organizations.
- Partnerships tend to be more horizontal, but also embrace vertical management structures.
- Collaboration and network theories are enhanced by partnership and partnership management theories.
- 'Publicization' is a functional outcome of Partnership Governance.
- Partnerships become partnerships through a process of implementing a four-part matrix: Agreement, Management, Commitment, and Accountability. This is an 'agreement system.'
- Agreement systems are more collaborative, performance oriented, and inclusive, utilize supportive competition, and are context oriented.
- Trust and social capital are real factors in partnership success, and therefore also of the four-part matrix.

REFERENCES

Agranoff, Robert (2006). Inside Collaborative Networks: Ten Lessons for Public Managers, Special issue, *Public Administration Review*, Vol. 66, pp. 56–65.

Agranoff, Robert (2011). Federalist No. 44: What Is the Role of Intergovernmental Relations in Federalism? *Public Administration Review*, Vol. 71, Suppl. 1, pp. S68–S77.

Agranoff, Robert & M.C. McGuire (2003). *Collaborative Public Management: Strategies for Local Governments*, Washington DC: Georgetown University Press.

Alchian, Arnen A. & Harold Demsetz (1972). Production, Information Costs, and Economic Organization, *American Economic Review*, Vol. 62, pp. 777–795.

Allison, Graham T. (2004). *Public and Private Management: Are They Fundamentally Alike in All Unimportant Respects?* Classics of Public Administration, 5th ed., Belmont, CA: Wadsworth/ Thompson Learning.

Axelrod, R. (1984). *The Evolution of Cooperation*, New York: Basic Books.

Bardach, E. (1998). *Getting Agencies to Work Together: The Practice and Theory of Managerial Craftsmanship*, Washington DC: Brookings Institution Press.

Becker, F. & V. Patterson (2005). Public–Private Partnerships: Balancing Financial Returns, Risks, and Roles of Partners, *Public Performance and Management Review*, Vol. 29, pp. 125–144.

Blessett, Brandi, Mohamad G. Alkadry, & Nadia Rubaii (2013) Management and Governance: 21st Century Implications for Diversity in Public Administration, *Public Administration Quarterly*, Vol. 37, No. 3, pp. 302–305.

Booher, David (2004). Collaborative Governance: Emerging Patterns and Democracy, *National Civic Review*, Vol. 93–4, pp. 32–46.

Bozeman, B. (1987). *All Organizations Are Public: Comparing Public and Private Organizations*, San Francisco: Jossey-Bass.

Brinkerhoff, D. W. & J. M. Brinkerhoff (2011). Public–Private Partnerships: Perspectives on Purposes, Publicness, and Good Governance, *Public Administration & Development*, Vol. 31, No. 1, pp. 2–14.

Bryson, John M., Barbara C. Crosby, & Melissa Middleton Stone (2006). The Design and Implementation of Cross-Sector Collaboration: Propositions from the Literature, Special issue, *Public Administration Review*, Vol. 66, pp. 44–55.

Carroll, P. & P. Steane (2000). Public–Private Partnerships: Sectoral Perspectives. In S. Osbourne (ed.), *Public–Private Partnerships: Theory & Practice in International Perspective*, New York: Routledge, pp. 36–56.

Chandler, Ralph Clark (1998). *Handbook of Public Administration, Public Administration Pedagogy: Another Look at Evolutionary Paradigms in Theory and Practice*, New York: Marcel Dekker, pp. 743–776.

Cousin, Victor (1854). *The True, the Beautiful, and the Good*. New York: D. Appleton & Co.

Darwin, Charles (1859). *On the Origin of Species by Means of Natural Selection, or the Preservation of Favoured Races in the Struggle for Life*, London: John Murray.

Denhardt, Robert (1993). *The Pursuit of Significance: Strategies for Managerial Success in Public Organizations*, Belmont, CA: Wadsworth Publishing Co.

Edelenbos, Jurian & Erik-Hans Klijn (2007). Trust in Complex Decision-Making Networks: A Theoretical and Empirical Exploration, *Administration and Society*, Vol. 39, No. 1, pp. 25–50.

Erie, Steven P., Vladimir Kogan, & Scott A. MacKenzie (2010). Redevelopment, San Diego: The Limits of Public–Private Partnerships, *Urban Affairs Review*, Vol. 45, No. 5, pp. 644–678.

Forrer, John, James Edwin Kee, Kathryn E. Newcomer, & Eric Boyer (2010). Public–Private Partnership and the Public Accountability Question, *Public Administration Review*, Vol. 70, No. 3, pp. 475–484.

Fredrickson, H. George (1971). Toward a New Public Administration. In F. Marini (ed.), *Toward a New Public Administration*, San Francisco: Chandler, pp. 309–331.

Fredrickson, H. George (1999). The Repositioning of American Public Administration, *PS: Political Science and Politics*, Vol. 32, No. 4, pp. 701–711.

Fredrickson, H. George (2012). Theories of Governance. In H. George Fredrickson, Kevin Smith, & Christopher W. Larimer (eds.), *The Public Administration Theory Primer*, 2nd ed., Boulder, CO: Westview Press, pp. 219–244.

Fry, B. R. & Nigro, L. G. (1998). Five great issues in the professionalism of public administration. (RHM Eds.), *Handbook of Public Administration* (2nd Ed), (pp. 1163–1208). Marcel Dekker, New York, NY.

Fukuyama, F. (1995). *Trust*, New York: Free Press.

Getha-Taylor, Heather (2012). Cross-Sector Understanding and Trust, *Public Performance & Management Review*, Vol. 36, No. 2, pp. 216–229.

Golembiewski, R. T. (1977). *Public Administration as a Developing Discipline*, New York: Marcel Dekker.

Golembiewski, R. T. & M. McConkie (1975). The Centrality of Interpersonal Trust in Group Processes. In C. L. Cooper (ed.), *Theories of Group Processes*, New York: Wiley, pp. 131–185.

Gray, Barbara (1989). *Collaborating: Finding Common Ground for Multiparty Problems*, San Francisco: Jossey-Bass.

Grossman, Seth A. (2008). *The Role of Entrepreneurship in Public–Private Partnerships: The Case of Business Improvement Districts*, PhD dissertation, Rutgers, The State University of New Jersey, School of Public Affairs & Administration, Newark, NJ.

Grossman, Seth A. (2010). Reconceptualizing the Public Management and Performance of Business Improvement Districts, *Public Performance & Management Review*, Vol. 33, No. 3, pp. 361–394.

Grossman, Seth A. (2012). The Management and Measurement of Public–Private Partnerships: Toward an Integral and Balanced Approach, *Public Performance & Management Review*, June 2012, Vol. 35, No. 4, pp. 595–616.

Gulick, Luther (1937). Notes on the Theory of Organization. In Shafritz and Hyde, *Classics of Public Administration*, New York Institute of Public Administration, pp. 3–13.

Hardin, Garrett (1968). Tragedy of the Commons, *Science #13*, Vol. 162, pp. 1243–1248.

Hartley, Jean, Eva Serensen, & Jacob Torfing (2013). Collaborative Innovation: A Viable Alternative to Market Competition and Organizational Entrepreneurship, *Public Administration Review*, Vol. 73, No. 6, pp. 821–830.

Heidegger, Martin (1927/1992). *History of the Concept of Time: Prolegomena*, Bloomington: Indiana University Press.

Hickman, Gill Robinson & Georgia J. Sorenson (2013). *The Power of Invisible Leadership: How Compelling Common Purpose Inspires Exceptional Leadership*, Thousand Oaks: CA: Sage Publications.

Himmelman, A. (1996). On the Theory and Practice of Transformational Collaboration: From Social Science to Social Justice. In C. Huxham (ed.), *Creating Collaborative Advantage*, London: Sage, pp. 19–43.

Hodge, G. A. & Greve, C. (2007). Public–Private Partnerships: An International Performance Review, *Public Administration Review*, Vol. 67, pp. 545–558.

Hodge, Graeme & Carsten Greve (2009). *PPPs: The Passage of Time Permits a Sober Reflection*, Institute of Economic Affairs, Oxford: Blackwell Publishing, pp. 33–38.

Holzer, Marc & Vatche Gabrielian (1996). *Cases in Productive Public Management*, Burke, VA: Chatelaine Press.

Holzer, Marc & Vatche Gabrielian (1998). Five Great Ideas in American Public Administration. In *Handbook of Public Administration*, New York: Marcel Dekker.

Huxham, C. (ed.) (1996). *Creating Collaborative Advantage*, London: Sage.

Huxham, C. (2000). The Challenge of Collaborative Governance, *Public Management*, Vol. 2–3, pp. 337–357.

Huxham, Chris & Siv Vangen (2005). *Managing to Collaborate*, New York: Routledge.

Kincaid, John & Carl W. Stenberg (2011). "Big Questions" about Intergovernmental Relations and Management: Who Will Address Them? *Public Administration Review*, Vol. 71, No. 2, pp. 196–202.

Koestler, Arthur (1967). *The Ghost in the Machine*, London: Hutchinson.

Kooiman, J. (1993). Socio-Political Governance: Introduction. In J. Kooiman (ed.), *Modern Governance: New Government-Society Interactions*, London: SAGE.

Kooiman, J. (2000). Societal Governance: Levels, Modes & Orders of Socio-Political Interaction. In J. Pierre (ed.), *Debating Governance*, Oxford: Oxford University Press.

Kooiman, J. (2003). *Governing as Governance*, London: SAGE.

Kort, Michiel & Erik-Hans Klijn (2011). Public–Private Partnerships in Urban Regeneration Projects: Organizational Form or Managerial Capacity? *Public Administration Review*, Vol. 71, No. 4, pp. 618–626.

Lee, Myungsuk (2003). *Conceptualizing the New Governance: A New Institution of Social Coordination*. Presented at the Institutional and Development Mini-Conference, May 3–5, Workshop in Political Theory and Policy Analysis, Indiana University, Bloomington.

Light, Paul C. (1997). *The Tides of Reform*, New Haven, CT: Yale University Press.

Linden, R. M. (2010). *Leading Across Boundaries: Creating Collaborative Agencies in a Networked World*, San Francisco: Jossey-Bass.

Linder, Stephen M. (1999). Coming to Terms with the Public–Private Partnership: A Grammar of Multiple Meanings. *American Behavioural Scientist*, Vol. 43, No. 1, pp. 35–51.

Lowndes, V. & C. Skelcher (1998). The Dynamics of Multi-Organizational Partnerships: An Analysis of Changing Modes of Governance, *Public Administration Review*, Vol. 73, pp. 313–333.

Lubell, Mark, Mark Schneider, John T. Scholz, & Mifriye Mete (2002). Watershed Partnerships and the Emergence of Collective Action Institutions, *American Journal of Political Science*, Vol. 46, No. 1, pp. 148–163.

MacDonald, John M., Robert Stokes, & Ricky Blumenthal (2010). The Role of Community Context in Business District Revitalization Strategies, *Public Performance & Management Review*, Vol. 33, No. 3, pp. 439–458.

Mauldin, Marcus (2012). A New Governance Explanation for the Creation of Minority Economic Development Public–Private Partnership in Florida. In *Public Performance and Management Review*, Armonk, NY: M. E. Sharpe, pp. 679–695.

Mendel, Stuart C. & Jeffrey L. Brudney (2012). Putting the NP into PP: The Role of Nonprofit Organizations in Public–Private Partnerships, *Public Performance & Management Review*, Vol. 35, No. 4, p. 617–642.

Miller, Gerald J., Justice, Jonathan B. & Illiash, Iryna (2002). Practice as Interpretation. In *Kahn and Hildreth's Budget Theory*. Newark, NJ: Rutgers University.

Moe, Terry M. (1984). The New Economics of Organization, *American Journal of Political Science*, Vol. 28, pp. 739–777.

Morse, Ricardo S. (2010) Bill Gibson and the Art of Leading Across Boundaries, *Public Administration Review*, Vol. 70, No. 3, pp. 434–442.

Navarro-Espigares, J. L. & J. A. Martín-Segura (2011). Public–Private Partnership and Regional Productivity in the UK, *Service Industries Journal*, Vol. 31, pp. 559–580.

O'Leary, Rosemary & Nidhi Vij (2012). Collaborative Public Management: Where Have We Been and Where Are We Going? *The American Review of Public Administration*, Vol. 42, pp. 507–522.

Osborne, D. & T. Gaebler (1992). *Reinventing Government*, Reading, MA: Addison-Wesley Publishing Co.

Ostrom, Elinor (1990). *Governing the Commons*, New York: Cambridge University Press.

Ostrom, V. & E. Ostrom (1971). Public Choice: A Different Approach to the Study of Public Administration, *Public Administration Review*, Vol. 31, pp. 203–216.

Policy Consensus Initiative (2005). *What Is Collaborative Governance?* http://www.policyconsensus.org/publicsolutions/ps_2.html [accessed January 17, 2014].

Pressman, Jeffrey L. & Aaron Wildavsky (1973). *Implementation*, Berkeley: University of California Press.

Purdy, Jill M. (2012). A Framework for Assessing Power in Collaborative Governance Processes, *Public Administration Review*, Vol. 72, No. 3, pp. 409–417.

Putnam, Robert D. (1993). The Prosperous Community: Social Capital and Public Life, *America Prospect*, Vol. 13, pp. 35–42.

Raadschelders, Jos C. & M. Rutgers (1999). The Waxing and Waning of the State and Its Study: Changes and Challenges in the Study of Public Administration. In Walter J. Kickert & Richard J. Stillman II (eds.), *The Modern State and Its Study. New Administrative Sciences in a Changing Europe and United States*, pp. 17–35.

Rhodes, R.A.W. (1996, September). The New Governance: Governing Without Government, *Political Studies*, Vol. 44, No. 4, pp. 652–667.

Salamon, L. M. (ed.) (2002). *The Tools of Government: A Guide to the New Governance*, New York: Oxford University Press.

Saranson, M. (1972). *The Creation of Settings and Future Societies*, San Francisco: Jossey-Bass.

Savas, E. S. (2000). *Privatization and Public–Private Partnerships*, New York: Seven Bridges Press.

Schlechty, P. C. & B. L. Whitford (1988). Shared Problems and Shared Vision: Organic Collaboration. In K. A. Sirotnik & J. I. Goodlad (eds.), *School-University Partnerships in Action: Concepts, Cases, and Concerns*, New York: Teachers College Press.

Schutz, Alfred (1966). The Problem with Intersubjectivity in Husserl. In *Collected Papers*, Vol. 3, pp. 51–83. The Hague: Matinus Nijhoff.

Searle, J. R. (1995). *The Construction of Social Reality*, New York: The Free Press.

Silvestre, H. C. & de Araújo, J.F.F E. (2012). Public–Private Partnerships/Private Finance Initiatives in Portugal, *Public Performance & Management Review*, Vol. 36, No. 2, pp. 316–339.

Simon, Herbert A. (1997). *Administrative Behavior*, 4th ed., New York: The Free Press.

Sirianni, Carmen (2009). *Investing in Democracy: Engaging in Collaborative Government*. Washington DC: Brookings Institution Press.

Stoker, Gerry (1998). *Governance as Theory: Five Propositions*, ISSJ 155/1998, UNESCO, Oxford: Blackwell Publishing, pp. 17–28.

Svara, J. H. (1985). Dichotomy and Duality: Reconceptualizing the Relationship between Policy and Administration in Council-Manager Cities, *Public Administration Review*, Vol. 45, pp. 221–232.

Taylor, F. (1911). *The Principles of Scientific Management*, Norton: New York.

Uveges, Joseph A. & F. Keller Lawrence (1998). One Hundred Years of American Public Administration and Counting: Moving into a Second Century in the Study and Practice of Public Management in American Life. In *Handbook of Public Administration*, New York: Marcel Dekker.

Velotti, Lucia, Antonio Botti, & Massiliano Vesci (2012). Public–Private Partnerships and Network Governance: What Are the Challenges? *Public Performance and Management Review*, pp. 340–365.

Vernon, Raymond, Debora L. Spar, & Glenn Tobin (1991). *Iron Triangles and Revolving Doors: Cases in US Foreign Economic Policymaking*, Westport, CT: Praeger Publishers.

Waldo, Dwight (1948). *The Administrative State*. New York: Ronald.

Waldo, Dwight (1964). *Comparative Public Administration: Prologue, Promise, Problems*. Comparative Public Administration Special Series No. 2, Washington DC: American Society of Public Administrators.

Wilber, Ken (2000). *A Theory of Everything*, Boston, MA: Shambhala Publications.

William, D. G. (1994). *Applying Public Management Concepts to Ourselves: Accreditation Under the New Master Degree Minimum Standards*, Washington DC: National Association of Schools of Public Affairs and Administration.

Wilson, Woodrow (1887). The Study of Administration, *Political Science Quarterly*, Reprinted in Shafritz, J, and Hyde, A (1997) *Classics of Public Administration*, 2nd edn, Chicago: Dorsey Press.

2

Trust in Partnership Development

In Chapter 1, Table 1.1 displays the function of trust in the Agreement-Management-Commitment-Accountability Partnership Model and explains how collaborative systems can be based on agreement and disagreement. Each system has its consequences. Agreement systems are more collaborative, performance oriented, and inclusive, utilize supportive competition, and are context oriented. Disagreement systems are derivative of agreement systems, attenuate agreements, utilize adverse competition, and are more compromising, ad hoc, and content oriented. It is the partnership model that corresponds to New Public Governance and the function of partnerships. We can't understand collaboration, let alone partnerships, without acknowledging the fundamental function of trust in these relationships. Partnerships, as well as collaboration and indeed governance, are unfocused without a thorough understanding of the fundamental and pervasive function of trust in these relationships (Barrett, Austin, & McCarthy 2000; Fukuyama 1995; Getha-Taylor 2012). A focus that has been building in recent times since Robert Putnam's works on the importance of and threats to social capital (1993, 2000) may reasonably be considered the same concern by Woodrow Wilson (1887) regarding the politics/administration dichotomy (or, as we see it, partnership), which he clearly indicates if unattended to can effectively erode trust and, therefore, the successful functioning of public administration.

This concern is at the heart of the New Public Governance because it is at the heart of a successful democratic society. Trust is not only a human behavior, but also a recursive social function. It is returned to and takes on new meanings and presentations with every generation. It marks the human condition and grows as we grow both conceptually and perceptually. Trust is a necessary skill that addresses maturity, leadership, strategy, organization, learning, and cooperation. It has been accurately 'the glue' of human social capability, but it is also as fundamental as gravity and affirms our basic organic beliefs. It is the basis of all capital and commerce, and our modern mode of rationality. It rises through the hierarchy of our needs and is the source of our desires to be more, better, and successful.

The Agreement-Management-Commitment-Accountability Partnership Model (Chapter 1, Figure 1.10a) explains new paradigms of capacity for public management. We would be quite accurate to sum these capacities up as known, developing, and unknown trust capacities between people and organizations. Trust and partnering, fundamentally, function together. Unification and integration are functions of trust, as is the erosion of such endeavors, i.e., distrust, as they represent firstly an erosion of trust. Trust is not to be assumed. It must be learned and managed. Due to trust, the utility of partnerships, as mechanisms of society and government, work to unite sectors and institutions, communities, professionals, sponsors, and volunteers around a shared vision of common value, the accepted direction that expresses those values, and the implementation of those values for growth and development. The power of partnering provides a significant competitive advantage and breakthrough results not easily available to independent and individual efforts. The combination is transformational. Public-oriented partnerships work by bringing people together to solve common problems, develop agreements, and manage those agreements with a commitment over time.

Certainly, New Public Management (NPM), with all its efforts to modernize government in the information age, has not engendered this recipe, nor did it specifically intend to. Unless privatization is the only form of partnership available, NPM tended to view governance not in terms of collaboration and partnerships, but as a limited stakeholder corporation. NPM flattens efficiency into effectiveness. This modifies trust to a cost-benefit ratio. But, of course, this is not the only way people transact political dialogue, the persistent background noise to all human activity. NPG recognizes the important contributions of NPM, such as technology transfer and professionalism. NPG views public effectiveness from quite an opposite perspective and in terms of infusing if not rebuilding public management with the intention of trust building and the talent and resources within communities. This expends trust to a value-adding process.

In general, public policy's chief aim would seem to be to cull out of human discourse resolutions to important problems (Cohen, March, & Olsen 1972; Kingdon 2003). This approach may be less efficient, a matter of muddling through, and time-consuming—yet, a necessary element of the democratic process, not least the pursuit of democratic accountabilities. "Muddling through" (Lindblum 1988) is muddled precisely because it is difficult to learn and manage trust across the modern pluralistic spectrum, let alone wade through a constantly evolving technological morphology. It's in our building of trust relationships and environments, particularly those that can be identified as partnerships, that the mud settles and the future becomes more discernible, therefore more actionable. When confusion is the new norm, we can perceive that trust is less formed. This leads to a structural disconnect between government and the people governed. Distrust and confusion are linked. Confusion by the citizenry in defining what the government does *and* how well it is doing it is a significant problem for government (Holzer & Zhang 2004; Light 1997; Pressman & Wildavsky 1973). Not surprising, "at the core of this confusion is trust" (Light 1997, p. 44). At a time when trust in government appears to be severely challenged, an increased interest in the topic of trust has bloomed in the form of a truly solid stand for New Public Governance in public administration and organizational studies as key to policy and performance (Salamon 2002).

Furthermore, the importance of trust has been cited in public performance (Bardach 1998; Cummings 1983; Gazley 2008; Getha-Taylor 2012; Holzer & Zhang 2004; Lung-Teng 2002; Pressman & Wildavsky 1973) and in collaborative studies (Agranoff & McGuire 2003; Forrer et al. 2010; Grossman 2008). "That trust enhances the value of a relationship is unanimously agreed among trust theorists" (Hwang & Burger 1999,

p. 118). According to Ouchi (1981, p. 5), "productivity and trust go hand-in-hand," and Jefferies and Reed state that management research on organizational trust is largely in agreement that "organizational trust is beneficial for performance" (2000, p. 873). "The relationship between public trust in government and government performance is a two-way track. These two factors interact with each other, especially in the long term" (Holzer & Zhang 2004, p. 226). The confusion regarding trust is the peculiar mixture of its cognitive and collective aspects. Trust feels personal, but acts social. In this way, we might see trust as the access we have to social sensibility, and consequently examine how this sensibility is constructed, exchanged, and maintained.

As discussed above, trust is prevalent throughout the partnership process. From a social constructionist perspective, trust is noticeable in the developmental process of partnerships at each stage. Trust examined by its social meaning appears to be instrumental in causing "the social meaning upon which political discourses turn . . . derived from moral and ideological positions that establish and govern competing views of the good society" (Fischer 2003, p. 56). A singular definition of trust is hard to come by because it has both internal and external referents, but a pragmatic attempt may reveal its everyday function as described in Figure 2.1. If we ask ourselves how implementation conforms to trust in partnerships, the answer appears to lie in human sociability, the inclination to be social, which explains in large part the linking of trust with social capital (Fukuyama 1995). The longer answer is the educational aspect of sociability in which trust is viewed as an acquired skill.

Both production and trust address social operations between people either as producers and consumers or as part and partner. There is general agreement that trust is a social discourse (Foucault 1972) that is both functional and phenomenological rather than a product of social interaction (Abramson & Finifter 1981; Bhattacharya et al. 1998; Bigley & Pearce 1998; Larzelkere & Huston 1980; Mayer et al. 1995). Trust is not simply behavior, but it is essential to implementation and production, and this may be a result of our human agency to be social rather than solitary creatures. Sociability is clearly an evolutionary advantage, and trust seems to follow. In order to be social, the cogent barriers inherent in our perceived and actual physical separateness must be dissolved in a manner that reconstitutes a greater collaborative advantage. This process of dissolution and reconstitution might be called trust even if it is arrived at frequently through argumentation (Fischer & Forester 1993). In many ways, trust is so ordinary that it is often unobserved; it is as basic as breathing. When it is observed, trust is epistemological; it is a form of learning with its stops and starts, trials and errors, struggles, and breakthroughs mimicking disjointed incrementalism (Simon 1955), or Etzioni's (1968) mixed scanning. It is an iterative process that works toward forging partnerships that transform human potential.

Not unlike concepts of truth, trust is a human agency that disrupts dichotomous concepts, acts as a door to human potential, and functions as the "social glue" between relationships (Coleman 1988; Fukuyama 1995; Putnam 1993, 2000), or a "moral glue that makes it possible for people to live together in communities of shared meaning"

(Wolfe 1999, p. 42). There are many definitions of trust; all require some form of dialogue between two or more people. If trust like truth is a social construction, a monologue will appear vacant because the "possibility of individualism is directly linked to the possibility of unsuccessful socialization" (Berger & Luckmann 1966, p. 171). Trust, therefore, operates in dialogue seemingly having partnership infused in its very meaning. Due to its dialectic nature, trust might be best described as constructing social reality, as its outcomes are attempts to find agreement on what is true (Berger & Luckmann 1966; Dahl 1989; Fernandez-Armesto 1997; Habermas 1973; Lindblum 1990; Searle 1995); therefore, it requires skill, which implies that it can be learned. Distrust, like disagreement, may be more a lack of skill than a personality trait. We can ascribe trust to all human relationships as fundamental to the function, or dysfunction, of the relationship. A lack of skill often leads to a lack of confidence and a lack of trust. As Galston points out, "much of the economic backwardness in the world can be explained by the lack of mutual confidence" (Galston 1996, p. 129), i.e., a lack of trust, and conversely much of social and economic achievement might be a result of the function of trust in social exchange.

To go further into the inquiries about trust and its role in human relationships, it is imperative that we accept as a basic assumption that human beings are essentially social creatures. Consequently, being social is what defines our most unique displays of humanity, and sociality is the logical purpose of our achievements. Collaboration among people, expressed by their production, leads to social enlightenment. The glue that sustains sociality appears to be what we call trust. The process that develops trust is collaboration, and the method of managing and sustaining collaboration over time is partnership. This is because trust has power: the power to adhere, and through this adherence trust has the power to forge and sustain or erode and destroy relationships.

Public policy is not simply an objectification of problems and their solutions, but a definition and guide to human relationships as well as to the relationship with the environment. Governance comprises the actions of policy implementation. To fully analyze public policy from problem identification to agenda setting to implementation, we must include the determination and function of perceived and evolving social context and the relationships that manifest context. On its own, the degree of trust can be argued to be a strong measure of the success of any policy. Trust operates as the adhesive of the constructed conventions of social reality, realities that change, the changing of which may be desired or feared. The anxiety regarding our success and failure to perform, achieve, and even show up on time is due to the fluidity, or lack thereof, of our trust environments (Fukuyama 1995; Galston 1996). Intrinsic in the trust environment is an intention to foster workable sociability; i.e., partnerships. "There is no social order without trust and no trust without truth or, at least, without agreed upon truth-finding procedures" (Fernadez-Armesto 1997, p. 3). If there is a social premise to human interaction, and that premise infers that social capability heightens individual capability (e.g., "united we stand divided we fall, two heads are better than one," etc.), then conversations about trust must be extraordinary expressions that leap past pure rational choice and exhibit a transrational choice; a pragmatic choice to create realities that work to support social endeavors. This is an everyday occurrence, as is the disintegration of constructed social realities, the meaning of which is held by higher and higher social capacities.

TRUST AND THE PROMISE/PERFORMANCE DIALOGUE

The function of trust, of which distrust is a subset (as stated in Chapter 1: distrust as an erosion, not an elimination, of trust is in conjunction with the concept that disagreement is an erosion, not an elimination of agreement), appears to be the production of reasonable stability and reduced uncertainty, the "reduction of complexity" (Lewis & Weigert 1985) in social constructs. Trust can "reduce anxiety" (Bhattacharya, Devinney, & Pillutla 1998; Goffman 1971; Zucker 1986) and risk and increase relative predictability and the "framing of outcomes" (Parks & Hulbert 1995). "Thus trust is an orientation towards others that is beyond rationality" (Jefferies & Reed 2000, p. 873). Deconstruction seems to occur when a social reality does not function according to its intention (Derrida 1973; Wilber 2000), which further explains distrust as the nonfunctioning of trust rather than an absence of trust. The functionality of trust also supports the learned aspects of trust. If we think of trust in this way, distrust can be observed as a matter of the lesser, or poorly acquired, skills of trust rather than as a social malady. If trust is a necessary component of the policy process, we can expect to see poor outcomes if trust is operating poorly. Partnership Governance, public decision making, and the policy process are also matters of skill. The skill may begin with trust.

If trust is a social construction, then it cannot produce an absolute reality; one in which nothing changes. It can only bind a created reality (a new partnership, or realities) (Fischer 2003) until it is fully actualized or discarded, and in so doing change the meaning of the intention of the trust dynamic as learning proceeds and sociability develops. Trust allows for growth and development and evolution and learning, and provides meaning and purpose to collaboration. It participates in a holistic learning process that produces a marginal reliability until the learning process is completed, fulfilled, and creates new opportunities (hierarchies of partnerships). The extraordinary expressions of reality engendered by trust are powerful enough to propel us into a sociability that creates environments that can be counted on and measured; i.e., things that are accountable. Pragmatically, a trust environment, therefore, refers to a field of accountability; it is a reciprocity in which we can be counted on by others and count on them. The reference for this social premise (the premise of sociability is society), in which measurement has a means and a purpose, is a declarative, functional, illocutionary expression and act; i.e., a promise. A promise is "a declaration or assurance that something will or will not happen, be done, executed, etc." (Random House Dictionary 1973). Consequently, there is no relevant performance without a promise (Grossman 2012). The intention of a promise is foremost one of trust and partnership building, and the competencies gained from that endeavor. A promise requires sociability—a promise and a promisor—and exhibits the necessary aspects of social construction: dialogue and argument. Trust functions in the social discourse of promises made, maintained, broken, restated, or destroyed. The social premises that trust acts on are maintained by expressed promises, and its evolution is tied to the management of the promise.

A social premise is experienced as a promise: the shared formal/spoken/written agreement between one or more people that cites a desired outcome and when that outcome will be fulfilled: a 'what by when' formula. Where you find a promise, you will find a partnership and the building blocks of a society. "Promises also have the world-to-word fit, because part of the point of the promise is to try to make the world change to match the words" (Searle 1995, p. 217) of the promise. It is social because a promise is most powerful as a shared language, a dialogue, between two or more people that establishes a known desired mutual reality. This implies that a promise invents or constructs a unique language transaction that intends a social functionality. That is, a promise intends a partnership.

The literature discusses the interpersonal and affected aspects of trust as well as the organizational aspects of trust, but it is weak on examining the mechanism of promise making and promise keeping in the establishment and maintenance of trust. Without this it is difficult to specifically identify trust, and may explain the profusion of definitions of trust. Trust is operationalized by the expression and maintenance of promises. Stronger measures of trust probe into the nature of promises. Consequently, if we are to effectively examine trust, we must measure the existence and maintenance of promises. Effectively creating, establishing, and maintaining promises produce higher levels of trust and sociability, and the perceived level of performance for both individuals and organizations.

The nature of trust appears to be the process of transforming "value designated outcomes" of individuals "to support the collective goals/vision" (Jung & Avolio 2000, p. 950) of social ability: partnerships, organizations, and communities. If this is true, it may establish a mechanism for public (communal/organizational) trust versus private (affected/interpersonal) trust. This is concerned with organizational trust; i.e., public trust. However, in practice there is a functional difference, as trust by its nature appears to transform the personal into the public. This phenomenon cannot be addressed fully in this book except to say that trust appears to be experienced, always, as personal. Trust is always perceived of as personal regardless of how public it actually may be. Because trust is a personal experience of being public—knowledge and skill building—we can further examine what trust is.

As discussed above, if trust is a social construction, then conversations that bind human potential as a mutual expression of purpose and action exhibit the social learning skills we call trust. Trust is an iterative hermeneutic process. Trust builds social competence and proceeds with the intention to maximize human potential through collaboration requiring a *transrational* breakthrough that moves the individual into and through social relationships as they grow and develop. We can only assume that evolution allows for this because it builds competency, prowess, and advantages special to our environment. Trust pervades the set of interactions and language that contain the reality we share with others. The purpose is to produce an intended outcome based on the potential identified in a mutual promise. This outcome is dependent on the articulation of the trust motive over time. Trust, then, can be understood as the binding mechanism in bounded rationality (Simon 1997): a partnership. Larue T. Hosmer sums up a definition of trust that pulls together the elements of collaboration, maximization of potential, and the self-centered to social-centered breakthrough:

> Trust is the reliance by one person, group, or firm upon a voluntarily accepted duty on the part of another person, group, or firm to recognize and protect the rights and interests *of all others* engaged in a joint endeavour or economic exchange.
>
> (Hosmer 1995, p. 393; my italics)

But, this does not imply that there are any fixed bounds or determined limits to human potential. Boundaries are the limits of a heterarchical partnership. Boundaries are determined, agreed upon, and managed to achieve *levels* of potentiality. Rational theories tend not to address this potential and are bounded by the idea that individual human thought is restricted by a retro-evolutionist position that posits mankind in a survival only mentality. Not untrue, but not the whole story. The boundaries of our *bounded rationality* may be boundless, established solely by our creative intent and practical application of social collaboration. Trust creates accountability for others as a social phenomenon that feedbacks and enhances the individual.

If we consider our understandings of time, we can arrive at a basic function of trust. Trust is a temporal experience, "a vivid present shared" (Berger & Luckman 1966, p. 28). This brings the element of time into understanding how trust is conceived. The difficulty in defining trust is less its social and economic consequences and more that it exists on various levels of temporal perception. The applicability of "now" can have different "time horizons" (Hwang & Burgers 1999) that extend the sense of time. Time is an integral element of trust; i.e., trust is gauged by a social occurrence happening at a specific time. A remarkable aspect of trust is that we integrate the various levels of our awareness as a general awareness of time that is socially accessible. This may be purely constructed in language; therefore different language systems may have different utilization and specificity of time, but once agreed upon it sets a basis for reality to be mutually perceived. Consequently, trust has specific time dimensions which can be measured beginning with "being on time"; however, the understanding of what that means in any social situation is obviously different, therefore a precursor to trust. The essential promise mechanism in building a trust environment might be said to be a promise to be on time. In this way, trust expresses a commitment to a social construction of reality: a construction that holds the potential of sociability in a temporal setting.

We might not be able to predict its maximum potential, but sociability implies that we are attempting something that requires more than ourselves to accomplish. We might understand trust to be further experienced as acceptance, the acceptance of another's potential and ability to deliver on that potential. It follows that trust may be practiced as the acceptance we have for others' pursuit of their maximum potential, and our promise to cause that potentiality and vice versa, by creating a reality that supports the agreed-upon promise. Potentiality is then linked to trust as a motivation to reach higher and higher potentials, the trigger of that motivation is acceptance, since the higher the potential desired, the higher the level of sociability is required. The reason why bounded rationality is not limited is that we can, if we choose, accept anything. This is an evolutionary imperative. That we chose not to accept something is not a requirement, but volition (Lindblum 1990). The ultimate promise of a trust environment is to express maximum potential in that environment (i.e., the partnership). Trust is something we generate, it is something we acknowledge, allow, and accept . . . or not. Trust is not a commodity, but the generosity we have to allow another to be fully expressed, or expressed at all. By expression, I mean being who we are and who we are not, and showing up just that way until we reach our maximum potential. Distrust looks a lot like the suppression of this generosity, and the experience we have is a scarcity of trust. Scarcity (Howlett & Ramesh 2003) models are akin to distrust and tend to assume that there is not enough product, space, place, or time, therefore the need for limitation. Distrust is based on an assumption that we live in a finite, quantum universe instead of an evolving universe.

If there are multiple realities (Fischer 1993, 2003) operating simultaneously, in synchronicity, competitively, and collaboratively, we might argue about the idea that "everything" potentially shows up all the time, even if we don't perceive or acknowledge it (everything may show up all the time, but not necessarily in the same finite determined space, even if everything is not immediately present in our finite space, because we filter it out, can't perceive it, or don't know its there). The purpose of sociability, such as partnerships, may be to expand our perceptions, therefore the potential to promote the capability of others to have more things becomes present to our field of consciousness, thereby expanding our boundaries and maximize our potential.

Scarcity (again, attributed to distrust and disagreement models) may well be true for human beings as individuals. An individual by definition has limitations, but partnership does not have similar limitations. As individuals, we are "bounded" by our individuality; limited rationality (Simon 1955). Maximizing potential may be unavailable to us except in partnerships. As individuals we are limited, but that limitation is broken down by effective sociability. Our limits are fairly obvious. For example, we all know that we cannot physically see ourselves completely without aids, and we cannot hear or feel ourselves in the environment or as the environment perceives us without a response from the environment. Therefore, we must trust the ability to better perceive ourselves to others. Our complete potential at all levels is unavailable to us except through others. The distrust model does not adequately grasp this. Distrust is adversarial and puts its faith "in compliance and the capacity to create and enforce deterrence" (Light 1997, p. 77). It limits itself to what is known by an individual.

The permission we give another to cause ourselves to be heard (thereby giving our expression purpose and meaning) is expressive or interpersonal trust (Jeffries & Reed 2000; Mayer et al. 1995). The permission we give ourselves to cause another to be heard is impressive trust, or organizational (Jeffries & Reed 2000). The term "permission" is used because it connotes a volitional capacity, which can be "either expressed in language or in action" (Lindblum 1990, p. 24). As stated earlier, the mechanism used to reveal or facilitate trust is a linguistic tool called a promise (Fukuyama 1995). In this way, trust can be experienced as a promise, a promise to honor the existence and partnership of another. That is, a promise begins with an acknowledgment that another exists (we acknowledge his/her presence and impact, or not), as a fundamental human potential and capacity. The degree to which we choose to allow a person to show up for us is the amount of trust we permit, or bestow upon that person, place, or thing.

The degree of trust becomes the capacity of the promise we make. Promise—promise making and keeping—is a skill. It enlists our ability to be what we say we are, do what we say we will do, at a specific place and time. A promise is unique because it requires the management of our intentions, abilities, and presence. It is a bold statement of a potential reality. The fulfillment of a promise relies on management; promises must be managed to succeed. Within a promise, "trust puts its faith in capacity and perfor-mance accountability" (Light 1997, p. 77). This skill can be measured by: (a) the abil-ity to promise in a manner that includes, augments, or affirms another's existence; (b) the clarity of the promise in terms of results: what will be accomplished or produced and by when; and (c) the fulfillment of the promise. This in turn measures the value given to a particular relationship. Faced with a compromised, inexperienced, or less expertly managed promise, we will experience an anxiety regarding our performance, and production will suffer, since we are not wholly available to perform (See Figure 2.1). High-level promises indicate promises that are well established and managed and equal higher levels of trust. Low-level promises indicate the presence of inarticulate or

Figure 2.1   **Promise Theory of a Trust, Performance, and Production Matrix**

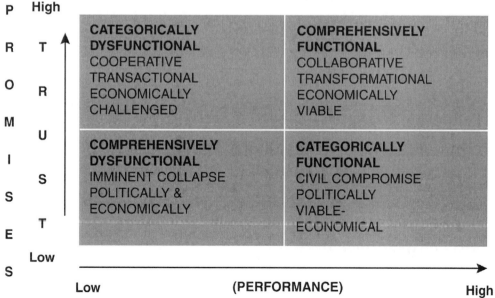

broken promises that are routinely obfuscated, functionally neglected, or destined to broker equally lower levels of trust.

Trust functions independently of market theories of supply and demand, since the demand for trust, collaboration, and partnerships is persistent and the supply inexhaustible. Trust is a form of human attention, an acknowledgment of the gift another has to cause the potential of another. This is a definition of how social capital functions; it empowers. Social capital is expressed as the power, inherent in us all, to transform our motives to survive the scarcity of our individuality in prospect of a social reality that allows for the growth and development of humanity and expands the horizons of human potential. Within social potential rests the realization of our individual potential. Trust may also then be measured by the potential-to-succeed that any one person perceives that he or she has in his/her community(s).

TEN TENETS OF TRUST

#1: **Higher levels** of trust are caused by high levels of promise making and keeping.

#2: **Higher levels** of trust cause higher individual and group performance.

#3: **Lower levels** of trust are a result of a lack of skill in making and keeping promises exhibited as an expression of suppressed expression; resignation of limited potential.

#4: **Higher levels** of trust occur in collaborative relationships that encourage and sustain promises.

#5: **Higher levels** of trust will occur in managed trust environments (partnerships) in which each individual is accountable for the environment. (A trust environment is an accountability environment [Dubnick 2005], or a domain of managed promises.)

#6: **Broken promises**, like broken agreements, result in lower trust levels.

#7: **Broken agreements** cause performance anxiety, further resulting in diminished performance and production; i.e., diminished effectiveness and efficiency.

#8: **"When trust and social capital** are destroyed, democracy becomes difficult or impossible" (Putnam 1993).

#9: **As trust** increases, so does human potential and the ability to solve problems.

#10: **Undeveloped trust skills** undermine access to higher levels of human potential.

A TRUST–PERFORMANCE CONSTRUCTION: FROM PROMISE TO PERFORMANCE

Trust is the human skill of sociability and is present in every stage of policy development; therefore, an analysis of policy is unfinished if it neglects an evaluation of trust. According to Tenet #9: As trust increases, so does human potential and the ability to solve problems. A lack of potential, therefore a lack of trust skills, will lower performance, have negative political consequences, and erode the promises that engender a civil society. A lack of trust causes performance anxiety, which devalues the policy process from its inception because (Tenet #10) the undeveloped trust skills undermine access to higher levels of human potential. Trust functions in the public realm as the result of the ability to accept social interaction as an opportunity to be accountable for another. Trust is operationalized as accountability for others, and this accountability is observed as a promise. Accountability is expressed in the nature and management of a promise: *What* will occur—*By When* it will occur. A promise is a language device, a linguistic negotiator that constructs a social reality around a perceived social potential. In other words, a promise is a managed dialogue. It's shared transmission, and in this mutuality all those involved in the promise participate. Its power alone can launch it more forcefully than non-intentional conversations, but it cannot sustain it. In order for a promise to be sustained (just like any linguistically constructed social reality), therefore achieve success, it must be structurally managed to fulfill its intention. In this way, promise-intention (planning) and promise-management (implementation) are equal performance (consequences)—consequences being the level of performance achieved as the fulfillment associated with the level of trust intended in the promise; i.e., promise fulfillment. If a promise is weak or distorted, then performance will suffer. This indicates that trust was low from the onset.

A promise has intention that requires mutual action in the implementation process: For human beings, this may be how reality is experienced. We might say that every meaningful action we have as an individual is a result of a promise, or promises made by or between someone in which we are one of the managers of the promise (this indicates that promise makers and promise keepers can be different people supporting a separation of political powers). Trust begins as a level of acceptance one person has for another and is extended to the desire and then intention to maximize one's potential through the benefit of another. The degree of trust determines the degree of performance in each setting. Trust is not an individual operation (even if an affected one). The statistical mean of a trust relationship will set its potential. This mean establishes the trust environment, which constructs an arena of potential. If we want higher potential, therefore higher performance, we must construct a trust environment that can accept a high potential.

CONCLUSION

We will assume that human beings can accept anything; therefore, we can promise anything. But a promise must be a dialogue, therefore have a trust mean, and that dialogue must be managed or it will disappear like any other form of conversation. The measurement of performance can not only be the performance itself, as performance cannot occur without a trust environment (even if that environment is extremely low, it must be present). Performance is the resulting consequence of the level of fulfillment of the enabling promise; i.e., the level of trust intended. Trust begets performance, not directly but through its progeny: promises. If we are to fully measure public performance, we must first measure the intention of the promise that allowed for the social interaction. Secondly, we can predict the performance and measure the actual resulting consequences against the prediction, which are generally twofold: minor and major consequences—the minor performance indicator: output consequences, and the major performance indicator: outcome consequences. Outcomes are the major indicator because the intention of any promise is to maximize human potential to the degree it is conceived and constructed. This means that performance must address the consequences of a quality of life promise. For instance, if our promise is to reduce crime 10% by the end of the year, we might fill one thousand more potholes in town to improve quality of life, but we might not have lower crime. The output (number of potholes filled) cannot indicate fully the performance of the promise. The consequence of a poor output result is an embarrassment. The consequence of a poor outcome is a political disaster.

The promise mechanism is essential to successful collaboration. It requires the four elements of the Agreement, Management, Commitment, and Accountability Model (Table 2.1) for its success:. The agreement describes the intention of the promise; management maintains the implementation of the promise; commitment provides the resources necessary; and accountability measures the fulfillment of the promise. It is both linear and a feedback loop. At each stage the level of trust can be evaluated as cited in Table 2.1 below. Low trust provides at best short-term objectives and low capability,

Table 2.1

Trust–Partnership Matrix

	LOW	(*TRUST*)	HIGH
AGREEMENT	Instant Gratification Output-only orientation Adversarial. Dichotomous		Real Change Outcome Orientation Partnership
MANAGEMENT	Ad hoc/Proxy Manipulative Exclusive Miscommunication		Professionalism Transparent Inclusive Communication
COMMITMENT	Deception Compromise Incompletion Short-lived		Commitment Collaboration Action Longevity
ACCOUNTABLITY	Disagreement Confusion Low-performance No measurement		Promises Clarity High-performance Balanced measurement

and perceives low potential. High trust provides long-term, ongoing, high-skill, and highly desired potential. Low trust at the agreement stage results in instant gratification and output orientation; high trust results in real change and an outcome orientation. Low trust at the management level results in ad hoc or management by proxy; high trust results in professionalism, sustainability, and perceived real performance. Low trust at the commitment level results in deception, compromise, and floundering; high levels result in completion, transformation, investment, and sustainability.

Trust functions in a feedback loop. It shifts the idea that government performance instills higher levels of public trust. It's not complete. Performance instills the trust that the promise of performance intended. Therefore, promise instills performance, which instills trust. The level of performance achieved is the level of potential understood and instilled in the promise. New levels of potential open up horizons of greater levels of potential and feedback, and can be addressed for further development at the promise stage.

KEY POINTS

- Partnerships are difficult to evaluate without a thorough understanding of the fundamental and pervasive function of trust, reciprocity, and social capital.
- Trust is not only a human behavior, but also a recursive social function.
- Trust is not to be assumed. It must be learned and managed. It is a skill.
- Trust feels personal, but acts social. It is an iterative process that works by forging partnerships that transform human potential and allow for growth and development.
- Distrust, like disagreement, may be more a lack of skill rather than a personality trait. Distrust is the nonfunctioning of trust rather than an absence of trust.
- Trust has power—the power to adhere—and through this adherence, trust has the power to forge and sustain, or erode and destroy social processes.
- A trust environment refers to a field of accountability, a reciprocity in which we can be counted on by others and also count on them.
- Intrinsic in the trust environment is an intention to foster workable sociability; i.e., partnerships.
- The social premises that trust acts on are maintained by expressed promises. The evolution of trust is tied to the management of the promise.
- A promise is "a declaration or assurance that something will or will not happen, be done, executed, etc." (Random House Dictionary 1973). Consequently, there the relevancy of performance requires a promise.
- A promise: the shared formal/spoken/written agreement between one or more people that cites a desired outcome and when that outcome will be fulfilled, a 'what by when' formula.
- Where you find a promise, you will find a partnership and the building blocks of a society.

- Trust is operationalized by the expression and maintenance of promises.
- Maximizing potential may be unavailable to us except in trust environments; partnerships.
- Trust functions independently of the market theory of supply and demand, since the demand for trust, collaboration, and partnerships is persistent and the supply inexhaustible.

REFERENCES

Abramson, Paul R. & Ada W. Finifter (1981). One Meaning of Political Trust: New Evidence from Items Introduced in 1978, *American Journal of Political Studies*, Vol. 25, No. 2, pp. 297–307.

Agranoff, Robert & M.C. McGuire (2003). *Collaborative Public Management: Strategies for Local Governments*, Washington DC: Georgetown University Press.

Bardach, E. (1998). *Getting Agencies to Work Together: The Practice and Theory of Managerial Craftsmanship*, Washington DC: Brookings Institution Press.

Barrett, D., J. Austin, & S. McCarthy (2000). *Cross-Sector Collaboration: Lessons from the Trachoma Initiative.* Working paper, Harvard Business School, Cambridge, MA.

Berger, P.L. & Luckman, T. (1966). *The Social Construction of Reality: A Treatise in the Sociology of Knowledge*, New York: Anchor Books.

Bhattacharya, Rajeev, Timothy M. Devinney, & Madan M. Pillutla (1998). A Formal Model of Trust Based Outcomes, *The Academy of Management Review*, Vol. 23, No. 3, July 1998, pp. 459–472.

Bigley, Gregory A. & Jone L. Pearce (1998, July). Straining for Shared Meaning in Organizational Science: Problems of Trust and Distrust, *Academy of Management Review*, Vol. 23, No. 3, p. 405–421.

Cohen, Michael, James March, & Johan Olsen (1972). A Garbage Can Model of Organizational Choice, *Administrative Science Quarterly*, Vol. 17, pp. 1–25.

Coleman, J.S. (1998). Social Capital in the Creation of Human Capital, *American Journal of Sociology*, Vol. 94, pp. 95–120.

Cummings, L.L. (1983). Performance Evaluation Systems in the Context of Individual Trust and Commitment. In F. J. Landy, S. Zedrick, & J. Cleveland (eds.), *Performance Measurement and Theory*, Hillside, NJ: Erlbaum, pp. 89–93.

Dahl, R.A. (1989). *Democracy and Its Critics.* New Haven, CT: Yale University Press.

Etzioni, Amitai (1968). *The Active Society*, New York: Free Press.

Derrida, Jacques (1973). *Speech and Phenomena*, Evanston, IL: Northwestern University Press.

Dubnick, Melvin (2005). Accountability and the Promise of Performance, *Public Performance & Management Review*, Vol. 28, No. 3, pp. 376–417.

Fernandez-Armesto, Felipe (1997). *Truth*, New York: St. Martin's Press.

Fischer, Frank (2003). *Reframing Public Policy: Discursive Politics and Deliberative Practices*, New York: Oxford University Press.

Fischer, Frank & John Forester (1993). *The Argumentative Turn in Policy Analysis and Planning*, Durham, NC: Duke University Press.

Foucault, M. (1972). *The Archaeology of Knowledge*, New York: Routledge.

Forrer, John, James Edwin Kee, Kathryn E. Newcomer, & Eric Boyer (2010). Public–Private Partnership and the Public Accountability Question, *Public Administration Review*, Vol. 70, No. 3, pp. 475–484.

Fukuyama, F. (1995). *Trust*, New York: Free Press.

Galston, W.A. (1996). Trust—but Quantify, *Public Interest*, No. 122, pp. 129–132.

Gazley, Beth (2008, Jan/Feb). Beyond the Contract: The Scope and Nature of Informal Government-Nonprofit Partnership, *Public Administration Review*, Vol. 68, pp. 141–154.

Getha-Taylor, Heather (2012). Cross-Sector Understanding and Trust, *Public Performance & Management Review*, Vol. 36, No. 2, pp. 216–229.

Goffman, E. (1971). *Relations in Public*, New York: Basic Books.

Grossman, Seth A. (2008). *The Role of Entrepreneurship in Public–Private Partnerships: The Case of Business improvement Districts*, PhD dissertation, Rutgers, The State University of New Jersey, School of Public Affairs & Administration, Newark, NJ.

Grossman, Seth A. (2012). The Management and Measurement of Public–Private Partnerships: Towards an Integral and Balanced Approach. In *Public Performance and Management Review*, Armonk, NY: M. E. Sharpe.

Habermas, J. (1973). *Legitimation Crisis* (T. McCarthy, Trans.), Boston: Beacon Press.

Holzer, Marc & Mengzhong Zhang (2004). Trust, Performance, and the Pressures for Productivity in the Public Sector. In *Public Productivity Handbook*, New York: Marcel Dekker, pp. 215–229.

Hosmer, Larue Tone (1995). Trust: The Connecting Link between Organizational Theory and Philosophical Ethics, *The Academy of Management Review*, Vol. 20, No. 2, pp. 379–403.

Howlett, Michael, Michael Ramesh, & Anthony Perl (2003). *Studying Public Policy: Policy Cycles and Policy Subsystems*, Oxford: Oxford University Press.

Hwang, P. & W. P. Burgers (1999). Apprehension and Temptation: The Forces Against Cooperation. *Journal of Conflict Resolution*, Vol. 43, No. 1, pp. 117–130.

Jefferies, F. L. & R. Reed (2000). Trust and Adaptation in Relational Contracting, *Academy of Management Review*, Vol. 25, No. 4, pp. 873–882.

Jung, Dong I. & Bruce J. Avolio (2000). Opening the Black Box: An Experimental Investigation of the Mediating Effects of Trust and Value Congruence on Transformational and Transactional Leadership, *Journal of Organizational Behavior*, Vol. 21, No. 8, pp. 949–964.

Kingdon, John W. (2003). *Agendas, Alternatives and Public Policies*, Reading, MA: Addison-Wesley Educational Publishers Inc.

Larselkere, Robert E. & Ted L. Huston (1980). The Dyadic Trust Scale: Toward Understanding Interpersonal Trust in Close Relationships, *Journal of Marriage and the Family*, Vol. 42, No. 3, pp. 595–604.

Lewis, J. David & Andrew Weigert (1985). Trust as a Social Reality, *Social Forces*, Vol. 63, No. 4, pp. 967–985.

Light, Paul C. (1997). *The Tides of Reform*, New Haven, CT: Yale University Press.

Lindblum, C. E. (1988). The Science of Muddling Through. In J. Rabin (ed.), *Handbook of Public Administration*, 5th ed., Belmont, CA: Thomson-Wadsworth, pp. 177–187.

Lindblum, Charles E. (1990). *Inquiry and Change: The Troubles Attempt to Understand and Shape Society*, New Haven, CT: Yale University Press.

Lung-Teng, Hu (2002). *Proposal for a Public Trust in Government*, Newark, NJ: Rutgers University.

Mayer, Roger C., James H. Davis, & F. David Schoorman (1995). An Integrative Model of Organizational Trust, *The Academy of Management Review*, Vol. 20, No. 3, pp. 709–734.

Ouchi, William G. (1981). *Theory Z: How American Business Can Meet the Japanese Challenge*, Reading, MA: Addison-Wesley.

Parks, C. D. & L. Hulbert (1995). High and Low Trusters' Responses to Fear in a Payoff Matrix, *The Journal of Conflict Resolution*, Vol. 39, No. 4, pp. 718–730.

Pressman, Jeffrey L. & Aaron Wildavsky (1973). *Implementation*, Berkeley: University of California Press.

Putnam, Robert D. (1993). The Prosperous Community. Social Capital and Public Life, *America Prospect*, Vol. 13, pp. 35–42.

Putnam, Robert D. (2000). *Bowling Alone: The Collapse and Revival of the American Community*, New York: Simon & Schuster.

Random House College Dictionary (1973). New York: Random House.

Salamon, L. M. (ed.) (2002). *The Tools of Government: A Guide to the New Governance*, New York: Oxford University Press.

Searle, J. R. (1995). *The Construction of Social Reality*, New York: The Free Press.
Simon, Herbert A. (1955). A Behavioural Model of Rational Choice, *Quarterly Journal of Economics*, Vol. 69, pp. 99–118.
Simon, Herbert A. (1997). *Administrative Behavior*, 4th ed., New York: The Free Press.
Wilber, Ken (2000). *A Theory of Everything*, Boston, MA: Shambhala Publications.
Wilson, Woodrow (1887). The Study of Administration. *Political Science Quarterly,* reprinted in 1997 in J. Shafritz & A. Hyde (eds.), *Classics of Public Administration*, 2d ed., Chicago: Dorsey Press.
Wolfe, A. (1999, Nov. 1). A Necessary Good, *New Republic*, pp. 37–42.
Zucker, L. G. (1986). Production of Trust: Institutional Sources of Economic Structure. In B. M. Staw & L. L. Cummings (eds.), *Research in Organizational Behavior*, Greenwich, CT: JAI Press, pp. 53–111.

3

Partnership Governance

The Role of Public Entrepreneurship and Social Capital

Throughout the world, partnerships in government are challenging and reshaping traditional assumptions of public management—its promises and performance—at the most local of government levels, the neighborhood and town center. Although public-public partnerships also exist and are finding resurgence, the key to this metamorphosis is the concept and application of public–private partnerships (PPPs) that merge public and private cooperative management technologies as well as public entrepreneurship, and social capital. This merger forges a distinctive form of public partnership management—public–private partnership management—an expertise within public administration—that brings together the knowledge and skills of business, government, planning, and community development in a collaborative manner and achieves a form of citizen-driven governance. When we look worldwide, PPPs are becoming mainstream policy and management tools for governments at the heart of community revitalization and economic development.

At the heart of a public–private partnership is the management of a new sense of community—one that is strategic, builds on its assets, sustains its values, and provides a place where people generate their livelihoods through participation. The profession of public–private partnership management and its key economic development affiliate—Business Improvement District (BID)—management is a pragmatic tale of emerging and evolving community spirit and democratic process (Grossman 2010). Within municipalities exist not only neighborhoods, but systems of communal interaction based on a variety of social and economic interdependencies that define the context of private investment and public accountability at the heart of the managed public–private partnership. Managed districts, both for business and residential areas, are unique PPP examples. In this way, managed districts fundamentally reinforce practices that support successful democratic governance and community and economic development, and provide the public sector asset management structure necessary to define and implement property investment maximization strategies.

The managed (special) district, and its public–private partnership, is first and foremost a vehicle for building successful communities. It relies on community organization and implementation practices. The public–private partnership manager is a change agent for a community, and a facilitator of public processes that engage individuals in developing and sustaining community competencies and competitive practices that draw out a community's potential and refine its assets. These "public managers" often rely more on intersectoral and interorganizational partnerships as complements for (and sometimes as substitutes for) authority.

ENTREPRENEURSHIP IN PARTNERSHIP BUILDING

Joseph Schumpeter, an economist and political scientist (the father of modern entrepreneurship) concluded that profit was not a chief motivator of entrepreneurship but "simply the doing of new things or the doing of things that are already done in a new way" (Schumpeter 1947, p. 151). That's a broad statement of a specific human desire to innovate. In this statement, the themes of organization, leadership, risk taking, and innovation are clearly expressed and must not be supposed as purely economic. Schumpeter points to the role of entrepreneur as a change agent in society.

Co-opted by the business community, 'entrepreneurship' does not define business prowess only, but essentially describes the ability to identify and create new things and/or enroll others in making something new happen. This may result in new strategies, partnerships, and organizations. In the arena of public–private partnerships, both public and private aspects of entrepreneurship converge to present a hybrid capacity that has proved successful in community development. As stated above, the field of entrepreneurship until recently has been dominated by positivist functionalism (Filion 1997; Pittaway 2003), and yet all definitions acknowledged that organization and contextual occurrences (Pittaway 2003; Weber 1946), culture (Goetz & Freshwater 2001), and climate (Goetz & Freshwater 2001) are necessary for the entrepreneur to thrive. If we accept organizational and contextual aspects of entrepreneurship, then we see that entrepreneurship and partnerships are aligned. Consequently, since the 1990s, the study of entrepreneurship has exploded into almost every field (Filion 1997) of social, economic, and political studies, and at the dawn of the 21st century it is redefining democratic governance. Due to this, or the complexity of human nature (Pittaway 2003; Schumpeter 1947), there was a great deal of confusion regarding a universal definition of entrepreneurship (Filion 1997; Kruger 2004; Pittaway 2003). Yet, there were two key aspects to which virtually every definition alluded: innovation and creativity. Entrepreneurship tumbled into the study of the entrepreneur, which at first was assumed to be a profit-motivated rationalist. But this assumption has changed as entrepreneurship became understood as an aspect of human behavior rather than solely a business orientation. Both Max Weber (1904), by addressing the cultural value system behind entrepreneurship, and Joseph Schumpeter (1947), who launched the modern assessment of entrepreneurship, associating it with innovation, made seminal contributions to economic and sociologic theory that inform both New Public Management (NPM) and New Public Governance (NPG).

From an individualistic point of view, entrepreneurialism appeared to be based on two factors: (1) individuals are the products of their environments and (2) people become entrepreneurs when they act, "entrepreneurs do not just plan. They act" (Carton, Hofer, & Meeks 1998, p. 5). People become entrepreneurs only by carrying out a new contribution accomplished by establishing a new organizational planning and implementation structure in their communities (Carton et al. 1998). The entrepreneurial process begins and ends with the observation, capturing, and implementation of the innovative enterprise. It disappeared in the maintenance stage (Schumpeter 1934), when the enterprise is no longer new and when creativity solidified opportunity and produced a real product or capability. When this occurred, it created a management/functional stage that was no longer entrepreneurial. This is why an entrepreneur and a small businessperson are not mutually inclusive. An entrepreneur might set up a business, project, or policy, but once it is established and operating, it becomes an ongoing enterprise (see Figure 3.1). In this way, entrepreneurship and business acumen are not the same thing because entrepreneurship expresses a human potential to develop opportunity rather than an economic technique to maximize production.

The missing piece in Figure 3.1 is that the process of Venture Formation is the entrepreneurial effort, and has an intermediary step: Venture Strategy, which formalizes the "Trigger Event" and directs entrepreneurial action. Management, venture performance, begins a production maintenance function (sustainability) that is not entrepreneurial unless a new venture is created.

Entrepreneurship does not exist outside of the conventional element only, but could occur in organizations because it is not a function but a process of human potential. The internal development of the entrepreneurial process and often a term to describe entrepreneurship in public organizations is *Intrapreneurship* (Carton, Hofer, & Meeks 1998; Kruger 2004). The Intrapreneur "represents a strategic form of corporate entrepreneurial activity and new venture creation within an organization" (Guth & Ginsberg 1990); therefore, it appealed to the corporate/bureaucratic nature of government where the public sector was urged to be more creative. Essentially, the entrepreneur is one who has direct ownership of an enterprise, while an Intrapreneur does not have direct ownership. In this way, the term Intrapreneur applies well to representative democratic systems.

The term Intrapreneur was devised initially as a way to encourage and reward competition within corporations. It allows departments to compete with each other as a way of developing product. Its chief aim is to encourage entrepreneurial behavior within

Figure 3.1 **The Entrepreneurship Paradigm (Carton, Hofer, & Meeks 1998) (*Management added*).**

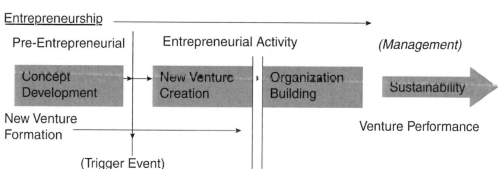

organizations. The essential aspect of an Intrapreneur is developing entrepreneurship. At the risk of the term Intrapreneur adding to a confusion in defining entrepreneurship, because it seems to appear as more of a euphemism, it can help to explain the evolving expansive understanding of entrepreneurship as "the pursuit of a discontinuous opportunity involving the creation of an organization (or sub-organization) with the expectation of value creation to the participants" (Carton, Hofer, & Meeks 1998, p. 1) and the entrepreneur as the "individual (or team) that identifies the opportunity, gathers the necessary resources, creates and is ultimately responsible for the performance of the organization" (Carton, Hofer, & Meeks 1998, p. 1). This leads us to not only a less private sector description of entrepreneurship, but to 'public entrepreneurship' a key aspect of Partnership Governance.

PUBLIC ENTREPRENEURSHIP

A uniform definition of public entrepreneurship is not established. But some aspects differentiate public from private entrepreneurship that make it easier to understand Partnership Governance and particularly public–private partnerships:

1. Public versus private information (Lewis 1984; Schneider & Teske 1992). The public entrepreneur must not only share (disclose) more information but should pursue information dissemination that is inclusive, while the private entrepreneur is more secretive and exclusive about information.
2. There is a "centrality of the social mission" (Mort, Weerawardena, & Carnegie 2002) in public entrepreneurship, and public entrepreneurs could be referred to as "collection action problem entrepreneurs" (Schneider & Teske 1992) motivated by a collectionist sentiment to maximize collective value. The private sector entrepreneur seeks to maximize financial profit and is motivated by rational choice theory (Lewis 1984) that inures profit to specific investors.
3. Public entrepreneurship works to create public value (Moore 1995), while private entrepreneurship works to create private profit (Weber 1904).
4. Private entrepreneurship is influenced primarily by the supply side of goods, while public entrepreneurship is influenced primarily by the demand side for goods (Thornton 1999).

The differences are intellectually stimulating, but the similarities of entrepreneurship across all fields of human endeavor are more compelling. There is little substantial difference in character, competence, and behavior between the private and public entrepreneur because entrepreneurship appears to be a unique human behavior that works to allow change, value reorientation, community building, and discovery (Thornton 1999). These attributes can be applied to every field of human endeavor and aptly function when ascribed to normative understandings of private and public sector entrepreneurship. The difference between the entrepreneur and the regular citizen is that the entrepreneur is on a mission to solve an identified social or economic problem, the solving of which creates new products, affiliations, and value possibilities as well as the organizational constructs to maintain them (Carland et al. 1984). The simplest definition of entrepreneurship is the strategic development of innovative value constructs (Schumpeter 1934; Thornton 1999). Strategy requires partnerships. This points us to an individualistic fallacy of entrepreneurship and toward a collaborative requirement of entrepreneurship. Throughout the literature in both private and public sectors, entrepreneurship shares many of the distinctions of partnerships:

- Innovation
- Transformation
- Risk taking
- Trust
- Value creation
- Organization and collective action
- Strategic manipulation
- Leadership

These distinctions identify the entrepreneur, both public and private (Baumol 1990; Carland et al. 1984; Huxham & Vangen 2005; Lewis 1984; McClelland 1987; Mort, Weerawardena, & Carnegie 2002; Schumpeter 1934; Thomas & Mueller 2000; Weber 1904). Human behavior that works to transform old concepts, values, and performance into new ones seems to be the telltale sign of entrepreneurial activity (Guth & Ginsberg 1990; Schneider 1992; Schumpeter 1934). The ideas of transrational behavior are also identical to the understandings of entrepreneurship because both are found in partnerships. Entrepreneurship like partnerships is pragmatic and transformational. Where there is the smoke of entrepreneurship, there is the fire of partnerships transforming approaches to problem solving. New Public Management contributed significantly to this understanding about entrepreneurship and, consequently, nonbusiness descriptions of entrepreneurship entered the everyday lexicon to the extent that entrepreneurship was beginning to have a public hue as it turned back and was applied to business and community development. This turn-around of publicly fused entrepreneurship prompted the New Public Governance movement, and inevitably brought us to Partnership Governance.

At its core, the concept of entrepreneurship is value generation (Weber 1904), whether it is financial, social, or political. Value generation is a pragmatic social construction. It is particularly human to attribute exchangeable and sustainable value to real objects and occurrences (James 1909). Value generation is a pragmatic and creative act elicited by inducing innovation and action, both individual and communal, that solves the ever-evolving question of what is valuable. Entrepreneurship flourishes when a society is stable enough to allow for innovation (Schumpeter 1934). A value generator, although social, often appears to the beholder as a leader who changes (Lewis 1984) the direction and flow of an entire community by:

- Defining a vision of value
- Enrolling others in that vision
- Organizing a strategic vision quest
- Developing a structure to manage the value obtained over time

Public entrepreneurship began to take on pragmatic public application in the 1990s with the NPM movement. PPPs and BIDs, consequently, also began to flourish. Eugene Lewis can be credited with establishing the term 'public entrepreneurship' in 1984 when he published *Public Entrepreneurship: Toward a Theory of Bureaucratic Political Power*. Coincidently, NPM took hold within five years. Lewis defined public entrepreneurship by concentrating on the public entrepreneur "as a person who creates or profoundly elaborates a public organization so as to alter greatly the existing pattern of allocation of scarce public resources" (Lewis 1984, p. 9). Immediately, individualistic notions of entrepreneurship broke down and revealed the collaborative context of entrepreneurship, and its transrational attributes that explain well how entrepreneurship actually succeeds.

Once again, we might experience a false dichotomy in the term 'public entrepreneurship' if we assume that entrepreneurship is only an individualist endeavor rather than a public activity. As discussed above, entrepreneurship is not confined to the rational choice model but also applies to a collaborative network (Lowndes & Skelcher 1998) and cultural models (Ozminkowski 2003). These models are transrational and each definition fluctuates between individualistic (personal/private) and collaborative (collective/public) descriptions of entrepreneurship. Roberts (1992) defined public entrepreneurship as "the generation of a novel or innovative idea and the design and implementation of the innovative idea into public sector practice" (p. 56). She also addressed the leadership qualities of public entrepreneurs as "individuals who generate, design, and implement innovative ideas in the public domain" (p. 56). This was echoed by Ozminkowski (2003), who described entrepreneurship as the ability "to find opportunities and to create opportunities" (p. 27), to facilitate the "entrepreneurial environment" (p. 24), and to function as an "agent of change" (p. 28). Roberts (1992) insinuated a link between social capital and public entrepreneurship by indicating that what enabled the public entrepreneur was the involvement of others in the policy process. This required participation and trust. Ozminkowski identified two key ideas that linked social capital and public entrepreneurship to public administration, furthering the cooperative aspects of public entrepreneurship as opposed to concepts of individual entrepreneurship:

1. The public realm, i.e., culture, matters.
2. Aspects of social capital are present in public entrepreneurship, such as trust, open mindedness, uncertainty avoidance, and public achievement (p. 59).

Due to its contextual nature, entrepreneurship is a driving force of political/economic change in society as it harnesses the charismatic aspects of strategic leadership (Mort, Weerawardena, & Carnegie 2002) in divulging human potential. Mort's description of leadership defined the individual *and* group entrepreneur and appeared reliant on the opportunities society presented in the pursuit of collective opportunity growth and value development. In this way, entrepreneurship is distinguished by its transformational directionality that points to collaboration and partnership.

THE PUBLIC AND SOCIAL ENTREPRENEUR
IN THE 21ST CENTURY

The term 'social entrepreneur' is almost the same as public entrepreneur. The distinction is that social entrepreneurs do not necessarily address change in government. Social entrepreneurship provides commercial entrepreneurs the advantage of going public without being public, apparently an important nuance for those who have an aversion to governance and faithfully connote the superiority of the market. Bornstein (2007) described social entrepreneurs as "people who solve social problems" (p. 1). The Ashoka website (2007) defined social entrepreneurs as "individuals with innovative solutions to societies' pressing social problems" (n.p.)—although virtually all definitions of entrepreneurship address correlations among environment, creativity, visioning, leadership, strategy, risk taking, being proactive, innovation, organization building, resource and asset realignment, sustained focus, and problem solving (Hitt et al. 2001; Miller 1983; Osborne & Gaebler 1992; Schumpeter 1934). Bornstein, in *Strategic Management Journal*, vol. 22, 479–491, 2003, discusses a clear distinction between social entrepreneurship and public entrepreneurship. The former addresses specific social problems and social change, whereas the latter encompasses the field of public administration and governmental processes. The literature notes that social entrepreneurship is not solely a public sector endeavor and is largely viewed as an alternative private sector movement, even though many social entrepreneurs seem to behave in political arenas adjacent to their concerns (Adler & Kwon 2002; Ashoka 2007; Bornstein 2007).

Emerging strongly in the late 20th century, entrepreneurship in the 21st century is equated with performance and public entrepreneurship, with obtaining solutions to public problems. This may be due to entrepreneurships' pragmatic problem-solving processes. However, most of the descriptions that we attribute to entrepreneurship actually refer to management. The distinction between the two is important but it does raise the issue of noticing the managerial necessity in evaluating the success of an entrepreneurial endeavor. Entrepreneurship has been considered both positively and negatively, but generally speaking, entrepreneurship is considered an important problem-solving attribute, which might explain its co-optation by the public realm. Its importance is due not only to its ability to tap into human potential, but also to its ability to open up managerial opportunity.

As stated earlier, entrepreneurship flourishes when a society is stable enough to allow for innovation (Maslow 1943; Schumpeter 1934) and appears to correlate with specific encouraging environmental factors. However, an entrepreneurial innovator appears to the beholder as an individual who changes the direction and flow of a community (Ashoka 2007; Lewis 1984) by:

- Defining a new synergistic vision of what is valuable
- Enrolling others in that vision
- Organizing others to develop and implement a strategic plan to build the potential of the vision and garner resources to support the plan
- Developing an organization structured to manage the value obtained over time

Definitions of the public entrepreneur are well suited to entrepreneurship in general. A public entrepreneur is "a person who creates or profoundly elaborates a public organization" (Lewis 1984, p. 11), and social entrepreneurs act as the "change agents for society" (Ashoka 2007). There is an overlap between public entrepreneurship and social entrepreneurship emphasized by "the fusion of public service with the private sector and civil society" (CSIS–GSI 2008, n.p.). This requires the compliance, if not intention, of the community at large. Social entrepreneurship is a function of groups inclined to or desirous of change and new value creation. The social entrepreneur, due to circumstance and traits, becomes the leader of the change action in a community. The public entrepreneur becomes a leader in governmental partnerships.

Due to its contextual nature, entrepreneurship is a driving force of social/economic change in society as it harnesses charismatic aspects of strategic leadership (Mort, Weerawardena, & Carnegie 2002) in divulging human potential. This leadership, more than any other trait, defines the individual and group entrepreneur and appears reliant on the opportunities society presents in the pursuit of collective opportunity, growth, and value development.

Entrepreneurship is distinguished by its direction. It points to future potential rather than reconciling deficiencies of the past. The entrepreneur, as leader, is forward thinking, where change creates a new construct rather than an incremental refinement. Public entrepreneurship is the practice of innovation, in which new elements of social action are created and sustained to achieve positive social and/or economic change.

Entrepreneurship is now an expansive term that illuminates the possibilities of other viable and fundamental sources of capital other than financial, such as: social, political, knowledge, information, cultural, and spiritual. It is difficult to find a definition of entrepreneurship that does not have the social implications of leadership and organization as mutually inclusive and virtually synonymous, particularly when viewed through the lens of society. Social entrepreneurship is distinct in that it elicits a sense of adventure and competence in the pursuit of new definitions and abilities of society as well as new opportunities for each member of that society to express himself or herself in a community-building function. Entrepreneurship appears not as an exclusive activity, but as a causal factor in society. In this way, social/public entrepreneurship is understood to grapple with the problems of governance by redefining purposeful inclusiveness in emerging and evolving cultures.

Entrepreneurship is not only a business, economic, or strictly personality trait. It expresses the human potential of exploration, curiosity, and organization. Fundamentally, it speaks to the ability to synthesize independent variables in the environment into something newly identified, enroll others to see this new potential, and have others commit to developing this potential in an organized manner. Communal potential is the dependent variable in entrepreneurship. Entrepreneurship produces a process of inquiry into human development and the potential of social capacity. If entrepreneurs are the explorers of human potential, then social entrepreneurs are the architects of society's promises.

Public entrepreneurship, which impacts governance systems, includes social, cultural, and other forms of human capital. The growing world of public entrepreneurs attests to the pervasiveness of social and governmental consciousness in entrepreneurial phenomena. Its encompassing and essential nature speaks pragmatically to the art of being a good citizen, an honest person, and an adult. Nonetheless, it is clear that entrepreneurship in social and organizational concerns is a growing phenomenon associated with those with the means or manner to provoke new solutions to stubborn social norms. The study of entrepreneurship requires catching practitioners in the field. The entrepreneur does not stand still for observation, but must be captured in flight, and this seems even more apt to entrepreneurs of the public persuasion.

SOCIAL CAPITAL AND PARTNERSHIP GOVERNANCE

Social capital was defined as an interactional process of networks and interrelationships (Nahapiet & Ghoshal 1998); as "a negotiated action taking place among individuals whose identities and decisions are shaped by their social roles" (Dubnick 2005, p. 388) in the process of account giving; as "dyadic sensegiving exchanges" (Maitlis 2005, p. 47); as "the invisible lever through which citizens collectively influence the quality of their shared public life . . . the shared resource produced by trust in others, which in turn enables individuals to participate in organized networks" (Pierce, Lovrich, & Moon 2002, p. 381; Putnam 1993); as "a collective dimension of society external to the individual" (Lochner, Kawachi, & Kennedy 1999, p. 260); as "a variety of entities with two elements in common: They consist of some aspect of social structures, and they facilitate certain actions of actors—whether persons or corporate actors" (Coleman 1998, p. 302); and as "a resource that actors derive from specific social structures and then use to pursue their interest; it is created by the changes in the relationship among actors" (Baker 1990, p. 619). Each definition struggled with the chicken or egg axiom. Which came first, the individual or the community? Pierce and Putnam recognized the contextual imperative of social capital, while Coleman, Lochner, and Baker seemed to dismiss it.

The concept of social capital was both compelling and enigmatic (Adler & Kwon 2002; Onyx & Bullen 2000; Portes 1998; Smith & Kulynych 2002). Every discipline and author offered a new description (Adler & Kwon 2002), and attempts to measure it were sparse and unsatisfying. This proposal deconstructs the notions and expressions of social capital as a term and proposes its operations at the heart of a new communitarianism (DeFilippis 2001; Onyx & Bullen 2000; Sobel 2002), which stated that "community is essential" (Etzioni 1968). From a public perspective, there was no such physical thing as social capital (Smith & Kulynych 2002) as a normative element. It was descriptive and acted as a metaphor for social processes rather than as a product or a stock, which could be traded. Yet, research indicated that it almost certainly influenced performance (Holzer & Zhang 2004). Nonetheless, a strong argument that social capital might, indeed, be a form of capital was made in the sense that it was an appropriable and convertible asset, even though it acted like a "collective good" (Coleman 1988) rather than private property. It seemed that "no one player has exclusive ownership rights" of social capital (Adler & Kwon 2002).

Social capital pointed to a capacity for exchange within a field of relationships where the sense of value for a community arose (Bourdieu 1985; Coleman 1998; Putnam 1993). Since that exchange was essentially a conscious act, it was often associated with organic social qualities like trust and reality building. As Fukuyama (1995) defined it, trust was a qualifying condition of social capital, not because it could be measured accurately but because it evoked an essential purpose of sociability. If trust was the lubricant of social exchange, then reality building was the glue. Both were socially constructed human phenomena (Berger & Luckman 1966). This dual aspect of social capital appears fundamental to the understanding of the term. Economic perspectives of social capital emphasize and value trust; whereas social perspectives of social capital tend to value reality. This proposal unites these often dichotomous perspectives by discussing the limits of the monological perspective and delving into a definition of social capital based on the collective nature of mankind. To this extent, it is considered that it is the community that defines the individual, not the individual that defines the community, and that individual expression is an expression of the community, both micro and macro, to which the individual belongs.

Social capital is a packaged paradox because its existence is causal rather than instrumental. Social capital is, like all forms of capital, descriptive of something of value. Social capital specifically refers to the value of sociability and infers its exchangeability as fundamental to all other forms of capital. Simply put, social capital infers that sociability is valuable. If this is true, the question becomes: How valuable is sociability? Social/public entrepreneurship suggests it is pervasive in every notion of humanity, as it defines who we are as human beings. It gives a sense of identity, both singularly and commonly, because it is a context-determining device. The attachment of social capital to the modern lexicon of the social sciences was a result of "the rise and evolution of this perspective . . . which . . . should be understood as a product of professional, cultural, and political forces, not necessarily of functional and economic needs" (Shenhav 1995. p. 557).

Public administration is at a point of reckoning regarding its co-optation by business administration, which has persuaded society that public administration is somehow inferior in theory and practice to business administration. New Public Management, in reinvigorating commercial fiscal and human resource efficiencies to public management, was at the point of completing this co-optation of the profession of public service and flattening it into a simple commodity exchange system (Denhardt 1993). At the heart of public service is accountability for progressive growth and development geared to maximize human potential through structural agreements, which translate into a civil society. When NPM builds its actions on the management of these agreements and their processes, a truer public administration paradigm is achieved. However, when governance is solely a broker of short-term cost/benefit ratio exchanges and the neglect of value determinations in the commons, public administration is simply a facet of business administration.

Because the concerns for democratic accountability remain unabated with regard to NPM, clearly something has been missing from NPM. DiIulio & DiIulio (1994) indicated that what was missing was a "moral factor" (Barnard 1938) as NPM relied on rational choice theory that ignored collective moralism. NPM's chief architects do tend to rely on business metaphor and theory to justify what appears to be a privatization of public service, rather than simply employing good business management practices and recognizing the need for citizen participatory processes. Ignoring these processes erodes one of the key premises of democratic societal public administration, which is, above all, to foster the progress of those very societal values. Assuming that market forces are correlated to democratic values appears to be NPM's clear, but unacknowledged, weakness.

Government services, NPM advocates say, will be better if allowed to function with market forces, a metaphor for individual, not communal, profit seeking. This sounds naïve, but the reason it is not is that NPM asserts that public processes are a function of politics, not management, and that politics is market driven in the same simplistic way that product development is driven. It is not, however (Derthick 1990; DiIulio & DiIulio 1994). NPM continues to ignore, or take for granted, the legal basis of a democratic society based on law, due process, and citizen participation. But this is exactly what public servants do not do. Yet, there was something to be said for the professional aspects of public administration versus the effect of elected and appointed politicians in government who attempted to be public managers and "leap into the dark" (Heclo 1977, p. 1) of public bureaucracies. Support of public sector professionalism may be NPM's strong card. The bottom line is, as professionals, public managers perform well and have their communities perform in a manner that even private sector market-driven analysts might admire. NPM can be too one-sided in its admiration for the private sector. Private sector admiration for the craft of management must be joined with public sector admiration in order to instill public trust.

It is within this dilemma that the arguments about social capital occur. This may determine that social capital is the battleground, which may determine the fate of public administration. Today, the term *social capital* often acts as a private sector Trojan horse penetrating the realm of public administration. It belongs to the field of economics, while coveting a public source of power and production. By attempting to co-opt the epistemology of social capital, its purpose is reduced to a functional commodity exchange. This takes the social out of the equation and, consequently, removes social processes that are the impetus of public action. Because of the social nature of social capital, it cannot truly be co-opted and may cause a reverse co-optation, which works to define values and the processes of human sociability essential to human action. In the final analysis, no other value system can exist without it, just as no system can function without the structures of governance.

Social capital, therefore, was not simply a function but a foundation of sociability (Portes 1998; Putnam 2000). It supersedes and encompasses all human social endeavor and production. In its unique convoluted way of mixing public and private sector metaphors, the concept of social capital is an attempt to define the process of social consciousness and the actions of human relationships at all levels, degrees, and functions. In this way, social capital is a modern term that places public processes at the source of human endeavor; therefore, its administration is the appropriate setting for other aspects of human expression, including business, culture, knowledge, technology, and of course government. Social capital may rightly be called community capital. Both refer to a source of exchange, not a commodity. Attempts to harness social capital are attempts to manipulate the exchange of value at its source. Paradoxically, this source appears as both singular and communal, but as the term (social capital) implies, the paradox is resolved by addressing its communal origins. In this way, an individual's capability in the social realm increases by an accountability to greater communal expressions. This accountability may point toward more appropriate measures of social capital.

The term 'social capital' evoked an air of mystery because it appeared to be "a feature of the social structure not of individual actors within the structure; it is an ecologic characteristic" (Lochner, Kawachi, & Kennedy 1999, p. 260), entirely interdependent and defining the mechanisms of human relations and the practice of humanity. At first glance, it makes sense but often reveals more about what it is not than what it may be. It cannot be seen or held but it is everywhere. "Social capital is a slippery but nonetheless important concept: slippery because it has been poorly defined, important because it refers to the basic raw material of civil society" (Onyx & Bullen 2000, p. 24). It cannot be bought or sold but its transactions increase value in many domains of capital exchange, describe social cohesion and community competence. It cannot be manufactured but it can be discovered and encouraged, and its accumulation enhances lives as a heuristic rather than rote phenomenon. Social capital was not a separate form of capital or commerce but a transformational mechanism of social context (Dubnick 2005).

The slipperiness of the term social capital lies in the word *capital*, which portrays a sense of individual propriety. The paradox that engenders this slippery metaphorical slope is that the words social and capital pull at opposite ends of the human condition. The term capital refers to a physical exchange mechanism, which can be possessed by anyone, but it may also point to a transformational process. In this way, "community characteristics ought to be distinguished from individual characteristics, and measured at the community level" (Lochner, Kawachi, & Kennedy 1999, p. 267). This is more difficult to do than it may seem because we live in a world with very little agreement or language regarding the nature of a human being from a community perspective. This means that whenever something is defined from a community perspective, it will necessitate using the language of individualism. That is the paradox of social capital that causes confusion and misguidance in its measurement.

Social capital is contextual. In line with Bourdieu (1985), social capital was defined as the actualized context of all values that comprise the potential of the common good, which might be "different at various levels of aggregation" (Lochner, Kawachi, & Kennedy 1999, p. 269). Therein lies the sticky wicket because human potential is understood differently by different societies and certainly not understood entirely by any. Separate, independent, or individual valuations occur within the value-making concept of social capital. Yet, one clear outcome of social capital, its discovery, applications, and investments, is the creation of community. This is another way of saying the creation of context. Social capital is, clearly, socially constructed. However, that construction involves real investments of time, trust, and determination in the process of relationship and network building.

Bourdieu (1985), who provided the first modern systematic analysis of social capital, defined the concept of social capital as "the aggregate of the actual or potential resources which are linked to possession of a durable network of more or less institutionalized relationships of mutual acquaintance or recognition" (Bourdieu 1985, p. 248). This outcome was not simply a matter of counting component outputs of social action but understanding that aggregate; consequently, Bourdieu (1985) did not propose investigating social capital using economic methodology. Social capital "is not simply a moderator . . . but also appears to have its own direct influence on both incremental and radical innovative capabilities of organizations [and] appears to be the bedrock of innovate capabilities" (Subramaniam & Youndt 2005, pp. 457, 459). Social capital, like the community outcomes derived from its exchange mechanisms, would aptly be the foundation of all commerce and the equity that arose in a field of social desire, impetus, and action.

Social capital was probably best viewed as value-laden discourse (Coleman 1988; Fukuyama 1995; Morrow 1999; Putnam 2000), and its performance as the result of the potential of these discourses that defined humanity within any community (Foucault 1972). Social capital was not difficult to perceive if experienced as the transformation of human capital into a functioning society (Coleman 1988).

According to Adler and Kwon (2002), the concept of social capital had become increasingly popular in a wide range of social science disciplines. Up against the long-standing theory of individualism as the rational social force, social capital peered into the "primordial feature of social life" (p. 17), our ties to one another and transcendence to a transrational force. Not unlike a fish in water, which does not perceive itself as being wet, human beings do not perceive that they are aspects of communities and their sociability is latently valuable. We cannot live without it. This is illustrated by noticing that human capital represents individual knowledge, which, by definition, is limited. Social capital represents community knowledge, which may or may not be limited and certainly is less limited than individual knowledge, while allowing for individual knowledge. Individual knowledge requires a community referent and does not exist without it. This referent is a result of the exchange mechanism of social capital. When society is structured, social and community capitals are released. What we perceive is the social referent that gives meaning to all other forms of capital. In this way, we understand social/community capital not as a product but as an ongoing process that produces social referents through social networks.

Social capital, as community capital, is available not as a personal commodity but as the matrix of human endeavor whose presence allows for a relationship of exchanges to make all other forms of capital express value. Social capital acts as accountability among different groups. Social capital can be measured by this transformation process and the outcome of social networks that manage the meaning, metaphor, and myths of human exchange. Separately, these can be described as forms of exchangeable or investable capital. Social capital, in describing general reciprocity, may be an "umbrella concept" (Adler & Kwon 2002, p. 18), in which social attributes such as organization, trust, culture, social support, social assets, relationships, and networks naturally occur. In this way, each form of capital, at its core, has the traits of social value and meaning. Social capital provided the exchange mechanism as a "negotiated action taking place among individuals whose identities and decisions are shaped by their social roles" (Dubnick 2005, p. 388). For instance, one might say the umbrella exchange mechanism in social capital humanizes economic processes, i.e., financial capital exchanges commitment and trust; physical capital exchanges power and performance; cultural capital exchanges self-expression and affinity; intellectual and knowledge capitals exchange contribution and curiosity; and human and organizational capitals exchange trust and security. Social capital embraces all of these forms of human exchange, each of which clearly is available at different levels of effectiveness and efficiency.

Social capital is different from the normal concept of "capital" because it does not solely transact information from one to another; it transforms concepts of human interaction into social phenomena. "An inherent characteristic of knowledge associated with social capital is its evolution" (Subramanian & Youndt 2005, p. 452). Social capital does not inform as much as it transforms. What it transforms is the potential each individual has to construct social reality with others. Consequently, it transforms each individual's conception of what is possible for humanity. Measures of social capital are congregate and holistic, rather than linear or fixed. These measures have qualitative results with quantitative symptoms.

Social capital and its chief variable, trust (Fukuyama 1995) in governance processes, may be at an all-time low while lamentations of its importance may be at an all-time high. Concerns regarding public trust certainly appear to be persistent over time (Holzer & Zhang 2004; Putnam 2000), as evidenced by Woodrow Wilson's (1887) concern about management ethics in an ideological politics/administration dichotomy; the 1939 Brownlow Commission's concern about financial accountability and executive management; Sen. William Proxmire's Golden Fleece Awards, highlighting a war on waste (1976–1982); Ronald Reagan's neoliberal rhetoric that "government is the problem" (1980–1988); and, most recently, Vice President Cheney's (2007) interpretations of the constitutional role of the office of vice president and his concern for secrecy and close ties to private corporations. Clearly in government, there is a problem with sabotaging public trust that looks more like congenital distrust.

Public trust and its processes and impacts on public performance may be the truest measure of a successful democracy but too often appears to be in peril. Does this mean that government is not performing well? Is the trust/distrust agenda a systemic and evolving aspect of the organic nature of a democracy? Perhaps Woodrow Wilson was implying that a more accurate dichotomy for understanding how public administration functions was not simply politics/administration but trust/distrust.

Economic, rational-actor theories go as far back as Adam Smith (1776), who noted that individual profit maximization, in both public and private interests, is the key motivator of human behavior. A motivation to promote a quality community, or contextual community environment, in which a "tragedy of the commons" (Elliott 1997) did not occur is not a persuasive or reliable indicator of human transactions. Yet, there is no evidence that business is more ethical, less political, or a better performer than government, particularly as measured against social impacts. Nonetheless, business management theory has pervaded public administration and organization theory since its modern conception.

Today, public administration cannot be separated from its business-oriented adaptations. In many respects, this has proven to be positive, chiefly in the areas of financial accountability, but muddled regarding accountability for policy development and implementation. Nor have business perambulations into the public sector achieved Woodrow Wilson's holy grail of democratic governance, a truer politics/administration dichotomy. One might safely say that since this dichotomous pursuit began almost immediately, the desired segregation backfired and forged a politicization of administration that inculcated a modern entrepreneurial-professional-political public servant. Furthermore, pushing past the anarchism that modern bureaucracy is a fourth branch of government (rather than the anchorage of government), a fifth branch of government may have emerged in the form of the private-sector/public-service provider, also known as *privatization* but which, in the case of PPPs, seems more a matter of publicization. This phenomenon appears not to disturb either liberal or conservative political ideologies, even though it is more constitutionally vague than proper public administration.

It is difficult to characterize the rational-actor (business) model as a trust model of governance. This is the limitation of the model as it veers toward disregard of democratic accountabilities, at times to such an extent that it nullifies a true sense of public responsibility. Odd as it may first appear, this may be a limitation imposed by representative democracy that may, at extremes (benevolent/malevolent), accept any form of representation as having more importance than the rights of the citizens on which it is based. Public potential can, indeed, be characterized as stemming from an essential trust in which not only relationships, networks, and the whole community are of primary importance, but this contextual adherence causes the very individuality that business admires.

Adam Smith (1776), by invoking a mystical concept of the "invisible hand" of socialization, inferred a transrational importance that overshadowed rational determination when he wrote about the individual in society as follows:

> He intends only his own security; and by directing that industry in such a manner as its produce may be of the greatest value, he intends only his own gain, and he is in this, as in many other cases, led by an invisible hand to promote an end which was no part of his intention. Nor is it always the worse for the society that it was no part of it. By pursuing his own interest he frequently promotes that of the society more effectually than when he really intends to promote it.
>
> (p. 1.1)

The inquiry this statement endorses and the trust we are to assume are misconstrued by the eternally positivist. The rational-actor business model, often labeled as positivist and scientific management, may explain immature individualism but cannot explain with much confidence the concept, implication, and practice of the more developed skills of trust. Without distorting its explanation toward distrust and its inherent limitations, it is anemic in explaining the most pressing concerns of governance: citizen-driven participation, citizenship, and community development. Midway through the 20th century, Waldo (1954/2007), Simon (1955), the Minnowbrook Conference of 1968, and George Fredrickson (1971) and in the 21st century Denhardt and Denhardt (2000) and others worked to correct this imbalance by addressing the social equity, citizenship, organizational behavior, and community development concerns of public service.

Business continues, by tradition and determination, to influence public opinion regarding the public sector and its practices. This may be due to the fewer constraints of the private sector in exploring new social and economic realms in globalizing humanity as well as impacting socioeconomic changes at the most local levels as evidenced in America's downtowns. Business is imbued with novel tendencies generally unaffordable to the public sector. This may explain why downtown revitalization, with its economic aspects merging private and public sector actors, is a chief motivator of community development. At the heart of the downtown revitalization movement are business interests, organized formally as improvement districts (Houstoun 2003), which bravely tangle with the merger of public and private sectors into workable community governance partnerships.

Although normally business motivated, BIDs exist as a form of public authority with quasi-governmental purposes. When the concept of trust is applied to the performance of BIDs, it shifts the entrepreneurial aspects of the BID. Its management interests describe less the profit maximization impulses of a private investor (Carton, Hofer, & Meeks 1998) and more the motivations of the public entrepreneur (Lewis 1984). The public entrepreneur manages the organization of people and resources in obtaining an agreed upon community vision or promise of what the community can be, i.e., community development as a maximization of communal assets.

Much has been said about the public entrepreneur by focusing on the individual who advances policy or programmatic solutions and takes advantage of political opportunity. However, little was said about public entrepreneurship (Kingdon 2003; Lewis 1984; Schneider & Teske 1992) as it defined the processes of public trust and the impact of these processes on performance. The term 'entrepreneur' suggests personal motivation and investment, whereas 'entrepreneurship' expresses a human potential to organize, develop opportunity, and address asset-and-values enhancement. Public entrepreneurship invokes a Gulickian transcendence of public and private motivations.

Business Improvements Districts, and other types of managed business districts, appear to endorse a form of pragmatic democratic accountability that decentralizes public authority toward a citizen-driven format. In a free enterprise economy, this alone might encourage entrepreneurship in the resolution of public problems. It emphasizes a classic trust dilemma between the private sector (business and private property owners) and the public sector (government and community values). BIDs, when they survive, thrive in this dilemma. How they do it may lie in the construction and reconstruction of private and public sector values and definitions and in the importance of social networks over strict performance. Being able to recognize and bridge vertical and horizontal relationships enables a BID manager to manage stakeholders in a supportive network that encourages self-reinforcing and cumulative increases in social capital using trust, norms, and networks. A BID manager could steer perceptions into recognition of collective achievement arising from stakeholder engagement (Justice & Goldsmith 2008).

PUBLIC ENTREPRENEURSHIP AND SOCIAL CAPITAL

Public entrepreneurship and social capital are the key attributes of public–private partnerships according to a 2008 Rutgers University study by Seth A. Grossman (2008).

Public entrepreneurship—A strategic process of organization and leadership that identifies, refines, improves, and capitalizes on communal assets to attain public goals.

Social capital—Social capital is considered an aspect of community development examined as social mechanisms fundamental to economic outcomes supporting the need for institutions of trust and sociability. Social capital is not difficult to perceive as it is experienced as the transformation of human capital into a functioning society (Coleman 1988). Social capital is not a separate form of capital or commerce, but a transformational mechanism of social context (Dubnick 2005).

What differentiates public from private entrepreneurship? The key differences seem to be the infusion and management of social capital in community-building processes:

1. Public versus private information (Lewis 1984; Schneider & Teske 1992). The public entrepreneur must not only share (disclose) more information but pursue information dissemination that is inclusive, while the private entrepreneur is more secretive and exclusive about information.
2. There is a "centrality of the social mission" (Mort, Weerawardena, & Carnegie 2002) in public entrepreneurship, and public entrepreneurs could also be called "collection action problem entrepreneurs" motivated by a collectionist sentiment to maximize collective value. The private sector entrepreneur seeks to maximize financial profit and is motivated by rational choice theory (Lewis 1984) that inures profit to specific investors.
3. Public entrepreneurship works to create public value (Moore 1995), while private entrepreneurship works to create private profit value.
4. Private entrepreneurship is influenced primarily by the supply side of goods, while public entrepreneurship is influenced primarily by the demand side for goods (Thornton 1999).

But it is the similarities of entrepreneurship that are intriguing and most compelling. There is no substantial difference in character, competence, and behavior between the private and public entrepreneur because entrepreneurship is a unique human behavior that works to allow change, value reorientation, and discovery (Thomas & Mueller 2000). The difference between the "entrepreneur and the regular citizen who takes an exploratory walk in the park is that the entrepreneur is on a mission to solve an identified social and/or economic problem, the solving of which creates new products, affiliations, and value possibilities, and the organizational constructs to maintain them. The simplest definition of entrepreneurship is: the strategic development of innovative value constructs (Schneider & Teske 1992; Thornton 1999). Throughout the literature in both private and public sectors, entrepreneurship shares the distinctions of:

- Risk taking
- Innovation
- Value creation
- Organizing collective action
- Strategic manipulation
- Leadership (Baumol 1990; Carland, Hoy, Boulton, & Carland 1984; Lewis 1984; McClelland 1987; Moore 1995; Osborne & Gaebler 1992; Roberts 1992; Schumpeter 1947)

Social capital shares the distinctions of:

- Trust (which to many may suggest risk taking)
- Value creation and enhancement
- Social and civic responsibility
- Organizing collective action
- Leadership (Coleman 1998; Fukuyama 1995; Galston 1996; Holzer & Zhang 2004; Portes 1998; Putnam 1993)

Behavior that works to transform the old into the new seems to be the telltale sign of entrepreneurial activity and social capital (Guth & Ginsberg 1990; Schneider & Teske 1992; Putnam 1993). Where there is the smoke of transformation there may be the fire of entrepreneurship buttressed by social capital creating public entrepreneurship (Grossman 2008). This may be applicable to many fields of endeavor, not only financial or product-oriented business transactions. This is because at its core the concept of entrepreneurship and social capital is value generation, be it financial, social, or political. Value generation is a pragmatic act that is elicited by inducing action, both individual and communal, that solves the question of what is valuable. Entrepreneurship flourishes when a society is stable enough to allow for innovation (Schumpeter 1947). The same is true for social capital in the emergence of public entrepreneurship (Grossman 2008). Innovation appears to the beholder as an individual who changes the direction and flow of a community by:

- Defining a vision of value
- Enrolling others in that vision
- Organizing a strategic vision quest
- Developing a structure to manage the value obtained over time

Public entrepreneurship began to take on pragmatic application in the 1990s with the New Public Management movement. This is the same time that BIDs begin to expand at a more rapid rate. Nancy Roberts describes a link between social capital and public entrepreneurship by indicating that what enables the public entrepreneur is the involvement of others in the policy process (Roberts 1992). This requires participation and trust (Fukuyama 1995). The term 'public entrepreneurship' has been around since at least 1984 when Eugene Lewis published *Public Entrepreneurship: Toward a Theory of Bureaucratic Political Power* (Lewis 1984). Lewis defines public entrepreneurship by concentrating on public a entrepreneur "as a person who creates or profoundly elaborates a public organization so as to alter greatly the existing pattern of allocation of scarce public resources" (Lewis 1984). It is not a great leap to conceive of entrepreneurship as a public attribute.

The dichotomy with the term lies in its economic origins that assume that entrepreneurship describes an individual's endeavors rather than (also) a public activity. Entrepreneurship cannot to be confined to a rational choice model, but applies correctly to collaborative networks (Carton, Hofer, & Meeks 1998; Lowndes & Skelcher 1998) and cultural models (Ozminkowski 2003). Roberts reinforces this understanding by defining public entrepreneurship as "the generation of a novel or innovative idea and the design and implementation of the innovative idea into public sector practice" (Roberts 1992). She also describes public entrepreneurs as "individuals who generate, design, and implement innovative ideas in the public domain" (Roberts 1992). This is echoed by Mariusz Ozminkowski, who describes entrepreneurship as the ability "to find opportunities and to create opportunities" (Mitchell 2008) and facilitate the "entrepreneurial environment" (Ozminkowski 2003) and public entrepreneurs as "agents of change" (Ozminkowski 2003). Ozminkowski identifies two key ideas that link social capital and public entrepreneurship to public administration, furthering the cooperative aspects of public entrepreneurship as opposed to concepts of individual entrepreneurship:

1. The public realm, i.e., culture matters.
2. Aspects of social capital are present in public entrepreneurship such as trust, open mindedness, uncertainty avoidance, and public achievement.

Due to its contextual nature, entrepreneurship can be a driving force of political/economic change in society as it harnesses the charismatic aspects of strategic leadership in divulging human potential. Mort's description of leadership seems to define the individual *and* public entrepreneur, and appears reliant on the opportunities society presents in the pursuit of collective opportunity growth and value development. Entrepreneurship is transformational and distinguished by its direction—pointing to a possible future rather than reconciling the past.

As community-based organizations with quasi-governmental functions and authority, Business Improvement Districts operate in the public entrepreneurship realm emphasizing economic development, decentralization, leadership, and cultural values. Without

Figure 3.2   **MATRIX: Public Entrepreneurship (P.E.) and Social Capital (S.C.)**

	LOW S.C.	**HIGH S.C.**
LOW P.E.	Broken promises, management of disagreements, highly unsuccessful socially and economically.	Compromised promises, management of agreements, successful socially, but less successful economically.
HIGH P.E.	Broken promises, business & residential discord, unsuccessful socially, but more successful economically.	Strong promises, business & residential affinity, management of agreements, successful both economically & socially.

argument, the general purpose of a BID is economic success, but success that can be measured not only on the individual level (demand), but also on the community level (supply) as improvements in the quality of life for a community. This statement is furthered by extrapolating that the general purpose of a BID is public entrepreneurial success. This insight supports the PPP as both nonlinear (quality of life—QOL) as well as linear perspectives (return on investment—ROI) on BID performance. As stated earlier, BIDs operate on the local level of governance acting as a link between the public and private sector, a broker of municipal services, and as a result become a potential technology and knowledge transfer mechanism with the aim of improving both sectors. The public administration argument is that public entrepreneurship (as exhibited by BIDs) takes on a somewhat different perspective when examined from a public, or cultural, standpoint rather than from a private, or individualistic, standpoint. Therefore, in determining the effect of entrepreneurship on the management of BIDs, we might look first at the level of benefit derived by its public (QOL) rather than private (ROI) expressions. We can do this by intersection of public entrepreneurship with social capital (See Figure 3.2).

PUBLIC–PRIVATE PARTNERSHIPS

One might say that the promise of democracy is not so great, thus permitting an interceding appropriation by economic mediums to quantify efficiency over effectiveness. This intercession may be the default of the democratic promise and we can expect to find a culture that exalts the individual and shifts public accountability from participation (citizens) to enlightenment (individuals). Democracy tells us that the mean of individual pursuits is apparently the efficiency of the majority. In a democracy, one cannot expect consensus, only a constructed majority. Here, we can expect to find definitions of the majority to be extremely conditional and in many cases statistically unreliable. Practical democratic effectiveness must rely on recognition if not on reasonable inclusion of a minority, but only one(s) that mathematically deduce the majority or create a cooperative political majority necessary to govern legitimately. Majority rule does not fully accommodate collective performance except by a subtraction or the tendency to marginalize the minority and ignore the silent. Concurrently and correspondingly, it must be remembered that regardless of personal charisma, "individual abilities do not automatically translate into collective performance" (Allison & Nicolaïdis, 1997, p. 39). This points us to the intellectual collision of individualism vs. community that forms the promise-performance paradox of democracy and is possibly the paradox of modernity. This offers a third option, a *third door*, rather than an *either/or* resolution of the paradox in which the resultant outcome is greater than the sum of its parts. The third door is partnerships, and particularly public–private partnerships.

Public–private partnerships are a growth field in government, for both project-specific public service contracts (design-build; design-build-operate-maintain; design-build-finance; design-build-finance-operate-maintain) and the establishment of ongoing and increased public management capacity such as BIDs, which are addressed in this book. The partnerships represent a continuum from almost purely public to almost purely private. In this dynamic arena, private investment and technology are transformed into public accountability. The private sector may look at these partnerships from the private end of the spectrum; however, public need and public actions bring forth and control the partnership and its methods of management, service delivery, accountancy, and finance structures. At the heart of Partnership Governance, particularly PPPs, is public entrepreneurship (also known as social entrepreneurship) and social capital. NPG assumes and converts public entrepreneurship from NPM within Partnership Governance. "The social entrepreneurship buzz phrase refers to the involvement of the private sector in aspects of the provision, maintenance, and sustenance of public or what should ordinarily be public owned utilities: transportation, water, electricity, health, information, sport, telecommunications, and other infrastructural assets. Most often these could be new or existing infrastructure services that have traditionally been provided by the government" (Somorin 2008).

There once seemed to be a clear difference between the public and private sectors and, for most, it followed that there was a difference between public and private sector management. Yet, no one could escape a sense that the differences were porous and becoming more so, the knowledge and experience of governance and business less reliable, and the mystery of what is private and the sanctity of that which is public was eroding (Allison 2004; Kettl 1993). By the 1990s, virtually worldwide, collaborations between the public and private sectors was heating up, eroding traditional epistemology of what was what and who was whom and merging, mutating, and evolving public management into something completely new. Our concept of entrepreneurship was at the core of this transformation and has enjoyed an expansion in its applicability from business to government. By the beginning of the 21st century, this transformation was a key success of NPM and has redefined public administration.

Since the Progressive era and the business applications of Frederick Taylor (1911), the public–private partnership distinction is displaying more and more advanced signs of slippage, or "mission creep" into traditional public arenas (Hoagland 1993). Despite the arguments of proponents of social equity and the concerns of market efficiency proponents on the other hand, a curious blur was settling over the public landscape. Private actors were becoming publicly active and accountable. In many respects, the dichotomous private vs. public sector discourse threatened to become a distinction without a difference. This was approved by some (Osborne & Gaebler 1992), who felt that the private sector had an advantage, and created dismay for others (Denhardt & Denhardt 2000), who felt that the public sector's advantage would become contaminated by business sector power elites. But the push for more partnering between public and private actors increased due to support of privatization (Savas 2000) or expanded public management, publicization, and governance (Grossman 2008). The modern era is notable due to a remarkable private/public integration that seems to have spirited away most reliable distinctions regarding management technology and has managed to sustain the distinction regarding profit and process. This has furthered an ongoing fusion of management technologies, particularly regarding the role of the public manager.

If "the market is a way of managing scarcity" (Kettl 1993, p. 206), conversely the public arena might be a way to manage human potential, which is abundant, growing, and not scarce. The private sector tends to attribute value from an individualistic perspective, and engages personal interest and competing market forces exhibiting limitations that are somehow overcome by an omniscient market administrator (Adam Smith's invisible hand) and/or the threat of a zero-sum game. The latter is evident, but the former, as witnessed by the economic collapse of financial markets (the Great Recession that began in December 2007 and ended in June 2009), requires a leap of faith.

The public sector attributes value from a communal perspective that causes the emergence and sustainability of responsive civil society and engages our collective interests. In order for this perspective to be realized, it requires pragmatism (Dewey 1925; James 1909), not prayer. The curiosity of what or which comes first, the individual or the society, is the crux of much modern argument, but the argument is settled; both come first. This divides the intellectual world into two camps: social realists who hold the individual as paramount, ascribed to the dignity of the Enlightenment (Newland 1997) to the point of self-absorbed disaster; and the social constructionists who stress that humanity's social nature is its most unique invention (Berger & Luckman 1967; Searle 1995), but often get stuck in peculiar dogmatisms. In the midst of this debate, the phenomenon of public–private partnerships emerged on the public administration scene. Having done little to ease the private vs. public debate, this phenomenon is a bona fide hybrid of the public and private sectors.

The dichotomy between the public and private aspects of society enjoyed vigorous debate in politics—that is, until the 19th century industrial economy was replaced by

20th century service and information economies, which required flexibility, integration, and adaptable external exchange. The dichotomy needed revision (Allison 2004). Service economies, both private and public, have similarities, most prominently because both serve rather than exploit. Necessity and interdependence blurred the boundaries between the public and private sectors (Bovaird & Löffler 2009; Briffault 1999; Kettl 1993). Areas of the economy that adapted to this interplay seemed to do well; those that did not, decayed. This was well illustrated in traditional urban areas with central business districts (economic generators) that deteriorated rapidly when they did not adjust to entrepreneurial and customer-oriented service models and held on to industrial models. Those that adapted or built on existing service models enjoyed better success. This is well documented in the BID movement (Becker, Grossman & Dos Santos 2011; Briffault 1999; Grossman 2010; Houstoun 2003; Hoyt 2001; Justice 2003; Mitchell 2008; Morçöl & Zimmermann 2006; Stokes 2002; Wolf 2008). "The BID phenomenon forces us to rethink our dichotomous conceptual foundation of public versus private on which traditional public administration is built" (Morçöl & Zimmermann 2006). The BID model formalized a concern that once might have been taken for granted. "They blend public management expertise with business acumen into a unique administrative form" (Mitchell 2001, p. 203) and "are rooted in the long privatist tradition of urban governance and politics in the United States" (Morçöl & Zimmermann 2006, p. 6).

At the edge of public administration, where the public sector meets the private and where free enterprise meets social capital, there used to be a no man's land of public policy. This may have been due to an allegiance to a private/public sector dichotomy. "As American governments pursued more public policy through nongovernmental partners, public policy increasingly became entangled in private goals and norms" (Kettl 2002). PPPs tend to operate in this no man's land, using both private entrepreneurial and community development approaches, synergistically. As entrepreneurial models, public–private partnerships are expected to "channel private-sector energy towards the solution of public problems" (MacDonald 1996, p. 42). Where government administration might be seen as bureaucratic and process oriented (Gingrich 2005), PPPs are viewed as entrepreneurial, management focused, and innovative. PPPs walk a fine line between traditional public administration and entrepreneurial public management, and things public and things private no longer are as meaningful as they once were.

At the PPP level of governance, two forces define benchmarks of success: citizen participation and professional management. If the definition of citizen participation is accepted as the role of self-governance in promoting institutional legitimacy, the formation of common understandings between public and private participants (Justice 2003), the role PPPs might play in furthering participation by citizens become evident.

PPPs require professional management to allow for the "facilitation of agreement" (Justice 2003) around compatible goals and committed resources (Schaeffer & Loveridge 2002). PPPs are a form of managed cooperation and an addition to democratic governance that operates at the defining nexus (Figure 3.3) of a private/public vs. social/economic dichotomy that defined and often transformed the term *community* in society. Stokes supports this in his 2002 dissertation, regarding BIDs, that a PPP "restores a

Figure 3.3   **Public–Private Partnership: BID Nexus**

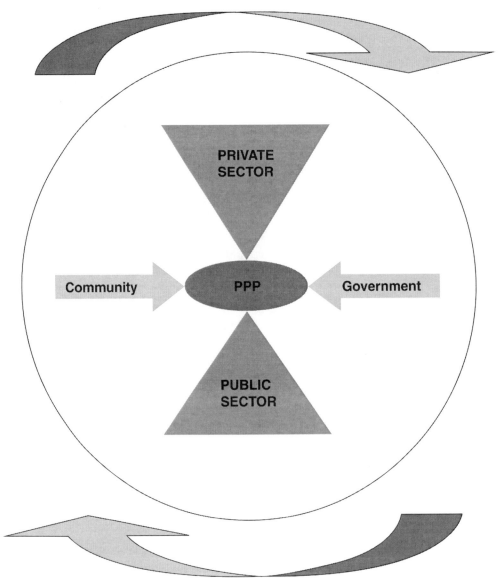

level of community faith in collective processes." Barry Bozeman goes a step further and makes a key point: All organizations are public (Bozeman 1987). In other words, the public–private sector dichotomy is false. The private sector resides within the public sector by virtue of being less public. (Not unlike disagreement and distrust existing by virtue of erosion not manifestation.) There is no private sector divorced of publicness, but there is publicness without privateness. Nonetheless, the concept of a public sector

Figure 3.4 **Multidimensional Theory of the Impact of Publicness on Organizational Behavior with Added Partnership (Bozeman 1987, p. 89, Fig. 6.1)**

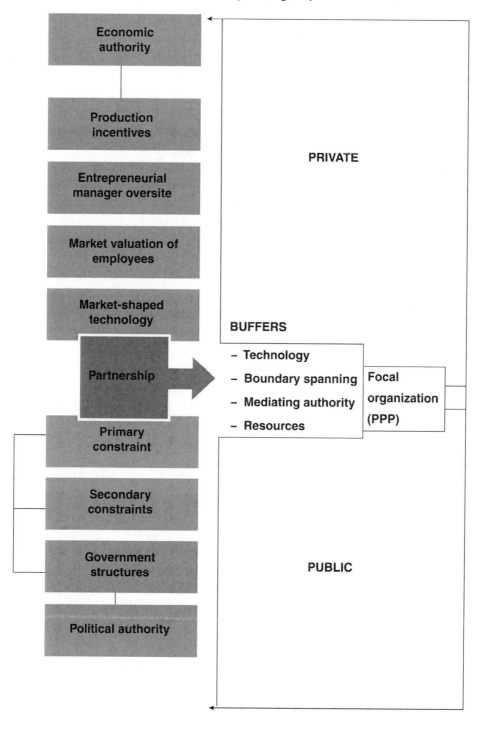

and a private sector are useful for analysis, but it is their multidimensional partnership that is most effective for producing results.

Bozeman's 1987 diagram (Figure 3.4) depicts a multidimensional theory of the impact of publicness on organizational behavior. It describes public–private partnerships and clearly illustrates the unifying role of PPP organizations as a "focal organization" (p. 91). Access to the processes of community appear to elicit perceptions of success, based initially on a sense that the quality of life is improved, which seems to be tied to the ability to invest personal time and energy into the development of the organization. Multidimensional theory could successfully be labeled the practice of public–private partnerships. Figure 3.4 depicts the entrepreneurial aspects of economic authority and the constraints that bind innovation and sustain its benefits through institutional structures and sustained agreements. PPPs are unique because they possess both economic and political legitimacy. It is clear from the design that the feedback loop caused by the focal organization, the PPP, works to impact both public and private processes so that political and economic authority are altered. The buffers represent the factual conditions that public and private forces must contend with to achieve the competency to operate. The diagram must be read so that all the buffers have both public and private attributes and the buffers act as equalizers to keep one sector from displacing another and eroding the partnership.

Buffers also act to protect each sector from itself or from excessive intrusions that would destabilize the partnership. In this way, buffers are the foundations of network capacity and act as confidence and trust builders by allowing the correct interpretation of each sector's assets. Improper or inadequate judgment of valued assets of one sector on another corrupts the rational process by attributing weakness or strength ineffectually. It creates a false adversity that promotes the idea that one sector is a problem, rather than an opportunity for the other. The buffers, in effect, reduce political adversity, an attribute necessary for functional partnering. For example, resources are both public and private; boundary spanning denotes not only movement across markets but political jurisdictions; technology must respect strengths and weaknesses of each sector, and mediating authority refers to constitutional law or enabling legislation. The focal organization acts as the fulcrum of the public–private partnership conferring the legitimacy of each sector.

PUBLIC–PRIVATE PARTNERSHIP MANAGEMENT

It is clear that the management of public–private partnerships is nontraditional, as its end goal is not to favor public or private sectors, but to create a working arena to exchange abilities and approaches by establishing hybridization in planning, policy, and implementation. The end goal is to manage change, but change that is pragmatic and synergistic; change that melds high levels of public entrepreneurship with social capital. If we are to understand the performance of public–private partnerships, then we must understand the attributes described in Figure 3.2 and see that the management of public–private partnerships provides better access to performance measurements. Management is the key to the success of everything, including public–private partnerships. Public-private partnership management is *an expertise that brings together business, government, planning, and community development knowledge and skills to solve public problems.*

Partnering is often nonlinear and transformational. That is its attraction. There is the traditional way of one agent either providing money for a project when requested or identifying some singular need or problem and organizing an effort to meet it or resolve it. These are ways to fix things. However, there is another way that strengthens and broadens that approach: *partnerships.* There is greater power available in communities, i.e., neighborhoods, towns, organizations, or corporations, than the people involved often realize. Partnership is the mechanism that unites communities, their sponsors, and volunteers around a shared vision. The special power of "partnering" provides a significant competitive advantage and is the way to achieve breakthrough results. Partnerships are a direct result of *bringing people together to solve common problems, developing agreements, and managing those agreements with a commitment over time* (Grossman 2008).

Successful PPPs can be identified by the quality, accountability, and transparency of the partnerships they keep. Achieving the ability to be an excellent partner is the result of focusing attention on the community rather than solely on the individual, and of seeing ourselves as being that community rather than only a solo entity (the term 'community' used here means PPPs, groups, organizations, families, or the society we belong to or are engaged in).

Partnerships require professional management to allow for the "facilitation of agreement" that fosters the partnership (Justice 2003). PPPs are an addition-to not separate-from democratic governance and exist at the defining point of private/public, social, and economic activities that define the term 'community.' PPPs dispel adversity in order to achieve progress and are measured politically by this ability. Achievement with this definition of community development will elicit perceptions of success based initially on a sense that the community's quality of life is improved. This seems to be tied to the ability to invest personal time and energy into the development of the community and to participate collectively in the activities that make a community viable, which are aspects of social capital. A successful PPP apparently "restores a level of community faith in collective processes" (Stokes 2002).

The services a PPP manager chooses "depends on the amount of agreement about goals and about the technology most reasonably suited to achieve agreed upon goals." PPPs that aren't moving ahead often have a lot of conversations about what to do, but not much actually happens. If something does happen, it is disjointed, out of step, or inadequate. People wonder how they are ever going to have their communities step up to the plate and take real initiative in making things better, and manage agreements not disagreements (Grossman 2008).

When the energy to move ahead is lost in a PPP, it often turns out that the PPP's attitude is one of managing its disagreements rather than its agreements. Unsuccessful PPPs may have no idea what to agree about, let alone what agreements to commit themselves to. On the other hand, PPPs that put their plans into action and achieve results seem to have discovered something important. They have learned how to discover their agree-ments and to manage their agreements with a *commitment* and accountabilities over time. This is a definition, described in Chapter 1, of partnerships in general and how they work to transform mutual interests into real improvements. A commitment may be credible not because contemporary politicians are themselves motivated to keep it, but because institutional or structural arrangements such as PPPs compel their compliance (Morçöl & Zimmermann 2006).

It has been noted that PPPs are often managed by private sector organizational enti-ties or not-for-profit corporations, possessing real public authority by offering a public/private partnership. Nonetheless, the effectiveness of a PPP is not that public goods are privatized, but that private capacities are utilized and managed as a public good. This definition of publicization infers public accountability. The PPP model allows the pri-vate sector to provide funds and technical expertise, and in turn receives from the public sector political legitimization and taxing powers. The public aspects of a PPP, particu-larly public taxes and/or assessments, allow a community to avoid the problem of free riders associated with volunteerism, address upkeep of common areas, and instill place management. "PPPs formalize the interests of the local community" (Stokes 2002). At the level of governance that PPPs represent, there are two forces that define benchmarks of success: citizen participation and professional management. If we accept as a defini-tion that citizen participation is "the role of self-governance in promoting institutional legitimacy, the formation of common understandings between public and private partici-pants" (Grossman 2008; Justice 2003), we can see the role PPPs might play in furthering participation by citizens. Institutional legitimacy is a hollow reward if it lies fallow.

The PPP manager is a different kind of animal in the public management field. For decades many have attempted to define the profession. It is not one that can easily be pigeonholed into a simple discipline. It requires not only public administration and organizational skills, but also business economics and development, public relations and marketing, personnel and project management, finance and budgeting, and political skills. (Grossman 2008; Mitchell 2001). PPP managers must adapt and use a variety of public and private management aspects (Mitchell 2008), described above, because PPP management is as much a venture in building community management capacity as it is in delivering business development services. The competencies of a PPP management expert are:

- Entrepreneurship
- Business retail development and marketing
- Public policy development, community development, and organization
- Personnel and group management
- Not-for-profit financing and budgeting
- Multitask project management
- Public relations and communications
- Urban planning and development (BDMCP 2008; Grossman 2008; Grossman & Ruffin 2007; Justice 2003; Mitchell 2001; Stokes 2002)

THE BUSINESS IMPROVEMENT DISTRICT PPP: EXAMPLE OF MULTISECTORAL PUBLIC ENTREPRENEURSHIP

As community-based organizations with quasi-governmental functions and authority, Business Improvement Districts (PPPs) operate as public–private partnerships in the public entrepreneurship realm, emphasizing economic development, decentralization, leadership, and cultural values (Justice 2003). The general purpose of a BID is economic success, success that is measured not only on the individual business level, but also on the community level at which the BID resides. Improvements in the quality of life for the business community directly impact the community encompassing the BID. Entrepreneurship becomes a public force for improvement. As a public force, public entrepreneurship participates in material and nonmaterial capital. It assumes that a community as a whole has economic value and that the co-joining of material and social wealth aspirations require a proficiency in the management of collective as well as individual potential, with the latter a subset of the former. Additionally, the public management in this process is expected to be an active partner in community and economic development. This describes the governance concerns of public–private partnerships. Government is no longer present to only help, but to be part of social/economic endeavors, and this participation is a management concern. As discussed earlier, public entrepreneurship takes on a different perspective when examined from a public or cultural standpoint, rather than from a private or individualistic standpoint. In determining the effect of entrepreneurship in Partnership Governance, examining its public, rather than private, expressions reveals a skill for public managers.

Business Improvement Districts, as formal public–private partnerships, operate in the realm of public entrepreneurship, emphasizing economic development, decentralization, leadership and cultural values. The goal of BIDs is economic success measured on the community level (Stokes 2002). BIDs, on the local level of governance, link the public and private sector and, as a result, become a potential technology and knowledge transfer mechanism with the aim of improving both sectors. The public administration argument is that social capital and public entrepreneurship (as exhibited by BIDs) take on a somewhat different perspective when examined from a public or cultural standpoint, rather than from a private or individualistic standpoint. In determining community needs, the success of a PPP must keenly be measured by determining its public manifestations as improvements to the quality of life.

BIDs are fascinating because they exemplify a new pragmatism in public management, working to unite the best functioning practices of public and private business. This pragmatism begins with a few intended promises of BIDs that are associated with creating formalized public–private partnerships, determining self-help approaches, and establishing a citizen-driven government forum. These promises examine and explore trust within the community: between people and groups; between government administration and the common man; and between what has been and what can be. At its heart is the examination of the importance of *professional* management by acknowledging its absence at the stages and local applications that are most crucial in maintaining agreement of direction, purpose, and value. Prior to a promise unfolding (performance), a mechanism to manage the promise is required; the operation of managing a promise is evidenced through the performance(s) it generates. The quality of the performance may then be tied to the precision and public nature of the promise. The intended promises of a BID appear to cause sustained collective action to maintain and improve community assets.

THE PERFORMANCE PARADOX OF PPPS—LESSONS FROM BUSINESS IMPROVEMENT DISTRICTS

Business Improvement Districts throughout the world were reshaping the nature of public administration, its processes, and performance (Hoyt 2008; Justice 2003; MacDonald 1996; Morçöl & Zimmermann 2006; Stokes 2002) at the most local of government levels, the neighborhood. The key to this metamorphosis is not only the public–private partnership but also the merging of public and private management technologies in such a way as to forge a distinctive branch of public management: business district management, an expertise within public administration that required a manager to bring together business, government, planning, and community development knowledge and skills pragmatically to achieve citizen-driven governance (Grossman & Ruffin, 2007).

Many small businesspeople and most people "do not really own much else" (Fishel 2001, p. 4) than their home, business, or business property. The small businessperson is Fishel's homevoter and, in the case of the small businessperson, the commercial voter. The 'homevoter' is linked to the small business commercial voter by the amount of personal investment in a single property and with a chief interest in "managing assets well" (Fishel 2001, p. 64). Both are also linked by their voting behavior, which aims to maximize their primary property asset. If this asset is exceedingly compromised, they both *vote with their feet* and purchase property or move their business to a better managed community (Tiebout 1956).

Home-based entrepreneurs seek governance that is accessible and directed toward maximizing their primary property asset. The enticement of real governance authority is a chief purpose of BID public–private partnerships, which represent a reaction to centralization and perceived government inaccessibility and indifference to economic maximization of property assets. Business Improvement Districts that focus on business communities work to equalize the relationship between the homevoter and the small business voter by emphasizing linked entrepreneurial interests. This is accomplished by extending the authorities of the municipal corporation to the business sector, defining a district community, and requiring stakeholder participation, both financially and managerially in the form of a partnership.

The recognition that within municipalities, there exist not only neighborhoods but also systems of communal interaction based on a variety of social and economic interdependencies that define the context of private investment is at the heart of the BID concept. In this way, BIDs fundamentally reinforce practices that support successful community development and provide the public sector asset management structure necessary to define and implement property investment maximization strategies. The BID concept is primarily a community governance movement and relies on community definition and implementation practices.

By seeking to embrace multisector organization, the home/commercial voter can be characterized as the community-based entrepreneurial voter. Entrepreneurial voters clearly comprehend the value of their personal property as a chief asset but must appreciate the impact of common property on this private asset. Addressing and managing common property as a linked asset to private property is less determinable unless a consistent and formalized structure, effective in identifying agreed upon mutual assets and managing these assets, is determined. Managing the assets of private property is often less complicated because it is frequently not democratic, but autocratic. Managing common community assets tends to be more complicated, particularly in a democratic process. In both private and public situations, without a management structure, investment potential is compromised. This requires additional attention at the public level. The successful entrepreneur pays attention to the internal private risks of an investment and, equally important, the impact of external public risks. In the case of the community-based entrepreneur, without a public asset management structure, the risk factor in managing the public impact of private investment may be too great and, eventually, would be relinquished to the few that are heavily capitalized by privilege or demeanor. This issue may propel many of the criticisms of BIDs (Briffault 1999; Ross & Levine 2001).

Management of assets, both private and public, is the key to success for the entrepreneur. The preferred method of management at the level of homeowner/small business was the localized municipal corporation and its antecedent, special assessment districts (Houstoun 2003) such as BIDs. Small business entrepreneurs and "homeowners will, at the local level, want to adopt the mix of policies that maximizes the value of their primary asset" (Fishel 2001, p. 6). Successful management is asset driven and maintains a close proximity to its charge. As private independent investment grew in the middle class following WWII, so did local government, which aimed at managing those investments.

In this way, the homevoter is partnered with the commercial voter, sharing a symbiotic entrepreneurial link and both behaving as entrepreneurial voters. Personal property assets at the scale of the modern homeowner and small businessperson function by the contextual framework of the community in which they are. The explosion in personal property ownership caused a fragmentation of community assets. This fragmentation creates a disturbance in the value of community assets because the level of small-scale private investment potentially interrupts communal identity, disrupting interdependent alliances through overemphasized independent alignments. "Once you've made the purchase, your only protection against community decline is watchfulness and activism" (Fishel 2001, p. 75), alluding to the purpose of municipal corporate strategies. The framework of the municipal corporation and its subagents (special districts) is to harness the exogenous assets that comprise the sense of contextual value (that is, value of the whole community), thus permitting fragmentation to sustain a rational purpose.

Zoning and other regulated land use designs are none other than the conceptual framework of asset valuation in the face of community fragmentation/individualized disturbance. A disturbance having no contextual relation withers away to meaninglessness, which is another way of saying it erodes contextual value. This is witnessed in situations of urban blight as well as in rural devaluation. However, a community fragmentation disturbance, if managed, can increase the overall value of the community by accentuating its constituent parts and managing them as assets.

Modern local government efforts are designed to identify and manage asset impactors (fragmentation disturbances) as they evolve in the successful development of real neighborhoods and extended communities. This includes PPPs. This sustains the value of contextual assets, of which the personal (privatized) asset is a part. The 'entrepreneurial voters' will vote with their feet and leave when contextual (community) assets are poorly managed and undefined. Community-based entrepreneurs and other localized investors tolerate property taxes (and special assessments) only when the public services financed by them are capitalized in their property and business values. The common assets when managed well become an added value and a capital gain for the individual. Because a home or small business property may, in fact, be most people's primary investment, this implies that the home-based entrepreneur is local. The investment is a locally generated motivator. Different from tribalism, the fragmentation of common goods in itself is disruptive to managing contextual assets. To counter this, "homeowners were becoming conscious that the attractiveness of the entire community, not just their own structure and those of their neighbours, made a difference in the value of their homes" (Fishel 2001, p. 216) and the same is true of the small business investor. The local municipal corporation balances the fragmentation disruption by effectively managing common assets and continuously interpreting their value over time.

The risk facing the modern civic (interdependent) entrepreneur is that the independent entrepreneur tended to an irrational abuse of the commons (Elliott 1997), which could disrupt the value of private investment by eliminating or reducing its contextual linkages. The rational response is to establish management structures that sustain contextual assets, i.e., partnerships, while recognizing private property assets through community fragmentation. This response notes that when the contextual asset is eroded, the value of the private asset also degenerates. Then, only attuned and sustained efforts to redefine and manage contextual assets will permit revitalization and investment maximization. Fragmentation is most effective when contextual assets are not valued at a premium. No fragment of a community can be a premium asset unto itself. If a trend toward fragmentation occurs and then makes a fragment of a community the premium contextual value, then each adjoining parcel value is at risk of degradation equal to the value of the primary fragment. This means that an entire community is at risk of being sufficiently devalued by reliance on one or more fragments of the community achieving the full asset value of the community. Company towns throughout the country are a testament to this axiom. When the company is successful, everyone wins; when it is not, everyone loses.

Municipal corporations are similar to private corporations but "different than private corporations because of the localized economic interests of the shareholders" (Fishel

2001, p. 30). Local municipal governments work to maximize stockholder assets just as private corporations. *Submunicipal* business and neighborhood improvement districts are extensions of this effort with often an even more articulated economic goal. It seems inevitable that decentralization will continue as long as private property is permitted because it empowers residents and local businesses to manage their chief assets. Again, the *homevoter hypothesis* can also be described as an entrepreneurial voter hypothesis that matches a fundamental model utilized by Business Improvement Districts to determine and maximize contextual assets through partnerships: Agreements, Management, Commitments, and Accountability. Although the entrepreneurial voter is initially motivated by the preservation of a private property asset, what has emerged by way of the municipal corporation is a clear understanding of the importance of contextual community assets arrived at by applying the PPP model. **Agreements** efficiently resolve the fragmentation problem when the "fragmentation of local government causes property owners, who are mainly homeowners, to see a mix of local services that maximizes the value of their holdings" (Fishel 2001, p. 223). **Management** resolves the erosion of achieved agreements by sustaining clear direction and recognizing that "the financing of local services from the property tax is a key element of this efficiency seeking activity" (Fishel 2001, p. 223). **Commitment** resolves fragmentation irrationality, the result of a process where business support and "homevoters will vote for property tax increases if the expenditures they finance will increase their home values" (Fishel 2001, p. 223). **Accountability** resolves performance confusion and asserts value equilibrium. This model defines the entrepreneurial advantage by equalizing public and private investment impactors, sharing common exogenous risk factors, and managing contextual community assets.

At stake in this process are the antecedent notions of democracy-in-action and its standard limitations: information asymmetry, particularism and exclusivity, and xenophobia of every hue that triggers a world economy based on distrust, disagreement, and conditional acceptance assumed as a broad and invisible discourse. The western arena of public service and its varied management apparatuses toil to extract the promise of democracy while human potential cowers to the mean of economic efficiency, clientelism, and more disastrously, economic tactics often misinterpreted as entrepreneurship.

There is often a noncontextual attitude about public performance that alienates the various public administration camps: management, policy, fiduciary, and political. It is a performance assumption, in which the components of human endeavor, let alone public human endeavor, are compartmentalized and examined as self-fulfilling and functioning. In other words, it is as if an individual part of the performance creation and performing process is unique and set aside as a function of the entirety of accomplishment by itself. This has worked to erode the purpose of public management, which may recognize aspects of its mission, but in fact is a functioning whole. As a whole, outcome measures that balance public, private, and partnership aspects are often more accurate measurements of PPP performance, which does not diminish, but rather places outputs in the supportive capacity they represent in the process of accomplishment.

Performance management and its measures begin with data collection but, ultimately, end with how those data are presented and used. In order to measure and monitor performance-based outputs and outcomes, a baseline data record must be established and a reasonable strategic goal stated. These two objectives (outputs and outcomes) offer primary assessment-driven choice (Wang 2002). However, in the public sphere, measuring outputs lean toward control, tactical production, and content orientation, where the goal is to function efficiently while the citizen remains purely advisory rather than managerial. Outcomes take us in the direction of public entrepreneurship (Wang & Berman 2000), in which strategic education/decision making and performance are the goal of transforming community capability and encourage the citizen as a management participant.

When we speak about public performance, we are speaking fundamentally (and ongoing) about how the promise of democracy affects the performance of tasks that are generated by public organizations (both informally and formally, although, in regard to business improvement districts, we are restricted to the latter): the planning process, the execution of projects and plans, the implementation of policy, and the evaluation of the endeavor. In every performance there resides a promise, or a set of promises, that guides the human endeavor, and this is true in both private and public environments. When we speak about performance in general, we are speaking fundamentally about measuring outputs and outcomes against inputs and implementation; therefore, we are assessing management processes. This process is the managing and evaluation of the inherent promise(s) in every performance. The chief differences between private and public sector management are the degree of inclusion and the fulfillment of outcomes, i.e., the promised levels of inclusion and envisioned contextual goal. If we are on the high end of either of these, we can safely presume that we are operating in a more public environment. If we are on the lesser end, then we are most likely operating in a private environment. The importance of this distinction is twofold:

1. Inclusion underwrites democratic functions and tends to diminish autocratic functions.
2. The often greater depth and breadth of the promises between people is imperative in public environments, due to:
   a. The extent of partnering needs places outputs as parts of outcomes.
   b. The performance process is nonlinear, so that input "A" may not directly impose upon or predict output or outcome "B."
   c. The timeline for expected results to occur and retain impact is expanded; it is long term (even short-term events often have lasting public effect).

The gap between public promise and performance is infused with the jujitsu of public and private partnerships. This is what BIDs seem to step into (Grossman 2007; Houstoun 2003). BIDs, as public–private partnerships, are subunits of government established to encourage a breakthrough in public and private sector behavior. These quasi-governmental partnerships are designed to transcend presumed adversarial relationships often experienced between government and business, and initiate a true partnership that utilizes the strengths and offsets the weaknesses of each sector. Public–private partnering presents an opportunity to bridge and unify dysfunctional and pathological social-economic situations. This allows the public sector to enjoy more vigorous entrepreneurship while allowing the private sector to utilize public authority and processes to achieve economic revitalization. The public sector takes on private aspects and the private takes on public responsibility. The increased knowledge of social, political, and economic processes benefits each sector but challenges established systems that have not achieved an institutional understanding of this unique partnership. The common discourse on public–private partnerships focuses on the privatization aspects of the partnership in which public services become privatized. But in a true PPP, we must equally consider the 'publicization' process in which private sector actors take on public accountabilities and begin to dissolve the public–private dichotomy to create a new hybrid capacity for community and business development. As stated above, this new capacity might act as a "third door" to economic and social stability.

The issue BIDs face has led PPPs to suffer the slings and arrows of political misfortune from both/many/all sides of the economic aisle. Public advocates get concerned about the undemocratic aspects of private government, and private advocates get concerned about tyranny at the thought of public businessmanship and governmental (public) entrepreneurship. Either concern is reasonable, but not generalizable. This argument provides us with a promise of democracy: tossing out notions of culturally defined public/private sector dualism and replacing it with the British and New Zealand approach of private, quasi-private (quango) quasi-government (quago) and government/public (Becker 2010), which all sound like forms of public–private partnerships. In the democratic promise, every citizen, regardless of persuasion and creed, may practice governance with his or her fellow citizen as it occurs to that person. But this would require the elimination of the cults of particularness, exclusion, and the system of closed privilege, which can ravage, contort, and betray even the basic justifications of democratic capability.

CONCLUSION

PPPs exemplify a new pragmatism in public management, working to unite the best functioning practices of public and private business. This pragmatism begins with creating formalized public–private partnerships, determining self-help approaches, and establishing a citizen-driven government forum. The promise system allows network actors to examine and explore trust within the community, between people and groups, between government administration and the common person, and between what has been and what can be. At its heart is the examination of the importance of "professional" management by acknowledging its absence at the level, stages, and local applications that are most crucial in maintaining agreement of direction, purpose, and value. Required prior to a promise unfolding is a mechanism to manage that promise. We experience the operation of managing a promise by the performance(s) it generates. The quality of the performance is tied to the precision and public nature of the promise.

The intended promise of a PPP is to cause sustained collective action to maintain and improve community assets (Justice 2003; Stokes 2002). PPPs address four fundamental themes (Grossman 2007; Grossman, Ruffin, & Reenstra-Bryant 2007; Houstoun 2003; Justice 2003; Mitchell 2001; Morçöl 2006; Stokes 2002):

1. Public Entrepreneurship:
   - Builds upon the assets of the community
   - Emphasizes organization and management to achieve a strategic vision
   - Utilizes business development technologies
   - Builds on comprehensive community development strategies
   - Unites public and private sector stakeholders
2. Social Capital:
   - Value derived from the social, cultural, and expressive assets of the community
   - Attained through an organized social network that achieves community goals and maintains community assets
   - A system that manages the articulation and fulfillment of community agreements, promises. and commitments for improvement
   - The primacy of goodwill, trust, and the strength of social accountability networks
   - Network governance that builds upon stakeholder engagement and applies strategic-planning and decision making
3. Comprehensive Community Development:
   - Unites organization, planning, economic, and social development
   - Citizen driven and managed
   - Is revitalization oriented
   - Community assets addressed by quality of life issues
   - Strategic and integrative planning
4. Cooperative Management:
   - Addresses common/collective customer concerns
   - Formalized in contracts
   - Attention to design
   - Customer service oriented—value added policy
   - Political aggregate

When accurately assessing and evaluating the performance of PPPs, we must do so by measuring within the contexts of these four constructs, referring to the pragmatic purpose of PPPs.

KEY POINTS

- Partnerships in government are challenging and reshaping traditional assumptions of public management. Public–private partnerships (PPPs) are an excellent example of this.
- Managed special districts, for both business and residential areas, are unique PPP examples.

- PPPs merge public and private management technologies as well as public entrepreneurship, and social capital.
- At the heart of a public–private partnership is the management of a new sense of community—as a partnership.
- Entrepreneurship is a human capacity for innovation, synergism, organization, collaboration, and partnership. It can be applied to every human endeavor.
- Entrepreneurship and management are complementary but different functions.
- Public entrepreneurship works to create public value (Moore 1995), while private entrepreneurship works to create private profit (Weber 1904).
- Organization and creative aspects of entrepreneurship are associated with partnership building.
- Social capital, by promoting partnership success, distinguishes private entrepreneurship from public entrepreneurship and is further distinguished as a primary outcome of partnerships.
- Entrepreneurship and social capital are key attributes of PPPs, and fundamental to partnerships in general.
- PPPs address four capacities: Entrepreneurship, Social Capital, Comprehensive Community Development, and Cooperative Management.
- PPPs reshape our notions of entrepreneurship and 'capital' by infusing public and social attributes and actions to these behaviors, capacities, and values.

REFERENCES

Adler, P. S. & S.-W. Kwon (2002). Social Capital: Prospects for a New Concept. *Academy of Management Review*, Vol. 27, No. 1, pp. 17–40.

Allison, Graham T. (2004). *Public and Private Management: Are They Fundamentally Alike in All Unimportant Respects?* Classics of Public Administration, 5th ed., Belmont, CA: Wadsworth/Thompson Learning.

Allison, G. T. & K. Nicolaïdis (1997). *The Greek Paradox: Promise vs. Performance.* Cambridge, MA: The Center for Science and International Affairs, John F. Kennedy School of Government, Harvard University.

Ashoka (2007). http://www.ashoka.org/files/2006_Summary_of_Results.

Baker, W. E. (1990). Market Networks and Corporate Behavior, *American Journal of Sociology*, Vol. 96, pp. 589–625.

Barnard, Chester (1938). *Functions of the Executive*, Cambridge, MA: Harvard University Press.

Baumol, W. J. (1990). Entrepreneurship: Productive, Unproductive, and Destructive, *The Journal of Political Economy*, Vol. 98, No. 5, pp. 893–921.

BDMCP [Business District Management Certification Program] (2008). Online program. National Center for Public Productivity, Rutgers University, Newark, NJ.

Becker, Carol (2010). Self-Determination, Accountability Mechanisms, and Quasi-Governmental Status, *Public Performance & Management Review*, Vol. 33, No. 3, pp. 413–435.

Becker, Carol, Seth A. Grossman, & Brenda Dos Santos (2011). *Business Improvement Districts: Census and National Survey*, Washington DC: International Downtown Association.

Berger, P. L. & T. Luckman (1966). *The Social Construction of Reality: A Treatise in the Sociology of Knowledge*, New York: Anchor Books.

Berger, Peter & Thomas Luckmann (1967). *The Social Construction of Reality*, New York: Random House.

Bornstein, D. (2007). *How to Change the World: Social Entrepreneurs and the Power of Ideas*, New York: Oxford University Press.

Bourdieu, P. (1985). *The Forms of Capital: Handbook of Theory and Research for the Sociology of Education*, Westport, CT: Greenwood.

Bovaird, Tony & Elke Löffler (2009). *Governance*, New York: Routledge.

Bozeman, B. (1987). *All Organizations Are Public: Comparing Public and Private Organizations*, San Francisco: Jossey-Bass.

Briffault, R. (1999). A Government for Our Time? Business Improvement Districts and Urban Governance, *Columbia Law Review*, Vol. 99, No. 2, pp. 365–477.

Carland, James W., Frank Hoy, Williams R. Boulton, & Jo Ann C. Carland (1984). Differentiating Entrepreneurs from Small Business Owners, *The Academy of Management Review*, Vol. 9, No. 2, pp. 354–359.

Carton, Robert B., Charles W. Hofer, & Michael D. Meeks (1998). *The Entrepreneur and Entrepreneurship: Operational Definitions of Their Role in Society*, University of Georgia, Terry School of Business.

Coleman, J. S. (1988). Social Capital in the Creation of Human Capital, *American Journal of Sociology*, Vol. 94, Suppl., pp. S95–S120.

CSIS-GSI online blog (2008, March 20). The Global Strategy Institute, Center for Strategic & International Studies. Message posted to http://forums.csis.org/gsi/index.php?page_id=89.

DeFilippis, J. (2001). The Myth of Social Capital in Community Development, *Housing Policy Development*, Vol. 12, No. 4, pp. 781–806.

Denhardt, Robert (1993). *Theories of Public Organization*, Belmont, CA: Wadsworth.

Denhardt, Robert & Janet Vinzant Denhardt (2000). The New Public Service: Serving Rather than Steering, *Public Administration Review*, Vol. 60, No. 6, pp. 549–559.

Derthick, M. (1990). *Agency under Stress*, Washington DC: The Brookings Institution Press.

Dewey, J. (1925). *Experience and Nature*, Chicago: Open Court Publishing.

DiIulio, J. D. & J. J. DiIulio Jr. (1994). Principled Agents: The Cultural Basis of Behavior in a Federal Government Bureaucracy, *Journal of Public Administration Research & Theory*, Vol. 4, No. 3, pp. 277–318.

Dubnick, Melvin (2005). Accountability and the Promise of Performance, *Public Performance & Management Review*, Vol. 28, No. 3, pp. 376–417.

Elliott, Herschel (1997). *A General Statement of the Tragedy of the Commons*, Gainesville: University of Florida Press, 1–12.

Etzioni, A. (1968). *The Active Society*, New York: Free Press.

Filion, L. J. (1997). *From Entrepreneurship to Entreprenology*, Montreal: University of Montreal Business School.

Fischer, Frank & John Forester, (1993). *The Argumentative Turn in Policy Analysis and Planning*. Durham, NC: Duke University Press.

Fischer, F. (2003). *Reframing public policy: Discursive politics and deliberative practices*. New York, NY: Oxford University Press.

Fishel, William A. (2001). *The Homevoter Hypothesis*, Cambridge, MA: Harvard University Press.

Fredrickson, H. George (1971). Toward a New Public Administration. In F. Marini (ed.), *Toward a New Public Administration*, San Francisco: Chandler, pp. 309–331.

Fukuyama, F. (1995). *Trust*, New York: Free Press.

Galston, W. A. (1996). Trust—but Quantify, *Public Interest*, No. 122, pp. 129–132.

Gingrich, Newt (2005). *Entrepreneurial Public Management as a Replacement for Bureaucratic Public Administration: Getting Government to Move at the Speed of the Information Age*, Gingrich Communications.

Goetz, S. J. & D. Freshwater (2001). State-Level Determinants of Entrepreneurship and Preliminary Measure of Entrepreneurial Climate, *Economic Development Quarterly*, Vol. 15, No. 1, pp. 58–70.

Grossman, S. A. (2008). *The Role of Entrepreneurship in Public–Private Partnerships: The Case of Business Improvement Districts*, doctoral dissertation, Rutgers University, Newark, NJ.

Grossman, S. A. (2014). *Business Improvement District Information Guide and Handbook.* Newark, NJ: Cooperative Professional Services.

Grossman, Seth (2007). *New Jersey Managed Districts Association (NJMDA) Handbook.* Retrieved April 2008 from NJMDA.com.

Grossman, Seth A. (2010). Reconceptualizing the Public Management and Performance of Business Improvement Districts, *Public Performance & Management Review*, Vol. 33, No. 3, pp. 361–394.

Grossman, Seth A. & Fayth A. Ruffin (2007). *Professionalizing the Field of BID Management*, International Downtown Association Conference, September, New York.

Grossman, S., F. Ruffin, & R. Reenstra-Bryant (2007). *Business District Management Certification Program.* National Center for Public Performance. Newark, NJ: Rutgers University.

Guth, W. D., & A. Ginsberg (1990). Corporate Entrepreneurship, *Strategic Management Journal*, Vol. 11, pp. 5–15.

Heclo, H. (1977). *A Government of Strangers: Executive Politics in Washington*, Washington DC: The Brookings Institution Press.

Hitt, M. A., R. Ireland, S. Camp, & D. Sexton (2001). Strategic Entrepreneurship: Entrepreneurial Strategies for Wealth Creation, *Strategic Management Journal*, Vol. 22, pp. 479–491.

Hoagland, Jim (1993). "Prepared for Non-Combat," April 15, and "Beware 'Mission Creep' in Somalia", July 20, *Washington Post.*

Holzer, Marc & Mengzhong Zhang (2004). Trust, Performance, and the Pressures for Productivity in the Public Sector. In *Public Productivity Handbook*, New York: Marcel Dekker, pp. 215–229.

Houstoun, L., Jr. (2003), *Business Improvement Districts*, Washington DC: Urban Land Institute.

Howlett, M., & Ramesh, M. (2003). *Studying public policy: Policy cycles and policy subsystems.* Ontario, CA: Oxford University Press.

Hoyt, L. (2001). Business Improvement Districts: Untold Stories and Substantiated Impacts, doctoral dissertation, University of Pennsylvania. *Dissertation Abstracts International*, Vol. 62, pp. 3961–4221.

Hoyt, L. (2008). From North America to Africa: The BID Model and the Role of Policy Entrepreneurs. In G. Morçöl, L. Hoyt, & J. M. Meek (eds.), *Business Improvement Districts: Research, Theories, and Controversies*, New York: CRC Press, pp. 111–138.

Huxham, Chris & Siv Vangen (2005). *Managing to Collaborate*, New York: Routledge.

James, W. (1909). *The Meaning of Truth: A Sequel to "Pragmatism,"* Amherst, NY: Prometheus Books.

Justice, Jonathan B. (2003). *Business Improvement Districts, Reasoning, and Results: Collective Action and Downtown Revitalization*, doctoral dissertation, Rutgers University, Newark, NJ.

Justice, J. & R. S. Goldsmith (2008). Business Improvement Districts: Research, Theories, and Controversies. In *Private Governments or Public Policy Tools? The Law and Public Policy of New Jersey's Special Improvement Districts*, New York: CRC Press, pp. 161–195.

Kettl, D. (1993). *Sharing Power: Public Governance and Private Markets*, Washington DC: The Brookings Institution Press.

Kettl, D. F. (2002). *The Transformation of Governance*, Baltimore: Johns Hopkins University Press.

Kingdon, John W. (2003). *Agendas, Alternatives and Public Policies*, Reading, MA: Addison-Wesley Educational Publishers Inc.

Kruger, M. E. (2004). *Entrepreneurship Theory & Creativity: Chapter Two*, Pretoria, South Africa: University of Pretoria.

Lewis, Eugene (1984). *Public Entrepreneurship: Toward a Theory of Bureaucratic Political Power*, Bloomington: Indiana University Press.

Lochner, K., I. Kawachi, & B. Kennedy (1999). Social Capital: A Guide to Its Measurement, *Health and Place*, Vol. 5, pp. 259–270.

Lowndes, Vivien & Chris Skelcher (1998). The Dynamics of Multi-Organizational Partnerships: An Analysis of Changing Modes of Governance, *Public Administration*, Vol. 76 (Summer), pp. 313–333.

MacDonald, H. (1996). BIDs Really Work, *City Journal*, Vol. 6, pp. 29–42.

Maitlis, S. (2005). The Social Processes of Organizational Sensemaking, *Academy of Management Journal*, Vol. 48, No. 1, pp. 21–49.

Maslow, A. (1943). A Theory of Human Motivation, *Psychological Review*, Vol. 50, pp. 370–396.

McClelland, D. C. (1987). Characteristics of Successful Entrepreneurs, *Journal of Creative Behavior*, Vol. 21, pp. 219–233.

Miller, D. (1983). The Correlates of Entrepreneurship in Three Types of Firms, *Management Science*, Vol. 29, No. 7, pp. 770–791.

Mitchell, J. (2001, June). Business Improvement Districts and Innovative Service Delivery, *American Review of Public Administration*, Vol. 31, No. 2, pp. 201–217.

Mitchell, J. (2008). *Business Improvement Districts and the Shape of American Cities*, Albany: State University of New York Press.

Moore, Mark H. (1995). *Creating Public Value: Strategic Management in Government*, Cambridge, MA: Harvard University Press.

Morçöl, Göktug (2006). Business Improvement Districts: A New Organizational Form in Metropolitan Governance, *International Journal of Public Administration*, Vol. 29, No. 1–3, pp. 1–4.

Morçöl, Göktug & Ulf Zimmermann (2006). Metropolitan Governance and Business Improvement Districts, *International Journal of Public Administration*, Vol. 29, pp. 1–29.

Morrow, V. (1999, November). Conceptualizing Social Capital in Relation to the Well-Being of Children and Young People: A Critical Review, *The Sociological Review*, Vol. 47, No. 4, p. 744.

Mort, G. S., J. Weerawardena, & K. Carnegie (2002). Social Entrepreneurship: Towards Conceptualization, *International Journal of Nonprofit and Voluntary Sector Marketing*, Vol. 8, No. 1, pp. 76–88.

Nahapiet, J. & S. Ghoshal (1998). Social Capital, Intellectual Capital, and the Organizational Advantage, *Academy of Management Review*, Vol. 23, pp. 242–266.

Newland, C.A. (1997). Realism and Public Administration, *Public Administration Review*, Vol. 57, No. 2, pp. ii–iii.

Onyx, J. & P. Bullen (2000). Measuring Social Capital in Five Communities, *The Journal of Applied Behavioral Science*, Vol. 36, No. 1, pp. 23–42.

Osborne, D. & T. Gaebler (1992). *Reinventing Government*. Reading, MA: Addison-Wesley Publishing Co.

Ozminkowski, M. (2003). *Culture Matters: Culture, Political and Economic Influences on the Formation of Public Entrepreneurship*, New York: iUniverse, Inc.

Pierce, J.C., N. Lovrich, & C. Moon (2002). Social Capital and Government Performance: An Analysis of Twenty American Cities, *Public Performance and Management Review*, Vol. 25, pp. 381–397.

Pittaway, L. (2003). *Paradigms as Heuristics: A Review of the Philosophies Underpinning Economic Studies in Entrepreneurship*, Lancaster, UK: Lancaster University School of Management.

Portes, A. (1998). Social Capital: Its Origins and Applications in Modern Sociology, *Annual Review of Sociology*, Vol. 24, pp. 1–24.

Putnam, Robert D. (1993). The Prosperous Community: Social Capital and Public Life, *America Prospect*, Vol. 13, pp. 35–42.

Putnam, Robert D. (2000). *Bowling Alone: The Collapse and Revival of the American Community*, New York: Simon & Schuster.

Roberts, Nancy C. (1992). Public Entrepreneurship and Innovation, *Policy Studies Review*, Vol. 11, No. 1, pp. 55–74.

Ross, B. H. & M. Levine (2001). *Urban Politics: Power in Metropolitan America*, 6th ed., Itasca, IL: F. E. Peacock Publishers.

Savas, E.S. (2000). *Privatization and Public–Private Partnerships*, New York: Seven Bridges Press.

Schaeffer, Peter & Scott Loveridge (2002). Toward an Understanding of Public–Private Cooperation, *Public Performance & Management Review*, Vol. 26, No. 2, pp. 169–189.

Schneider, M. & P. Teske (1992). Toward a Theory of the Political Entrepreneur: Evidence from Local Government, *American Political Science Review*, Vol. 86, No. 3, pp. 737–747.

Schumpeter, J. A. (1934). *The Theory of Economic Development*, Cambridge, MA: Harvard University Press.

Schumpeter, J. A. (1947). The Creative Response in Economic History, *The Journal of Economic History*, Vol. 7, No. 2, pp. 149–159.

Searle, J. R. (1995). *The Construction of Social Reality*, New York: The Free Press.

Shenhav, Yehouda (1995). From Chaos to Systems: The Engineering Foundations of Organization Theory, 1877–1932, *Administrative Science Quarterly*, Vol. 40, pp. 557–585.

Simon, Herbert A. (1955). A Behavioural Model of Rational Choice, *Quarterly Journal of Economics*, Vol. 69, pp. 99–118.

Smith, Adam (1776). *An Inquiry into the Nature and Causes of the Wealth of Nations*, London: Methuen & Co. Ltd.

Smith, S. & J. Kulynych (2002). It May Be Social, But Why Is It Capital? The Social Construction of Social Capital and the Politics of Language, *Politics and Society*, Vol. 30, No. 1, pp. 149–186.

Sobel, Joel (2002). Can We Trust Social Capital? *Journal of Economic Literature*, Vol. XL, pp. 139–154.

Somorin, Kinle (2008). *Demystifying Public–Private Partnership,* Leadership Nigeria, April 29, Abuja, Nigeria (Internet posting).

Stokes, R. J. (2002). *Business Improvement Districts: Their Political, Economic and Quality of Life Impacts*, doctoral dissertation, New Brunswick, NJ: Rutgers University.

Subramaniam, Mohan & Mark A. Youndt (2005). The Influence of Intellectual Capital on the Types of Innovative Capabilities, *Academy of Management Journal*, Vol. 48, No. 3, pp. 450–463.

Taylor, F. (1911). *The Principles of Scientific Management*, New York: Norton.

Thomas, A. S. & S. Mueller (2000). A Case of Comparative Entrepreneurship: Assessing the Relevance of Culture, *Journal of International Business Studies*, Vol. 31, No. 2, pp. 287–301.

Thornton, Patricia H. (1999). The Sociology of Entrepreneurship, *Annual Review of Sociology*, Vol. 25, pp. 19–46.

Tiebout, Charles, M. (1956). A Pure Theory of Local Expenditures, *The Journal of Political Economy*, Vol. 64, No. 5, pp. 416–424.

Waldo, Dwight (1954/2007). *The Administrative State: The Study of the Political Theory of American Public Administration*, New Brunswick, NJ: Transaction Publishers.

Wang, X. H. (2002). Perception and Reality in Developing an Outcome Performance Measurement System, *International Journal of Public Administration*, Vol. 25, No. 6, pp. 805–829.

Wang, X. H., & E. Berman (2000). Hypotheses about Performance Measurement in Counties: Findings from a Survey, *Journal of Public Administration Research and Theory*, Vol. 11, No. 3, pp. 403–428.

Weber, Max (1904). *From Max Weber: Essays in Sociology*. H. H. Gerth & C. Wright Mills (eds.), London: Routledge & Kegan Paul.

Weber, M. (1946). Selected Works. In H. H. Gerth & C. Wright Mills (eds.), *From Max Weber: Essays in Sociology*, New York: Oxford University Press.

Wolf, James F. (2008). Business Improvement Districts' Approaches to Working with Local Governments. Chapter 12 in *Business Improvement Districts: Research, Theories, and Controversies*, New York: CRC Press/Taylor & Francis Group.

4

Business Improvement Districts—Formal Public–Private Partnerships

In Chapters 1 through 3, we looked at governance through the lens of partnerships as well as the underpinnings of partnerships, particularly as they apply to public administration. In this chapter (and the following chapters), we look at public–private partnerships (PPPs) through the application of special districts, specifically Business Improvement Districts (BIDs), which have become a worldwide phenomenon. BIDs are public–private partnerships, and we will look at how they are structured, managed, and measured in the field of community and business development. From the beginning of this book, we identified PPPs as intriguing, formal, and expansive aspects of Partnership Governance that significantly alter the way government behaves, therefore, the role of public management. In many ways, PPPs are the taskmasters of Partnership Governance. It is in this arena that government (public sector), the private sector, and the citizenry must adapt and create new ways of to determine policy, political interaction, and planning and management capacity. On one hand, public advocates are wary of private intrusion of any kind, let alone management of public goods, as it often occurs as private government: an anathema to democratic accountability. On the other hand, private advocates warn of collectivism, bureaucratic delays, and an erosion of the free market through overregulation and procedure. Both concerns reflect the dynamics of our society and our relationship to government and public processes. As averse as it may seem, it reflects a whole and cooperative system; in fact, an inherent aspect of democracy: partnership. PPPs do challenge our basic assumptions about private and public governance. If we look through history, this has always been the case. In the 21st century, we are again reviewing how this system works, and, consequently, why PPPs are at the forefront of challenging our assumptions about government.

Alan Reeves summing up the impetus of BIDs in Britain as town center management (TCM) writes, "TCM's principal modus operandi has acquired certain respectability because of the general acceptance in other areas of public life of the partnership ethos" (Reeves 2008, p. 427). We cannot separate BIDs from this partnership ethos. In these chapters, our examination of public–private partnerships is conducted at the municipal level of government by exploring the Business Improvement District movement particularly in the USA, where it has made a major impact on downtown and community development and transferred private and public technology throughout the world. BIDs are results-oriented ventures, but also serve as a 'laboratory' of PPP development. Unlike transportation PPPs, which are well-known PPPs and chiefly transactional, BIDs go beyond projects to the redefinition of the community itself, and the functions of government. Originally conceived of as an urban (downtown) revitalization strategy in the 1970s, within thirty years BIDs have evolved from downtown into wholesale neighborhood improvement districts, tourism improvement districts, industrial improvement districts, and multi-use improvement districts furthering the growth of special district government as a subtheme of changes in modern governance. As the postmodern world has become more globally interactive and economically connected, there has been a—special district and PPP—counteracting movement toward localization and economic immediacy. They are not adverse, but complementary and part of the same event.

Globalization makes the world smaller, that is, more accessible and more homogeneous, but in that process it also illuminates niches, differences, and the desire of expository determination. People want to be heard and known, and now they can more than ever. We have an immediate complementary and declarative world forcing us outward and pulling us inward. As we delve into Business Improvement Districts, we grapple with the economic and political policies of our generation. As identified in Chapter 3, partnerships in government, PPPs, and especially BIDs reshape our notions of entrepreneurship and 'capital' by infusing public and social attributes and actions into these behaviors, capacities, and values. We do see specialized public services; those that the private sector initially found too risky or unsupportable, becoming acceptable to the private sector and functional in that field, which we call privatization. We also see one of the more intriguing aspects of democracy; private and public business and citizens adapting to, obtaining, and applying public accountability and authority to their environment, which we call publicization. Often both capabilities are utilized, sometimes synthesized in one venture. They are always conducted in some type of partnership. These partnerships give rise to a necessary and adaptive public manager with skills that are partnership derived. We are left with the realization that it is the 'partnership' in PPPs that is not only most important and where the action is, but easily overlooked.

When we discuss BIDs, we can accurately substitute PPP and reveal the true intention of this movement. BIDs, because they are PPPs, have a number of key attributes that make it difficult to label them in one way; i.e., in one sector. Jonathan Justice and Robert Goldsmith in discussing New Jersey (USA) BIDs argue that "BIDs can best be understood as genuine public–private partnerships in that they serve simultaneously as policy tools through which state and local governments seek to advance general public interests and as self-help entities to further the more particular interests of local business communities" (Justice & Goldsmith 2008, p. 163). Everything in a BID is multisectoral and equitable, but not always equal. It is necessary to reinforce that BIDs are subunits of government, special districts, and agents of the municipality even if business-led organizations practicing both privatization and publicization (Hochleutner 2008). PPPs neglect the public side at their peril. This is the most significant reason PPPs, including BIDs, fail. BIDs are also, of course, PPPs, collaborative networks, asset and destination managers, organizations, and community development agencies. However, these private attributes are always embraced by public accountabilities and the nature of the partnership. BIDs are all these things and it has been misleading not to notice it, even as it appears contradictory. The contradictions reside in a functioning democracy representing a system of public accountability derived from private value. This is the challenge of public–private partnerships, and their most uncanny operatives: Business Improvement Districts. "The BID phenomenon forces us to rethink our dichotomous conceptual foundation of public versus private on which traditional public administration is built" (Morçöl & Zimmermann 2006). BIDs are much more than self-help business service organizations.

BUSINESS IMPROVEMENT DISTRICTS: A PRIMER

"BIDs have come to be embraced by their host cities as providing focused services that facilitate publicly defined benefits to the broader community" (Levy 2001a, 2001b; Stokes 2008, p. 264). The premise for BIDs is based on a governance problem: Without reliable resources and strong administrative support, volunteer and ad hoc efforts are limited. This limitation stifled competition and led to the decline of downtowns worldwide. This observation also defines a key determination of the progressive age and ushered in public administration in the modern age (Wilson 1887). It defines the need for the public sector as a distinct organizing tool of society and calls forth the skills necessary to manage that sector. It considers the possibility of a separation between politics: the processing of social norms, and public administration: the business of government. Simply being a nonprofit community organization, or a nongovernmental organization, is not enough to sustain long-term revitalization. Also, inadequate legal structures do not sustain hard-earned plans. They require informal and formal governance of public partnership processes, and eventually government. "A tight working partnership between BID and the local authority," according to John Ratcliffe and Brenda Ryan discussing the Dublin, Ireland BID governance process (Ratcliffe & Ryan 2008, p. 479). Government builds lasting management capability to sustain the infrastructure of social agreements, but is often held responsible for economic trends it cannot control, services that are poorly designed, and service delivery systems that do not meet the day-to-day requirements of dynamic and changing environments. BIDs are designed to remedy this problem, particularly in traditional downtown business areas, although this is not the only application of this model (Mitchell 2008).

BIDs are a common decentralization practice (Lloyd & Peel 2008) and part of a special district movement (Grossman 2008; Houstoun 2003), which merges the political will of a municipality with a commitment to participate by its business community. Decentralization is a unique and formative aspect of American democracy beginning with strong states' rights, thereby creating an institutionalized movement of government away from a centralized federal core (federalism) and at the same time defining the need for such a core. "Institutions consist of cognitive, normative, and regulative structures that provide stability and meaning to social behavior," through "multiple levels of jurisdiction" (Scott 1995, p. 33). Decentralization is not an end in itself, but an intention to put the reach and practice of government in the hands of the citizens through sustained action and agreement. It is a service delivery and governance method. Decentralization often leads to legal public–private partnerships, which expand local management capacity.

The intention of Business Improvement Districts is first and foremost to create a formal public–private partnership to manage a special district business community— typically, but not always, a designated downtown, commercial, or industrial area in a municipality. Because BIDs "are public–private partnerships between government and the private sector to foster the growth of commercial districts" (Becker, Grossman, & Dos Santos 2011, p. 4), every "BID model is based on a partnership between the BID, the local council, property owners and tenants (including local employers), the local community, and other BIDs" (Hernandez & Jones 2008, p. 417). BIDs throughout the world manage themselves as a PPP along a public–private continuum; some very privately managed, others very publicly managed, most somewhere in between (Becker, Grossman, & Dos Santos 2011; Briffault 1999; Grossman 2010; Hernandez & Jones 2008; Meek & Hubler 2006). Fundamentally, BIDs are functions of local government based on special assessment forms of public financing that create a formal public–private partnership (Savas 2000, Stokes 2008) and a local self-help mechanism to address revitalization and economic development needs of a designated business area (Hoyt 2001; Justice 2003; Mitchell 2001; Morçöl 2006; Stokes 2002). Göktug Morçöl, Ulf Zimmermann, and Patricia Patrick resolve the issue of whether a BID is a public or private enterprise by explaining succinctly that "by definition, BIDs are self-assessment districts" (Morçöl & Patrick 2008, p. 307). BIDs blur the line between the public and the private so much that they are termed (Morçöl & Zimmermann 2008, p. 28) "quasi-governmental entities" (Ross & Levine 2001). They are public entities and often managed by private entities, primarily private nonprofit organizations. "It is this combination of governance by private commercial actors with the compulsory special-assessment based financing arrangements that is generally considered the cause of BIDs' presumed distinctive effectiveness in selecting and accommodating revitalization goals" (Justice & Goldsmith 2008, p. 165). "Critically, BIDs are also influenced by contemporary attempts to better integrate and 'join up' public service delivery as part of a wider commitment to modernize service provision and realign resource availability in submunicipal governance" (Lloyd & Peel 2008, p. 89).

BIDs are 'of but usually not in' government (however, sometimes they are), and they are always subunits of government that establish a legal public–private partnership. Again, the public foundation of BIDs cannot be ignored, the ignoring of which has led many good-minded researchers and questionable consultants astray. The PPP is what separates BIDs from other revitalization efforts, including community and economic development corporations, enterprise zones, the Main Street Program, or redevelopment authorities. BIDs are not designed to replace municipal services, but enhance them and provide specific business-related activities, services, and planning to promote, revitalize, and develop business at a subgovernmental level. The primary focus of a BID is to provide competitive services that manage assets and address customer needs. This viewpoint is not the specific job of the municipal government, although the government can encourage, support, and partner on these activities. BIDs as subunits of local government operate with significant local government oversight requirements such as a required yearly audit and reports, annual approval of their budgets, ordinance reviews, and representation by elected officials on the BID management organization's Board of Directors as voting members (Becker, Grossman, & Dos Santos 2011).

With this is mind, the purpose of a BID is to promote business development in a businesslike manner, institute business infrastructure improvements, manage assets, and upgrade customer service standards in a designated business district. Business development on the local level is a joint economic, community, and social service concern. This purpose is immediately intermingled with community development concerns, as the community the BID resides in is its fundamental asset. Asset management becomes a primary BID focus, a consideration that underlines all PPPs. BIDs manage community assets, and PPPs do as well. Asset management research regarding PPPs is a solid approach, but generally neglected.

BIDs are created because it is abundantly clear, through not only land use laws but actual commercial activity, that business standards are different than and special in relation to local government, which is responsible for the overall (general) standards of an entire community. Generalities (collective and common concerns) lend themselves to general-purpose government, whereas specialization lends itself to business. PPPs fall in-between. They address generalities in the infrastructure of economic development, and specialization regarding the market and its customers. BIDs are responsible for the standards of the business community, including promotions, cleanup, design, business recruitment, development as appropriate, and maintaining professional business practices. First and foremost, a BID allows *the business community* to be competitive in the market and professionally managed (not unlike other retail-commercial cooperatives such as suburban malls and shopping centers) and to determine services it specifically needs in order to maintain acceptable business standards, leverage funds with accountability and integrity, and to be a good partner with a variety of different entities in the community at large.

BIDs are not as difficult to establish as one might think, but they do require a strategic partnership building process. This is because businesses know that management is the key to their success. Once the concept of a 'business community' is established and customers are seen not only as personal but also as collective, it is a rational transition to understanding that the conglomerate also needs managing. Secondly, it is not the job of general purpose government to manage business districts. It is the appropriate job of special purpose government, BIDs, to do this, and generally speaking BIDs are acknowledged as a successful form and method of accomplishing this within the legitimacy of public processes (Briffault 1999; Houstoun 2003; Justice 2003; Mitchell 2008 Morçöl & Zimmermann 2006; Stokes 2002). Many business communities are not managed at all. Those that are seem to thrive. Those that aren't seem to struggle. This is why BIDs are managed professionally and at the highest standards possible. Their success, like all PPPs, consequently relies on the quality of their management. This is why we spend time on this subject. Management is a deliberate statement of accountability and intention to be successful at meeting and exceeding customer needs. As we know, BIDs are managed by the municipality, a municipal commission, or most usually by a designated nonprofit management corporation comprising key stakeholders in the BID (Becker, Grossman, & Dos Santos 2011; Mitchell 2008). That means they are not out to make a profit for themselves, but to support higher profits and a better business environment for all businesses in the district.

BIDs are service oriented, and their orientation is to the business community's collective clients and customers. Essentially, BIDs are successful because they consciously increase the level of customer service in a district by managing common concerns, issues, needs, and assets of the business community. Increasing the level of customer service can mean many things, such as increasing a sense of safety and cleanliness, making parking more accessible, having appropriate stores that are inviting, marketing the district so customers know what is there, and most importantly ensuring that the district is enjoyable. Business districts need to be designed as social gathering places where restaurants, culture, and entertainment are available and cause people to mingle. This adds value to customers' experience, giving them a sense of obtaining a better value; literally "a bigger bang for their buck." They not only buy products, but also have a valuable social experience.

BIDs do not replace the work of the municipal Public Works Department, Redevelopment Authority, Economic Development Corporations, Offices of Community and Economic Development, or Enterprise Zones. BIDs enhance where necessary and appropriate, bring new ideas where needed, and manage common business concerns, collective customer services, and agreements. The BID works in partnership with the local government and other entities both public and private to target and enhance services where needed. BIDs are known by a variety of names throughout the world:

- Business Improvement Areas
- Business Improvement Zones
- Community Benefit Districts
- Community Improvement Districts
- District Management Corporations
- Downtown Improvement Districts
- Economic Improvement Districts
- Enhanced Municipal Service Districts

- General Improvement Districts
- Improvement Districts for Enhanced Municipal Services
- Local Improvement Districts
- Local Improvement Taxing Districts
- Maintenance Assessment Districts
- Municipal Improvement Districts
- Municipal Management Districts
- Municipal Service District
- Municipal Special Service Districts
- Neighborhood Improvement Districts
- Principal Shopping Districts
- Property-based Business Improvement Districts
- Public Improvement Districts
- Self-Supported Municipal Improvement Districts
- Special Assessment Districts
- Special Benefit Assessment Districts
- Special Business Districts
- Special Community Benefit Districts
- Special Improvement Districts
- Special Service Areas
- Special Service Taxing Districts
- Special Services Districts
- Tourism Improvement Districts
- Voluntary Business Improvement Districts

"BIDs have to be understood against the government's main objectives for public service reform and the modernization of local government. . . . [W]ithin this context there has been a concern with enhancing quality and creating choice for the consumer" (Lloyd & Peel 2008, p. 83). Most BIDs are business-led, business-oriented organizations with real authority through the municipal ordinance and a designated management corporation to accomplish the agreed upon goals of the public–private partnership that it represents. This partnership is represented by nongovernmental stakeholders (business, citizens, nonprofits, etc.) and the government stakeholders (local elected officials and government administrators and staff). The BID works to unite the business community in an equitable and honest fashion to make a real impact on customer satisfaction, quality of life, and physical infrastructure, and promote and advance better business practices and plans throughout the district. BIDs also allow the business community to be a true partner with the larger community and address common needs effectively while working with other businesspeople. This means businesspeople do not have to work alone as independents but can work together as a team with government and the greater municipality. The BID also helps businesspeople do what they do best but on a community basis: solve business problems and infuse the public process with an entrepreneurial spirit.

Figure 4.1 **Some typical questions regarding BIDs (Grossman 2014)**

QUESTION	ANSWER
1. IS THE BID A PRIVATE OR PUBLIC ENTITY?	A Business Improvement District is a public agency (Kennedy v. Montclair Center Business Corporation Business Improvement District, NJ, 2014) often managed by a private nonprofit management corporation or a municipal commission that assumes public responsibilities. BIDs are true, legal public-private partnerships between the local government and the business district community, and are subunits of local government with real authority and accountabilities. The purpose of a BID is to manage the partnership, the public agency, encourage entrepreneurship and organization to accomplish comprehensive and positive changes.
3. WHO GOVERNS THE BID?	The BID is a public-private partnership governed by the municipality, which designates a private nonprofit management corporation, or sometimes a municipal commission to manage the BID. BIDs are often required by state statute to have a local elected official on the board of directors as a voting member, and that the board be composed of a majority of business and property owners.
4. WHO DETERMINES THE BID BUDGET AND HOW DO BIDs ENHANCE THEIR BUDGETS?	The BID Management entity determines the budget of the BID, not the local government; however, the municipal council must approve the budget annually by resolution. The first and foremost job for a BID is to manage its public-private partnership systematically and not in a haphazard manner. Secondly, the BID can leverage its funds, and within two-three years most BIDs do begin to leverage two-four times their budget through grants, loans and fees. They can do so because of their legal authority, nonprofit status (to receive funds), leveraging potential, and reliable publicly authorized source of funds.
5. WHO COLLECTS THE BID ASSESSMENT?	The chief partner of a BID is the local government which provides legislative oversight and acts as collector of the BID's funds. It is the municipality's responsibility to bill and collect the funds as a special assessment and ensure that 100% of the funds are given to the BID.
6. HOW MUCH IS THE BID ASSESSMENT AND WHO IS ASSESSED?	This is determined locally by each BID. As an example: BID assessments on average in New Jersey (USA) are equivalent to an increase of approximately 7.5% (between 4% and 11 %) of the total property tax bill.
7. DOES THE BID REPLACE ANY MUNICIPAL SERVICES?	No. Most state BID statutes are designed to "enhance and not replace" municipal services. The BID can provide many services to enhance business and development, but it can not be used to pay for existing municipal services. However, a BID can operate in the public right of way and obtain public funds. In this case, the BID is usually subject to local public financing rules.
8. DOES THE BID REPLACE ENTERPRISE ZONE PROGRAMS OR REDEVELOPMENT AUTHORITIES?	No. enterprise programs and BIDs are designed to complement each other with the BID acting as a business constituency focused on improvements and customer satisfaction, and the enterprise zone on business recruitment and job creation. Both are intended to revitalize activity business in commercial, retail and industrial areas. Redevelopment is project-driven and a focused business endeavour usually involving business and policy elites. Revitalization is management-driven and a comprehensive approach to community development that enhances community and citizen participation at the neighborhood level. Redevelopment builds and revitalization manages. After something is built through a redevelopment effort, it is revitalization that manages the ongoing process of success.
9. IS THERE MUNICIPAL OVERSIGHT OF THE BID?	Yes. There are usually four substantive oversights; 1. **Legislative oversight:** through the enabling ordinance and contracts; 2. **Partnership oversight:** BID statutes generally require at least one elected person to be a voting member of the BID Board of Directors; 3. **Budget oversight:** the municipal council must approve the annual BID budget and be presented with an annual report; and, 4. **Audit requirements:** the BID must conduct an annual certified audit, which must be submitted to the municipal government.

PLANNING AND IMPLEMENTING: A BUSINESS IMPROVEMENT DISTRICT PPP

Creating a Business Improvement District requires a consensus-oriented planning process that emphasizes the inherent dignity, values, and assets of the community. People who work on a BID need to:

1. *Know:* (a) the facts about the Business Improvement District legislation and (b) what cooperative commercial management is as a technology for business success.
2. *Agree:* (a) that working together in a committed and organized manner is appropriate; (b) that establishing a Business Improvement District provides the remedy for revitalizing, improving, and maintaining community and business standards; and (c) that managing the service plan arrived at through this process is to be conducted at a highest professional level possible.
   A community education/planning process is inclusive and may take time until consensus is reached on the vision, values, purpose, and functions (budget, boundaries, and business) of the district (Grossman 2014).

- *Consensus:* *Consensus* is a process that is designed to identify and support agreements rather than an orientation toward resolving disagreements. It is helpful to have a facilitator who understands this process and identifies agreement when it is arrived at. Practicing agreement-management is the basis of asset-based planning strategies, goals and objectives, and ultimately the services rendered by the district.
- *Dignity:* *Dignity*, in current community development approaches, is a result of providing people with real authority and self-determination. Dignity is built upon: a value system that respects the capabilities, time, and energy people in our communities possess; and, by acknowledging the inherent assets of the community and its people, the value each point of view and life experience brings to create the community we work, live, and conduct business in.

PHASE ONE—FEASIBILITY

Step One: **Establish a general agreement** to study and plan a BID by holding community meetings and introductions on what a BID is, and determining feasibility: tentative boundaries of potential BID (if appropriate) budget potential, service needs, and community support.

Step Two: **Establish an official Steering Committee (often by resolution of municipal council *(see attached).** Identify well-respected leaders (stakeholders) from the following groups: property owners; business operators; media residents; financial institutions; consumers; educators; civic leaders; police; public transportation officials; local governing body, etc.

The purpose of the Steering Committee is to guide the BID education and planning process, conduct meetings and community information forums, present a report and proposal for the BID to the governing body including a proposed ordinance and budget, and support the preparation and passage of the BID ordinance.

PHASE TWO—PLANNING

Step Three: **Hire a downtown revitalization and management professional** to act as staff to the Steering Committee, conduct necessary research, and educate the community about cooperative management technology and Business Improvement District legislation (consider visiting other established BIDs).

Step Four: **The Steering Committee conducts an education and training process** to learn about: BIDs as an institution; and Business Improvement District technology that the community agrees is best for downtown business in light of what is the potential for an improved business district. Include:

- BID training, conflict resolution techniques, strategic planning, visioning and team building, analysis of other plans and existing services

Step Five: **The Steering Committee plans the BID.** There are three required areas of concentration for the Steering Committee:

1. *Governance*: Boundaries, type of assessment, and style of management
2. *Service*: Budget capability, service priorities and estimated costs, general budget, and planning requirements
3. *Public Relations*: Community notices, press releases, and informal and formal public meetings on the BID process

Each concentration may be expanded to include additional research as needed, such as: security/cleanliness; public relations/ promotions; transportation and infrastructure; and business recruitment and retention.

Step Six: **Develop and present a BID report** to include the results of Step Five and include the following:

1. Description of the district with accurate maps and boundaries
2. A vision and values-based mission statement
3. Explain why the district is beneficial
4. The assessment method and contributors
5. General budget
6. Type of management
7. Structure of the Board of Directors of the BID
8. By Laws of management corporation (if appropriate)

Step Seven: **Conduct a community meeting** to present committee findings and receive community input.

Step Eight: **Present a revised BID proposal** to the governing body and include a proposed Business Improvement District Ordinance and Budget Resolution.

- The ordinance establishes the district and its boundaries, designates the nonprofit management corporation, and may contain guidelines for the minimal makeup of the Board of Directors, and the special assessment method.
- A resolution is enacted separately to approve the annual BID budget and proceed with collection of the BID assessment.

PHASE THREE—IMPLEMENTATION

Upon the successful acceptance of the proposal and consequent passage of the BID ordinance and budget, the following initial steps are necessary to establish the management corporation according to the enabling legislation.

Step Nine: **Incorporate management entity** as a nonprofit corporation, conduct first organizational meeting and election of officers, establish financial accounts, and appoint special committees.

Step Ten: **Organization: Implement a working committee structure** as a comprehensive administrative and policy development approach to Board of Director development and a means to keep in touch with your community. With the following committees:

- Executive Committee (Management)
- Environmental Maintenance (Cleanliness, Security, and Transportation/ Parking)
- Promotions and Public Relations
- Architecture and Design
- Business Recruitment and Retention and Business practices and support services

Step Eleven: **Hire professional management.**

- Downtown revitalization and management is a professional field combining (at minimum) public administration, business administration, and planning. Obtain the best manager you can afford and realize this as the primary aspect of the district's success.
- Look for someone, or a firm specializing in BIDs, that is self-directed, organized, and competitive, is likable and has energy. The strengths of your manager should match the needs of your district. Skills to look for are: public relations, knowledge of government, planning, marketing, public administration, design, business advocacy, and economic development.

Step Twelve: **Board Policy and Procedures Manual and Training:** The BID Board of Directors is accountable both financially administratively. A thorough manual of the duties, roles, and responsibilities of the Board is necessary. Also, this manual should contain work plans, plans of each committee, and legal and fiduciary guides. If the Board has not had strategic Vision and Values training on the role of the BID Board, this should be conducted. Also, each year as new members arrive, the Board is advised to conduct a retreat to build team skills and review its mission, vision, and standards.

Step Thirteen: **Long Range Strategy:** After the first- or second-year organizational operations are complete, and effectively budget for and develop a three- to five-year strategic redevelopment and business plan. The following are included in a plan:

1. Business and real estate market research analysis
2. Comprehensive inventory/survey of the condition of the district environment, infrastructure, transportation/ parking, and properties in the district
3. Agreements with the municipality and other governing agents, other community development entities, and adjoining BIDs
4. Strategic delivery of services to enhance business, maintain values, and meet customer needs
5. Benchmarks for measuring success
6. Ongoing Board training

Business district management succeeds by merging the best aspects of a comprehensive approach to community development with professional management. The committee structure within the Board of Directors is a means of coordinating planning, managing various essential facets of a successful district comprehensively, and assuring necessary community input.

In summary, downtown business district revitalization and management encompasses:

1. Professional business management
2. "Mining" of social capital and providing a dignified experience to volunteers
3. A comprehensive, asset-based community development process
4. Strategic planning (Visioning & Values)
5. The provision of effective services that communicate the community's goals and vision geared to increasing customer services by providing enhanced value to the customer's shopping or business experience.
6. Enhance and sustain the historical community identity.
   a. BIDs provide services that take advantage of these disciplines utilizing their unique authority, cooperation, and a community-based planning and management approach.

BID CASE SUMMARIES

Business Improvement Districts vary in size, services, cultural orientation, and organization. They are designed to address specific local markets and community needs, but also have specific similarities. To illustrate this, below are summaries of three diverse BIDs: the

Ironbound BID in Newark, NJ, USA; the Charlottestown BIA in Charlottestown, Prince Edward Island (PEI), Canada; and the Times Square BID in New York City, NY, USA. Each has significantly different budgets. Budgets for BIDs (worldwide) range from as low as $20,000 a year to over $16,000,000 a year. The median BID budget is closer to $350,000 a year. Nonetheless, all BIDs manage public–private partnerships, enhance customer service capability, advocate for the community, and are allowable and created by government. All BIDs address the public management of the district, marketing and communications, environmental improvements, business development, and safety and cleanliness issues. The Times Square Alliance's motto, "Creating Partnerships, Changing Perceptions," illustrates the purpose of BIDs.

Ironbound BID, Newark, NJ, USA

Located in the East Ward of the City of Newark (population: 275,221), the Ironbound is an area that encompasses over 45,000 people located at the vortex of major regional rail and international air travel. Newark, over the past five years, has had success in revitalizing its downtown areas with the success of the New Jersey Performing Arts Center (NJPAC) and a new minor league baseball stadium. Newark is the insurance, finance, and banking capital of the state, and hosts six colleges and universities. Additionally, professional sports franchises have expressed a strong interest in locating to Newark in areas adjacent to the Ironbound. Prudential Insurance Company has remained in the city and has proven to be a committed resident and a key developer of the downtown area, which is adjacent to the Ironbound. The Ironbound is well known for its Portuguese, Spanish, Brazilian, and Latin restaurants and ambiance, and a vibrant retail corridor on Ferry Street.

The Ironbound Business Improvement District (IBID) is a Business Improvement District created, under NJ state statute, in December 2000 by local ordinance. The IBID is a public authority designed to improve economic conditions in the Ferry Street & Wilson Avenue business areas of the Ironbound neighborhood. Originally the IBID comprised approximately 420 businesses in the Ferry Street business area. In May 2003, the district was expanded to include an additional 230 businesses providing a current total of 650 businesses from Penn Station to Lexington St., from the Passaic River to Lafayette St. Its spine is Ferry Street. And, in May 2013, the district again was expanded to include Wilson Avenue and another 200 businesses. The IBID is a mile long and a quarter mile wide. The Board of Directors consists of 23 members representing business owners, landlords, residents, professionals, and government officials. All commercial properties are assessed in the IBID.

IBID 2013 BUDGET

The 2014 IBID assessment budget is $825,000. This budget does not include any grants, gifts, contributions, or other public funds such as Urban Enterprise Zone (UEZ) or city funds. The budget reflects an expanded sidewalk cleaning crew from 5 to 8 staff, more in-depth promotions and marketing such as the "Meet Me in the Ironbound" campaign, and *NewarkBound* magazine, purchase of street furniture and equipment, streetscape and gateway designs, and façade improvement programs are increased in this budget. (Ironbound BID website 2014, goironbound.com, Newark, NJ).

INCOME

BID assessment	**$825,000.00**
Expenses	
Administration & management	**288,650.00**
Programs:	
Business development	25,000.00
Promotion & special events	37,000.00
Marketing & communications	214,350.00
Quality of life	260,000.00
Total programs:	**536,350.00**

Downtown Charlottetown Inc., Prince Edward Island, Canada

The City of Charlottetown is a flourishing community of over 34,562 people located on the south shore of Prince Edward Island. Charlottetown is the capital city of Prince Edward Island, and is called the "Birthplace of Confederation" after the historic 1864 Charlotte-town Conference, which led to Confederation. Downtown Charlottetown Inc. (DCI) is a nonprofit organization established in 2004 with the mandate to work with businesses to create and maintain a vibrant downtown through an established Business Improvement Area (BIAs are BIDs). There are approximately 450 businesses within the geographic area, 330 property owners. Working with these businesses, DCI will focus on projects that will improve living and commerce in downtown and rejuvenate the city core into an exciting place to live, work, and play—the centre of business, government, culture, and entertain-ment. If you own commercial property within our BIA (between Prince and Pownal Streets and from Euston Street to the Water), then you are a DCI Member. The 2013 budget is $200,000. The Board is made up of 12 City Stakeholders, property and business owners, who share in executive duties and act as Chairs for our committees which focus on Business Development and Recruitment, City Enchantment, Parking, Marketing, and Advocacy.

THE SPECIFIC OBJECTIVES FOR THE ASSOCIATION ARE:

1. To motivate and encourage business development
2. To promote and support urban residential living
3. To market downtown Charlottetown as a place to live, work, and play
4. To represent property and business owners

PROGRAMS

Downtown Farmers' Market Open

Graffiti Removal Program

Parking Tokens—Reward valued customers when they visit businesses.

The award-winning Adopt a Corner Project (winner of the 2009 IDA award of Distinction)

This program is a great example of the benefit of partnerships.

Clean Sweep—The event serves as an opportunity for business members to get outside and contribute to a cleaner, more beautiful downtown

Winterdine, Charlottetown dining festival

The Downtown Value Card Program—A discount card which encourages shoppers to purchase downtown and in doing so receive a discount up to 20% off.

Co-op Marketing Campaign—Downtown Charlottetown "Make It Your Own This Christmas," TV ads with tag reimbursed (25% of advertising cost reimbursed to a maximum of $1000)

Heritage Wayfinding Project—This project saw new street blades (issues have been resolved), information kiosks, gateway and directional signage placed throughout the core.

Christmas lights and window decorating project—enhance the downtown for the festive time of the year.

The Annual Downtown Barbeque—thanks downtown workers who support our businesses all year.

Clean Team—Clean Team Members will create and maintain a clean, welcoming and safe environment for the Downtown Charlottetown core area Municipality residents, visitors, and tourists.

Special Project—Design Charrette—a new vision for a redesign on the Historic portion of University Avenue

Special Project—Light and Sound Show

Business Development—Recruitment—focus on financial institutions

Parking—"Park Free" ads

Streetscape and Capital Projects—The redevelopment of University Avenue, Euston to Grafton

Marketing Campaigns

The Spring and Fall Marketing Campaigns primarily purchase and produce TV commercials which highlight features of our downtown. "What Brings you Downtown?" (Downtown Charlottestown, Inc website, 2014, Charlottestown, PEI, CA)

TIMES SQUARE ALLIANCE, NEW YORK CITY, USA: CREATING PARTNERSHIPS, CHANGING PERCEPTIONS

The Times Square Alliance manages the Times Square Business Improvement District, founded in 1992, which works to improve and promote Times Square—cultivating the creativity, energy, and edge that have made the area an icon of entertainment, culture, and urban life for over a century. In addition to providing core neighborhood services with its Public Safety Officers and Sanitation Associates, the Alliance promotes local businesses; encourages economic development and public improvements; coordinates numerous major events in Times Square (including the annual New Year's Eve and Broadway on Broadway celebrations); manages the Times Square Museum and Visitors Center; and advocates on behalf of its constituents with respect to a host of public policy, planning, and quality of life issues. The Alliance's district covers most of the territory from 40th Street to 53rd Street between 6th and 8th Avenues, as well as Restaurant Row (46th Street between 8th and 9th Avenues). The Alliance is a 501(c)3 not-for-profit organization, accepts tax-deductible gifts, and is governed by a large, voluntary 54-member Board of Directors. We have a 30-member staff. The total 2013 budget (see below), including assessments, grants, and revenue, is approximately $16 million.

REVENUES

Assessment $ 11,685,440
Contributions and Sponsorships 2,783,750
Museum and Visitor Center 437,428
Program Service Revenue 1,001,849
Interest Income 20,000
Total revenues 15,928,467

PROGRAM EXPENSES

Administration 716,845
Events and Programming 3,483,334
Museum and Visitor Center 993,972
Public Safety 3,741,135
Sanitation 4,056,083
Policy, Planning, and Design 884,356
Communications 286,209
General Operations 1,432,983
Total program expenses: $15,594,917

Clean, safe, and friendly were the three most important words during our first decade of work. Many partnerships brought great progress in the face of enormous challenges. Every sign of progress was celebrated and amplified in the face of enormous skepticism that anything could ever change. With the effective use of partnering, the Alliance has worked closely with businesses, nonprofits, and, most of all, the leadership and agencies of New York City government to address some of the most complex and high-profile urban problems facing this city. (Times Square Alliance Website, 2013, http://www.timessquarenyc.org, New York, NY)

AT THE HEART OF A BID: A PPP

At the heart of a BID is its partnership between the business community and the local government (Grossman 2008; Justice & Goldsmith 2008, Meek & Hubler 2008, Ratcliffe & Ryan 2008). This public–private partnership is determined by state statute and the consequent passing of local laws that enable and describe the partnership. The controversies that surround BIDs tend to travel along the continuum of the partnership. From a social constructionist perspective, Greg Lloyd and Deborah Peel view BIDs as "the plurality of interrelations and interactions in the public domain [that] are continuously negotiated and renegotiated, and are differentiated across time and locale" (Lloyd & Peel 2008, p. 72). There are those who are unsure of the privatized conveniences of profit seekers at the private end and the generalization proclivities of government at the public end. BIDs are not a strict form of privatization and may be better understood as preliminary, albeit primitive, forms of democratic process that call the private citizenry to become publicly involved and accountable as well as creative in solving immediate social and economic problems (Stokes 2008). Public–private partnerships are poorly evaluated when the aim is to diminish either party in the partnership. It would be expected that the spectre of diminishing attribute contributes to diminishing results, and the practice of mutually expanding attribute in such partnerships are not only intended, but functionally successful. "It is evident that regulatory frameworks have to be sensitive to the composite uses, users, behaviors, activities, and social constructs that crisscross the commercial, public, private, and imagined spheres of the public domain. . . . BID initiatives operate in a particularly negotiated environment" (Lloyd & Peel 2008, p. 73).

BIDs tend to be pragmatic rather than ideological. BIDs are evaluated on their ability to translate municipal (local) to neighborhood (sublocal) capacity (Morçöl & Zimmermann 2008). In this way, BIDs translate general public capability into specific public practice. The practice usually has very specific and measurable determinants of success: Is the community's quality of life improved and are businesses thriving? These questions, derived from a melding of local-GDP-Gross Domestic Product (private) and GDH-Gross Domestic Happiness (public) indexes, reflect a fairly straightforward measurement by the community: Is our community better off today than it was yesterday? Because BIDs are usually small business oriented, the horizon of this measurement is often within days or week rather than months or years. On a daily basis, these questions tend to define the conversations about the BID among BID partners, Board of Directors, and communications between the BID management entity and the local government. BIDs are oriented toward public response and therefore are responsive to public measurements, even as businesses reconcile daily cash receipts. At the end of the day, bills must be paid, but in order to live another day the customer must be happy (Houstoun, 2003).

"The dynamic and volatile character of the town center sets the evolutionary context to specific urban management and development initiatives such as TCM and BIDs. . . . [P]art of the argument for . . . BID initiatives is that they enable local differentiation in design and remit" (Lloyd & Peel 2008, pp. 75, 78; TCM is Town Center Management, a European reference to business district management). Often in comparison to surrounding communities and after years of planning, BIDs are eventually established on the premise that the community needs improving, and improvements require everyone and all sectors of society to achieve it. Facing great anticipation by a community that has seen this light and enacted a BID, the BID management entity (assuming the mantle of "the BID") is faced with the job of interpreting and implementing comprehensive strategies that satisfy political, economic, and social concerns that help the community understand and communicate its specific identity and purpose within its regional markets.

The BID is generally successful if it can be trusted to deliver the economic and social promises of the community without promising too much. Therefore, BIDs must be politic about expectations and even more practical about the promises the community makes based on its inherent assets, funding, political will, and competitive nature. The assets are economic, cultural, physical, and social. Concisely understood, 'the BID's job' is to best understand these assets and develop them competitively. Community development in BIDs attends not only to quality of life improvements, but also to how quality of life improvements uniquely generate the economy of the community.

The most replicated public management model that incorporates place management ideas with customer satisfaction appears to be the business or neighborhood improvement district. This model is often referred to as "place management" (Berk 1976; Mant 2007), a term that denotes or revitalizes community as an outcome of a real place to live and work (in the modern world suburban locations may only be a place to live, urban places only a place to work, this constitutes a function not a place), or business district management (Grossman 2008). Customer orientation is the new twist on the place management model that BIDs provide. The articulation of "live" and "work" merges public and private concerns. The BID model formalizes this concern that once may have been taken for granted. "They blend public management expertise with business acumen into a unique administrative form" (Mitchell 2001, p. 203) and "are rooted in the long privatist tradition of urban governance and politics in the United States" (Morçöl & Zimmermann 2006, p. 6).

At the edge of public administration, where the public sector meets the private, where free enterprise meets social capital, there is a struggle in terms of allegiance to a private/public sector dichotomy. "As American governments pursued more public policy through nongovernmental partners, public policy increasingly became entangled in private goals and norms" (Kettl 2002). BIDs tend to operate in a professional 'no man's land' using both private entrepreneurial and public management models. As entrepreneurial models, BIDs are expected to "channel private-sector energy towards the solution of public problems" (MacDonald 1996, p. 42). Where government administration may be seen as bureaucratic and process oriented (Gingrich 2005), BIDs are seen as entrepreneurial, management focused, and innovative. BIDs walk a fine line between traditional public administration and entrepreneurial public management. Consequently, the boundary between what is public and what is private is no longer as meaningful as it once was. (Menzel 2000).

The BID model merges private sector funding and management expertise with the public sector political legitimization and taxing powers. In this way, a BID avoids the problem of 'free riders' associated with volunteerism (Justice & Goldsmith 2008), addresses upkeep of common areas, and provides place management (Berk 1976; Houstoun 2003).

The commitment to partner and assume public authority is general, consequently everyone pays their fair share and no one gets a free ride. BIDs are not like Chambers of Commerce where voluntary dues are paid. The level of commitment is higher, so that services are more accountable. "BIDs formalize the interests of the local community" (Stokes 2002). At the level of governance that BIDs represent, there are two forces that should define benchmarks of success: citizen participation and professional management. If we accept as a definition that citizen participation is "the role of self-governance in promoting institutional legitimacy, the formation of common understandings between public and private participants (Justice 2003, 2006), we can see the role BIDs might play in furthering participation by citizens. Robert Stokes points to this in his 2002 doctoral dissertation on BIDs and found that a BID "restores a level of community faith in collective processes" (Stokes 2002) because through the BID those processes are professionally managed. BIDs require professional management to allow for the "facilitation of agreement" (Justice 2003).

BIDs are an addition to democratic governance and tend to be at the defining point of a private/public social and economic dichotomy that defines and often transforms the term 'community' in society. Access to the processes of community definition appear to elicit perceptions of success based initially on a sense that one's quality of life is improved, and this seems to be tied to the ability to invest personal time and energy into the development of the community and to participate collectively in the activities that make a community viable. Today, older urban markets must compete within their regional areas, which do not automatically sustain and manage mutual interests. BIDs reexamine the localization of mutual interests and adopt retail commercial cooperative technology utilized by suburban malls to establish self-reliant service-sector economic generators. "We are evolving to the point of realizing that where we have the BID, we have the vehicle to make the street what it can be in response to different markets and different mixes of clientele" (Barbara Wolff interview, 1996, from Gross 2008, p. 226). Service-sector economies are based on convenience, and area malls excel at this in a mobile society. However, convenience and ease can become monotonous. Suburban malls tend to excel in standardization and are consequently monotonous. Traditional downtowns tend to excel at diversity and niche opportunities but suffer when poorly managed and inaccessible. "The ensuing demise of town centers may therefore be seen as a consequence of a passive management attitude of government" (Lloyd & Peel 2008, p. 79), but also of the business community.

PUBLIC–PRIVATE PARTNERSHIP MANAGEMENT: BUSINESS DISTRICT EXECUTIVE MANAGEMENT

Business communities and the municipalities in which they are located seek and find ways to build successful organized approaches to development, revitalization, and improvements by creating Business Improvement Districts that forge unique public–private community-based partnerships (Briffault 1999; Hoyt 2001, 2006; Justice 2003; MacDonald 1996; Mitchell 2001; Morçöl and Zimmermann 2006; Stokes 2002). Most studies of BIDs focus on the concept of defining *place* (definable geography, market, and sense of community) and the legal structure of the BID. However, the role of business district management and the professional aspects of the managers of BIDs are virtually ignored. It cannot be done when we look at only one sector of the partnership. It becomes clearer when we realize that business district and place managers manage PPPs.

The idea of professionalism in public administration has its controversies, starting with the nagging question of accountability to democratic processes. This controversy extends to all forms of public administration and is less an issue when the task being assigned is strictly technical, such as: building inspector, postal clerk, soldier, garbage collector, police, firefighter, economic development, etc. These task positions are aptly described as being "professionals in government," while those that provided the task of managing government services are "professionals of government" (Gargan 1998, p. 1092). PPP managers tend to be both in and of government, but also professionals of business administration, specifically *cooperative* retail/commercial management. It is odd that we may have to argue for the profession of public administration in its various forms when we rely every day on these professionals. As to PPPs, including BIDs, it is the professional manager that defines the PPP's success.

In either case, the term *professional* not only describes a recognized mastery of a particular and useful skill or technology, but also ascribes to itself a sense of mission, ethics, and purpose. It is derived from the establishment of collective order and purposeful public action. Public administration is a profession, and the practices, both in and of government, certainly are. It describes more than it prescribes a sense of humanity, of human behavior, and a set of outcomes achieved by good management practices. Public administration is an outcome of a need for collective action and communal identity that is naturally evolving. The outcomes of public administration derive from this (communal) need and the actions necessary to translate the need into real activities, products, and processes.

Professional attributes, alive within the realm of public administration, have those components and are transacted by the role of management, which implies that there is a business of government. The business of government, as opposed to the private sector, trades in the realm of public values, ethics, and interests that are simply not measurable by market forces. Both produce services, products, and possibilities. Government has a "focus on interdependence" (Bozeman 1987, p. 149) created by legitimate political authority rather than on the independent aspirations of the individual. Although leadership and political identity may promote one individual over another, it is the public trust, not personal interest, which chiefly advises the government.

The public sector professional is the focused aspirant of the community, representing core values and managing those values as assets to produce a healthy economic state. Communal values are derived by a pursuit of that which promotes growth and development for all, essentially, an entrepreneurial drive. The paradox in public administration professionalism is the balancing of one's personal values with those of the community. An assumption that they are automatically aligned will result in inequity. The professional public administrator's task then is to eliminate assumptive values and work to discover, reveal, and sustain agreements. The questions are: 1) Where do we draw the boundaries of community? 2) How do we bridge between boundaries? 3) What establishes context of bridging? and, 4) How do we determine agreements that build bridges? The nature of agreements may lead to the answer and provide a better science of administration.

BUSINESS IMPROVEMENT DISTRICTS IN THE 21ST CENTURY

Participating in, caring for, and being committed to our communities are time-honored concerns, and this certainly includes business communities. There is a rational purpose for transrational activities; where the individual supports the community, a publicization process. We have clichés that speak to us of this purpose: United we stand divided we fall, Two heads are better than one; a good rising tide lifts all boats.

More communities are looking for and finding ways to build successful organized approaches to development, revitalization, and improvements by creating Special (Business) Improvement Districts. BIDs began in Toronto, Ontario, Canada in the 1960s and in New Orleans, Louisiana in the United States in the 1970s. However, it was not until the late 1980s and early 1990s that BID creation accelerated and in the mid-1990s that BIDs began to be exported around the world at the same time as New Public Management (NPM) was gaining global acceptance. It is noted that as of 2011, within the USA, BIDs are allowable in 49 states (excluding Wyoming) and established in 48 states (South Dakota has yet to create a BID, according to Mitchell (2008). Identifying BIDs is an exploratory process based on looking into nonstandardized state programs, advocacy agencies such as the International Downtown Association (IDA), and similar networks that are not necessarily focused on BIDs. Prior to 2007, only 574 BIDs were verified chiefly by Jerry Mitchell (2008), and in 2008, there was an estimated 650 plus BIDs in the United States, 400 plus in Canada, 1000 plus BIDs in North America, 350 plus in Europe and over 60 BIDs in the United Kingdom (Grossman 2008). There are at minimum "1,200 non-American downtown management corporations in countries around the globe: Australia (185), Canada (347), Japan (261), European Countries (225), New Zealand (140), and South Africa (42)," according to Lorlene Hoyt (2008, p. 116). In 2010, Carol Becker and Seth A. Grossman conducted a USA BID census for the International Downtown Association and found 1002 BIDs (Becker, Grossman, & Dos Santos 2011, p. 10), but because some states had poor records regarding BIDs it is suspected that there may be as many as 20% more, plus it is speculated that 2.7% of BIDs established have been terminated.

The premise for BIDs is based on the observation that without reliable resources and strong administrative support, volunteer efforts are limited. Simply being a nonprofit community organization or a nongovernmental organization is not enough to sustain long-term revitalization. Inadequate legal structures do not sustain hard-earned plans. Government needs to work with communities to build lasting local management capability, but it is often held responsible for economic trends it cannot control, services that are poorly designed, and service delivery systems that do not meet the day to day requirements of dynamic and changing environments. Business Improvement Districts are designed to remedy this problem, particularly in traditional downtown business areas, although this is not the only application of the model.

Business Improvement Districts are a common decentralization practice for downtown revitalization, which merges the political will of a municipality with a commitment to participate by its business community. Decentralization is a unique and formative aspect of American democracy, beginning with strong states' rights, which creates an institutionalized movement of government away from a centralized federal core (federalism) and, at the same time, defines over time the need for such a core. "Institutions consist of cognitive, normative, and regulative structures that provide stability and meaning to social behavior [through] multiple levels of jurisdiction" (Scott 1995, p. 33). Decentralization is not an end in itself but an intention to put the reach and practice of government in the hands of the citizens through sustained action and agreement. Decentralization often leads to legal public–private partnerships because the negotiations of these partnerships are at the core of democratic processes. Decentralization accomplishes two fundamental democratic goals: 1) the assumption of the people into governmental processes and 2) the support and protection of minority populations in a manner that brings them into the collective process.

Decentralization in the form of BIDs has developed (over time) a true (and necessary) offshoot profession of public administration that, in practice, tends to dissolve the private/public (politic/administration) dichotomy and is applicable universally. Decentralization is a process of bringing government closer to the people. This certainly happens with BIDs, and BIDs can properly be labeled as citizen-driven governmental units. The administrative politics that permit such a process require a resolution of the conflict between traditional principal/agent versus network political structures. Business Improvement Districts represent this resolution because they require an orderly transfer of political power and the legitimate power to emerge from a centralized model to a decentralized partnership model.

Business Improvements Districts are acknowledged as creative, pragmatic, and effective mechanisms for solving intractable problems of community revitalization in threatened but viable areas. Much of this success is due to formalization of a public–private partnership among the local citizenry, business, and the local government (Morçöl et al. 2008). BIDs, as a new form of governance, do face concerns regarding public accountability (Hoyt 2008; Ross & Levine 2001), community participation, and representation; and accountability to local government (Briffault 1999). It must be noted that criticisms are not generalized, but are usually in reference to a specific incident in a specific BID. Additionally, BIDs represent a minority population (the business community) in a community often politically disenfranchised because although they have their business in the community, they often do live in the community. To date, this has been almost entirely missed by BID researchers. Minority communities by their nature have special interests and/or attributes that divide them from the general community (the majority). They tend to be initially overwhelmed with sustaining and meeting their most basic needs, as well as fitting into the larger community. This tends to be true of business communities that become BIDs. The initial result is a somewhat insular presentation, but over time this appears to dissipate and the PPP becomes a normal institution in the community, which is a primary intention of community development PPPs.

The importance of context is necessary when determining local issues regarding BIDs and community development PPPs. The concerns raised above are also symptomatic of government in general when it addresses specialized interests. Accountability controls are readily available to government in regard to BIDs, since bonafide BIDs are universally established through ordinances. The ordinances control everything. Much of the problems faced in understanding and formulating BIDs is in the evolution of the contractual arrangement of the public–private partnership. It is often the inexperience of the government partner that creates political and managerial issues that could have been avoided had the planning and ordinance process contributed to better arrangements. There is a learning curve regarding the function and authority of a BID that seems to be resolved in mature BIDs, as evidenced in the *2nd Roc-Jersey Associates, et al. v. Town of Morristown, et al.* (Justice & Goldsmith 2008), in which the state had to reaffirm that the public financing mechanism for BIDs was an assessment, not a tax. This would seem obvious, as most special district public financing is in the form of a special assessment, not a generalized tax. These types of misunderstandings contribute too many of the early confusions regarding the function of BIDs nationwide. BIDs are distinct because they are special districts that utilize special assessment forms of financing (Justice & Goldsmith 2006; Morçöl & Zimmermann 2008). In the 1998 Kessler case, the New York court decided (and most jurisdictions agree) that the GCP-District Management Corporation (and by extension, other BIDs) is a limited purpose institutional design because its services are: 1) supplemental and secondary to municipal services; 2) quantitatively dwarfed by those of the municipality; and 3) qualitatively different from core municipal functions (*Kessler v. GCPMA* 1998). All existing state BID legislation empowers a District Management Corporation to provide business management and economic development activities, including administering district affairs (adopt by-laws), purchasing and managing property, and managing the provision of specific services and standards (design, promotions, marketing, rehabilitation, cleanup, security).

Business Improvement Districts provide services to encourage and support retail/commercial economic activity similar to shopping malls. BID legislation is designed to provide municipalities with the ability to focus, elevate, and manage services specifically designed to enhance the economic viability of business areas and downtown business centers. The services that are provided by a BID are specific and unique to that business district. Business Improvement Districts are public agencies (Kennedy v. Montclair Center Corporation Business Improvement District 2014), but are managed utilizing cooperative retail/commercial management technologies similar to shopping malls as well as destination marketing technologies. It is a reasonable comparison to describe BIDs as "malls without walls" (Grossman 2014), since the cooperative technologies that malls utilize are the same, except malls have leases and are autocratic, and BIDs have ordinances and are democratic.

Today, BIDs are not targeted solely for downtown revitalization efforts but extend into multi-use districts and industrial and purely residential neighborhoods, which shifts the definition toward broader community revitalization. This is chiefly seen as a reaction to the problems of suburbanization (Morçöl & Zimmermann 2006) and an increased interest in smart growth strategies that emphasize urban development around existing mass transit hubs. For example, the Pennsylvania BID statute (2000) describes the districts as "neighborhood improvement districts," which includes every form of neighborhood from industrial to commercial to multi-use to residential, urban to suburban and, potentially, rural. "BIDs are an evolving phenomenon" (Morçöl & Zimmermann 2006, p 8). Morçöl, Hoyt, Meek, and Zimmermann argue that although BIDs are not general purpose governments, they "become like general-purpose governments" (Morçöl et al. 2008, p. 7). BIDs, they argue, challenge the sovereignty of governments in urban/metropolitan areas and force us to rethink the traditional distinctions between public and private realms. Justice and Goldsmith (2006) and Hoyt (2008) note the precocious policy transfer that is occurring with BIDs, as they become the community development method of choice internationally. There are a number of explanations as to why BIDs began to take off as a substantive form of community development. Much was attributed to the privatization movement in response to the Reagan administration's privatization policies and political rhetoric (Briffault 1999). Certainly, the upsurge of public choice arguments during the 1970s–1990s supported this claim. But other key motivations can also be found in the serious deterioration of urban retail and commercial economic generators (downtowns) and, with it, an important tax base. Downtowns once represented the mainstay of American retail commerce as well as its social life. Yet, by the 1950s, downtowns were seriously losing their prominence, a condition that contributed to Robert Putnam's concern in diminishing social capital in many these communities (Putnam 2000, "Bowling Alone"). This decay extended beyond urban areas to small towns. No one was immune to the erosion of the downtown.

The culprit was clear to see: the suburban mall. The suburban mall summarized the conflicts between urban and suburban, social rest and unrest, political fight and flight, middle class and lower class, and modernity and the mundane. The first attempt to design a BID was to emulate the physical structure of suburban malls, and many BIDs were extensions of state statutes that permitted what were called *pedestrian malls*, in which the heart of the downtown area was cordoned off and paved like a piazza, emulating European and South American town center plazas. The pedestrian mall concept did not have long-lasting value as a created urban space. It tended not to have a sense of a real place but rather a forced socialization.

However, almost all pedestrian mall projects failed for two fundamental reasons: 1) the town they were in was never designed to block traffic at such a strategic location, therefore the mall was poorly engineered to support the community's real needs; and 2) the benefits of an enclosed environment of a suburban mall were never realized, thereby letting in and not preventing urban transgressions (such as safety and cleanliness problems). As the false spectre of competition from the suburban mall muddled urban revitalization planning, competition continued to increase from other sources with the advent of big boxes—the store as mall (WalMart, Home Depot, etc.) and by the Internet and online purchasing (such as eBay), signaling forms of competition unheard of a half a generation earlier or less. As the urge to emulate the successful suburban mall proved less than successful, what did prove successful was the organizing of the business and property-owning communities around common issues.

This indicated that downtown decline was not specifically suburban mall–induced but caused by other, even greater social and economic factors. By the 1960s, downtowns had gone from virtually no competition to global economic warfare. The simple rule for BIDs was not to engage in direct competition with suburban malls but to offer better customer service, organization, and niche marketing. Downtowns, through their BIDs, began to address the special retail and social-entertainment aspects of their immediate markets. This was, and remains, a transformation of the existence of downtown from being the only game in town to being a professionally managed economic generator that addresses the cooperative needs of customers and consumers as a value enhancement for the entire town.

BIDs emphasized collaboration-management similar to Stone and Sanders' (1987) urban regime theory with heavy social capital attributes plus innovation planning similar to Molotch's (1976) growth machine theory with even heavier entrepreneurship attributes. Both theories emphasized organization through formal institutional coalitions of the like-minded (Molotch 1976) or local economic desire and the informal acquiescence of neighborhood interests to elite economic agents. Stone and Sanders (1987) call these agents *urban regimes.* Traditionally, only one of these aspects was needed to further a community development effort, but both elements, entrepreneurship and social capital, are synergistic where needed to drive the Business Improvement District movement while "embracing a vision of community governance" (Lowndes & Skelcher 1998). Placed in the role of political and entrepreneurial activists, "BIDs are the essence of innovative thinking" (Mitchell 2001, p. 201).

BIDs also represent a political shift. With the advent of suburbanization and, later, globalization, the trend of business and commercial property owners no longer living in the towns in which their businesses were located plus the lack of management were the leading causes of urban downtown decay, not competition. Chiefly, downtown business communities that once were political elites became political minorities without the ability to vote because suburbanization removed business leaders from urban areas and traditional downtowns to the suburbs. They no longer could vote where they had a business. This caused a tremendous (and poorly recorded) political power shift from commerce to residential concerns, particularly in urban and small town areas. Consequently, following the suburbanization of the 1950s and the social unrest of the 1960s, more mayors and legislative members of local government seemed to have a social agenda rather than a traditional business agenda. Additionally, business faced the status of taxation with no representation, which exacerbated a fundamentally adverse relationship between business and the community at large.

The business community lost its essential voting power because its members resided outside the urban and business municipality and lived in suburban "bedroom" communities. This was certainly less politically effective regarding their business interests.

For the same reasons, Kiwanis, Rotary, Lions clubs and even Chambers of Commerce began to lose political power, which was previously quite substantial. (Local Chambers of Commerce are resurging when they become more regional.) Additionally, the business community could not field political candidates to advance their concerns. Robert Putnam and others seem to have missed this essential political phenomenon of declining social capital caused by the loss of political capability within the business community in traditional economic generators. Although this is not the thrust of this report, BIDs restore the social capital that formal and informal political effectiveness engenders, that which was lost to suburbanization. BIDs are largely successful because they recreate formally, by ordinance and the logic of collective action (Justice 2006; Olson 1971), the special interest of business, thereby giving them not only a political forum but the means to manage it. In this way, we see an injection (or transmission) of suburban political power into the urban and downtown realm.

BIDs are created formally by municipal ordinance, which is the chief aspect of what makes BIDs different from other economic and community development efforts. No other effort, whether it is a business association, economic development corporation, redevelopment authority, or civic association, is created to extend the capability of government in such a manner, gives private sector control to legitimate public sector processes, and extends the public trust to the business and investment community with the ability to self-finance through public assessment in quite the manner that BIDs enjoy. In the 2nd Roc-Jersey Associates case, the NJ court found that assessments did not amount to a "taking without just compensation [because] the BID provides sufficiently identifiable benefits to the subject properties, and . . . that the special assessments are measured reasonably and fairly in proportion to the benefits conferred" (*2nd Roc, 1999, np*). This included management and organization.

Due to their formal nature, BIDs are a function of government at the level of the neighborhood, affecting an immediate form of civic engagement aimed at community improvement. "BIDs have the additional advantage of being an institutional design that explicitly binds the local government into the groups of collective actors we know well, by involving it in revenue collection" (Justice 2003). The BID functions as both a collective unit of subgovernance and an economic collective. Additionally, BIDs are true public–private partnerships in which the contract is defined in the enabling ordinance. The partnership can be initially sought by either the public or private sector but retains its public persona and extends public authority to traditional private interests.

The BID represents an invitation by the public sector to act in partnership, not in a solely advisory or diplomatic capacity, but as an exchange of public authority for economic technology without reducing the effectiveness of either party. In other words, the private sector assumes a public trust, which extends to the entire community, and the public sector defers some of its authority to the economic interests of the neighborhood.

Although mandatory financing does eliminate free riders as it establishes fiscal equity in the BID, the method of financing a BID does not seem to determine whether a BID is a BID. A mandatory tax or special assessment seems more precise and equitable and requires the sort of direct commitment that legitimates a partnership. It is important to note that BID property owners and business owners are not taxed, but assessed. A special assessment was defined as a form of public financing that provided "a combination of services and improvements that are intended and designed to benefit particular properties and demonstrably enhance the value and/or the use of function of the properties that are subject to the special assessments" (2nd Roc, 1999, np). Since BIDs generally utilize assessment forms of public financing and not taxes, BID residents and any other defined entity can be exempt from assessments (Justice & Goldsmith 2006; Ruffin 2008). However, the type of financing appears to be more of a nuance than a determining factor. The financing formula does not alter the legal status of a BID. Incidentally, there appears to be nothing in BID statutes that requires a BID to have an assessment or a budget, although some would argue the practicality of a BID that has no public assessment. This indicates that BIDs have public authority and that authority and how it is organized and managed is what indicates whether a BID is present. Additionally, a BID could get financing from alternative private or public sponsors or have a unique fundraising scheme that would satisfy its financial needs. Both of those alternatives do not require mandatory public financing but could finance a BID.

Although public and private funding have different regulatory concerns, what determines the legal status of a BID is not so much the funding, or whether it utilizes public or private management, but how the BID is created and for what public purpose. If it were created by ordinance that passes enumerated powers of the state to a new public entity and it intends a public–private partnership and is called a BID (or something equal), we are compelled to identify it as a BID.

This indicates that what fundamentally makes a BID a BID is that it is a unit of government with a public–private partnership framework—one that offers the private sector a reasonable entrée into government processes. This is accomplished through the ordinance. In this way, BIDs are *public–private partnerships* in name and practice because they openly fuse distinct and descriptive public and private societal constructs.

But it is arguable that these are invented distinctions and not organic agents. Examining the way in which these distinctions are constructed in a democracy, one can say that essentially all societal agents are intended to be public to one degree or another. Privateness is not considered a separate aspect of human behavior; it is derivative of publicness (Bozeman 1987). In other words, privateness is the degree of removal one has from public accountability, a deviation ascribed to cultural nuance, not an innate characteristic. Absolute removal or pure privateness is unachievable, although there is a possible absolute public responsibility. This is because all citizens are potentially 100% sovereigns even if their motives are less communal. This sovereignty cannot be denied in a democracy even if it is ignored. It is prudent that we are primarily public people with public responsibilities and our private aspects are negotiated after the public welfare is determined, not before. Privateness is a deviation ascribed to cultural nuance. The intersection of private property law and eminent domain is a good example of this process.

Regarding BIDs, the management entity (private or public) is not the BID. The BID is a public trust (owned by the people). The authorized agents of that trust, municipal legislatures, determine, by decree, the management entity, contractually, through the local ordinance and sometimes through other attached contractual devices. Additionally, the financing of the BID always requires municipal legislative oversight, whether direct financing (assessments) or indirect tax increment financing (TIF) are employed. Unless a management entity is specifically designated in the enabling local ordinance, it is not authorized to use its budget for BID supplemental services per se unless it is approved by the municipal legislature. The municipally approved budget is an approved spending plan for the BID public trust. This further emphasizes the public nature of the BID, and this designation is what distinguishes BIDs from other revitalization efforts, like the Chambers of Commerce (private advocacy group) and Main Street Program (a private consulting service of the National Trust for Historic Preservation).

As we have pointed out in this book, what occurs in a BID, as in many PPPs, is not strictly privatization but *publicization*. The public purpose does not actually become more private. Private attributes become more public even if normative private sector attributes like entrepreneurship are driving forces. Those aspects also become public as in public entrepreneurship. But this should not be a surprise, as in democracy, as stated above, the social imperative is to be more public. This is more often than not overlooked and generally misunderstood by BID practitioners. The public–private partnership that a BID represents is another name for the localizing process of democratic governance. The intention is to enhance citizen investment.

BID-PPPS ARE COMPLEX

Business Improvement Districts are "highly complex" and must be looked at "from perspectives of public administration and policy, economic development, urban politics and policy, and policy transfer and diffusion . . . from rational (public choice) to social constructionist and structural theories of power" (Morçöl et al. 2008, p. 4). BIDs are distinctive, formalized partnerships between the public and private sectors operating as functional units of (sub)government (McCool 1990). BIDs have begun to take "on the character of a downtown city government" and have become "established players in governance" (Wolf 2008, pp. 285, 286). "For some, BIDs are a funding tool; for others, a service delivery tool; for others, a common interest tool; and still for others, a development tool" (Meek & Hubler 2008, p. 217). "There has been an important shift in approach that has progressively witnessed a rethinking of governance around management and partnership . . . to a reforming of governance around the more formalized and contractualized concept and arrangements of BIDs. . . . The introduction of BIDs has effectively institutionalized what were relatively more informal and localized partnership-working arrangements" (Lloyd & Peel 2008, pp. 86, 88).

Growth in BIDs may be attributed to the understanding that "[t]own centers represent increasingly competitive arenas that demand ever more sensitive and appropriate forms of governance, management, and regulation" (Lloyd & Peel 2008, p. 72). BIDs are special assessment districts established at the local level of government to bring together public, private, and civic actors to address necessary revitalization, economic development, and quality of life improvements in a designated business area. BIDs are unique because they are established by local ordinance, usually managed and overseen by private as well as public agents, and funded through a special assessment. "The challenge for BIDs is how to help make the renewal of cities a reality, to tip them into prosperous modern agoras" (Mitchell 2008, p. 9). BIDs offer an avenue of public impact, participation, and organization for invested private actors. However, "a major challenge in studying BIDs academically is to conceptualize their nature and functions" (Morçöl et al. 2008, p. 3).

"BIDs have been given the financial and managerial capacity to make a difference" (Mitchell 2008, p. 38). The BID manager is strongly identified as a "public management entrepreneur (Grossman 2008; Hoyt 2008) representing a pragmatic form of public administration that is well suited to hybrid management techniques necessary for public–private partnerships to succeed (Grossman 2008). "BID organizations act as an 'entrepreneurial holding company' . . . a means of governing the center of communities through a partnership involving public, private and civic actors" (Segal 1998).

But entrepreneurial activity, as progressive as it may be, does not come without concerns (Hoyt 2006) regarding public accountability, gentrification, conflicts with residential advocates, service provision, and policy influences (Hoyt 2001; Justice 2003; Stokes 2002). There is virtually no evidence that BIDs are exceptional in these ways. "The caricatures of BIDs—that they are too consumption-oriented, undemocratic, and unaccountable—are likewise criticisms of city administration in many policy areas. . . . BIDs work within an economic development policy arena encompassing the public, private and nonprofit sectors" (Mitchell 2008, pp. 14, 51). BIDs may get involved in local political controversies but seem to act as vehicles for accelerated citizen involvement and dialogue. Unlike purely economic agencies, BIDs are so localized that they are extensions of the community and their true nature is community development. "A primary mission of most BIDs is to provide a safe environment for shopping, workers, residents, and tourists" (Mitchell 2008, p. 84). Their positive impact on quality of life issues that affect everyone in the community may be the reason for their popularity and persistence.

"A development related to the convergence of business and government organizations attributes and practices is the rise of hybrid organizations which are partly public and partly private" (Bozeman 1987, p. 31). In a democracy, public administration often evolves when new aspects of private society become the normal practices of government. This transformation in government is best described as the private sector taking on public sector accountabilities rather than the public sector deferring to private practices. Public–private partnerships at "the edges of government" (Becker 2007) have traditionally been the method of governmental transformation. The most formal and localized PPPs to emerge as a reaction to the social fragmentation caused by suburbanization and the consequent neglect of America's downtowns are Business Improvement Districts (Berk 1976; Houstoun 2003; Hoyt 2001; Mitchell 2001; Morçöl 2006; Stokes 2002). BIDs infuse community development processes with a new entrepreneurship based on community ownership of the process. "The use of BIDs in San Diego and their encouragement to be entrepreneurial organizations has increased the program reach of these organizations, while lessening their need for public subsidy" (Stokes 2008, p. 265)

The subgovernmental special business improvement district movement formalizes this partnership (Houstoun 2003), and in the past 30 years Business Improvement Districts have emerged to challenge the private/public dichotomy. Justice and Goldsmith (2006) discussed the dichotomous nature of BIDs that is often systemic of all "genuine public–private partnerships" that operate in a "twilight zone" between public and private policy and implementation practices. As public entities, BIDs take on what has been assumed to be much of the private sector function of community-based entrepreneurship: "the BID model initially materialized in response to suburbanization, and this condition remains the primary incentive for its proliferation" (Hoyt 2008, p. 127). As private entities, BIDs have public authority and accountability for community development. But the emerging result is not just a quasi-governmental form of governance, but a public organization that utilizes entrepreneurial capability with a distinctly social aim. Consequently, traditional public administration must assimilate the concrete functions of interdisciplinary public managers who embrace entrepreneurship (Grossman 2008).

Efforts to understand the merger of public and private sector management behavior in business and community development appear to be a challenge to both normative public and business administration practices (Hoyt 2001; Jeong 2007; Justice 2003; Morçöl 2006). Both sectors express independence, but often act interdependently. A problem in determining the capacity of public management arises when public administration is within a public–private partnership (Savas 2000). There is a natural confusion regarding with which sector the partnership is chiefly aligned. As we have noted, this "blurring of sectors" (Bozeman 1987, p. 5) extends to the professionals who manage these partnerships.

Recent research has examined the role of entrepreneurship (Grossman 2008; Hoyt 2008) in these partnerships and seeks to understand the management of a private-public partnership in the context of government without diminishing either sector. Jerry Mitchell noted in his book *Business Improvement Districts and the Shape of American Cities* that "creative entrepreneurs often start BIDs" (Mitchell 2008, p. 119), and as BIDs and their managers act as public/policy entrepreneurs, we are reminded that this may be due to the levels of risk necessary to explore, establish, and implement a policy of public–private partnering, let alone act upon it. Jeffery Pressman and Aaron Wildavsky reminded us of this back in 1973, explaining that "policy implementation is hypothesis-testing: it is exploration" (Pressman & Wildavsky 1973, p. 254). The public–private partnerships that BIDs represent are exploratory elements at the community level and assume that risk.

Over the past thirty years or more, entrepreneurship has been more and more vigorously attributed to public sector behavior. Prefixes to entrepreneurship have been added to describe its social and public potential (social, public, policy, political, etc.). Definitions of entrepreneurship consistently and universally disavow a strict profit motive for entrepreneurship and support a definition that speaks of exploration, creativity, and the ability to organize others around new notions of what is valuable (Lewis 1984; McClelland 1987; Newbert 2003; Schumpeter 1947; Thornton 1999). Entrepreneurs are notable because they identify and exploit opportunities that others do not observe or act upon (Schumpeter 1947). Contrary to common assumption, entrepreneurship seems to stem from as much a social as an economic interest (Ashoka 2007; Wiklund & Delmar 2003), and it is this interest to serve, promote change, and/or make a difference that bridges public and private domains.

Entrepreneurship, both theoretically and practically, suggests a synergy between the traditional management purposes and practices attributed to both public and private sectors. In recent times entrepreneurship has been used to examine the role of public management (Grossman 2008). The BID partnership represents a movement past a traditional adversarial relationship (Grossman 2008; Justice 2003; Stokes 2002; Wolf 2008) often experienced between government and business, and the beginning of a legal partnership that utilizes the strengths and offsets the weaknesses of each sector. BIDs are "intertwined with local government . . . joined at the hip" (Wolf 2008, p. 286) and can "afford the creation of public benefits through privately funded services and planning activities" (Stokes 2008, p. 250). Such partnerships allow the public sector to enjoy more vigorous entrepreneurship while allowing the private sector to utilize public authority and processes to achieve economic and community revitalization. The public sector takes on private aspects and the private sector takes on a measure of public responsibility. In a case study of five Los Angeles BIDs and their relationship to the local government, Jack Meek and Paul Hubler pointed out that "it is apparent that BID leadership and city leadership share mutual respect for the operational efficiencies of BIDs. . . . [T]he clear hallmark of BIDs is that they have the advantages of specific focus and stabilized funding" (Meek & Hubler 2008, p. 216)

We cannot understand the emergent phenomena of the BID process without understanding why and how private sector actors take on public accountabilities and begin to dissolve the public–private dichotomy to create a new hybrid capacity for mutually beneficial community and business development. This new capacity is notably entrepreneurial and acts as a functional third option for achieving economic and social stability and success. Business Improvement Districts represent a worldwide evolution in the capacities of government to develop and transform local communities and their cooperative economies by encouraging entrepreneurship supported by public legitimacy and real public financial commitment. BIDs represent a relatively new form of subgovernance that relies on a functioning partnership between the public and private sectors at the neighborhood level. "The unusual position of BIDs between private and public domains, together with their increasing numbers and powers, raised concerns among the general public and academics about their role in a democratic society" (Morçöl et al. 2008, p. 10). But BIDs appear to extend functional aspects of democracy by inviting and permitting traditionally business and private citizens into the formal processes of community development and governance.

BID MANAGEMENT—A PARTNERSHIP APPROACH

"With the growth of business improvement districts (BIDs), the focus in many communities has been directed to the management of downtown" (Bradley 1995, p. 11). BIDs are initially found in traditional commercial areas (downtowns, neighborhoods, city centers, industrial areas, etc.) that have not adapted to current competitive trends. These trends are consumer and employment standards: cleanliness, pedestrian accessibility, signage, modern store display, advertising, dining, entertainment, automobile safety, operable public leisure space, definable destination (Brodeur 2003). Each business area is distinct, and BID management must be innovative. Innovation as the cutting edge of governance often embodies the blending of private and public sector practices; entrepreneurial with public choice; market-driven with accountability; and self-interest with public good. "BIDs may serve a less tangible social capital function for the local business community by creating trust among property owners, businesses, and residents (Gross 2008, p. 228). Jerry Mitchell (2001) describes three BID management aspects that blend (to one degree or another): "a) an entrepreneurial approach focused on independent decision making and creative thinking; b) a public service approach centered on the development of political relationships and the need to work with alternative stakeholders to advance particular objectives; and c) a supervisor approach concerned with efficient management of day-to-day activities" (Mitchell 2001, p. 206). Entrepreneur, public servant, and supervisor address the themes of the BID manager.

With prescience toward Business Improvement Districts, in 1955 Luther Gulick wrote, "it is therefore highly probable that public administration and private administration are part of a single broad science of administration" (Gulick 2003). In this vein, the BID manager is a different kind of animal in the public management field. For decades many have attempted to define the profession. It is not one that can easily be pigeonholed into a simple discipline. It requires not only public administration and organizational skills, but business economic and development, public relations and marketing, personnel and project management, finance and budgeting, and political skills. BID managers must adapt and use all of the three management aspects Mitchell (2001) describes above because BID management is as much a venture in building community management capacity as it is in delivering services. The competencies of a BID management expert are generally agreed to be:

- Business retail development and marketing
- Public policy development, community development, and organization
- Personnel and group management
- Not-for-profit financing and budgeting
- Multitask project management
- Public relations and communications
- Urban planning and development

Mitchell ranks nine knowledge and skill requirements for the management of Business Improvement Districts based on a questionnaire mailed to 404 BIDs nationwide in June 1999 (Mitchell 2001, p. 213):

1. Speaking effectively to audiences
2. Financial analysis and budgeting
3. Planning for and designing projects
4. Situation and political analysis
5. Bargaining and negotiating methods
6. Writing policy statements and reports
7. Impact analysis and evaluation
8. Research methods and data analysis
9. Job analysis and performance evaluation

In short, a BID manager is a blended public administrator with an economic development focus "combining practical business skills with community knowledge and consciousness" (Stanford University 2005). However, at the risk of obscuring these competencies, the BID manager must be looked at first and foremost as a change agent; a facilitator of public processes that engage individuals in developing and sustaining community competencies and competitive practices that draw out real potentials and refine assets. "Public managers need to rely more on interpersonal and interorganizational processes as complements—sometimes as substitutes for authority" (Kettl 2002, p. 169). This is why BID managers, as public managers, transcend strict expertise even while accomplishing necessary competencies, which define a key aspect of the public entrepreneur (Lewis 1984). The chief expert capability of a BID manager is a fundamental pursuit of interdependent-cooperative functionality. This does not rely on the interest of individual actors, but on the sensibility of aggregate determination. The competency missing in the above charts is that of the transrational actor, one whose self-interest is communally based.

The BID movement is a new governance axiom (Osborne & Gaebler 1992) that reinvents and redefines the functionality of our communities, which derive economic relevance through social investment. In many urban and transitional communities, economic relevance seems marginalized in large part to a process of disinvestment in social norms and shifting global relationships. Communities must be reinvented by the citizenry and the expressed agreements managed effectively to avoid social erosion, blight, or economic decline. This shifts government to more localized formats such as BIDs. BIDs operate in a context of emerging governance and are "increasingly important actors in the network governance in metropolitan areas" (Morçöl & Patrick 2008, p. 315). BIDs are decentralized government structures; however, decentralization does not only depart from centralized structures, but also works back to formalized government and is most successful when that is accomplished. BIDs are generally designed as legal public–private partnerships (Houstoun 2003). These partnerships predict not only required BID management competencies, but also dictate an essential accountability to provide legitimate financial and organizational capability to emerging communities. In this way, the BID model is adaptable to many public forums.

Teamwork, collaboration, and coordination allow the entrepreneurial spirit to evolve (Schumpeter 1947). "In a consumer society, BIDs symbolize the desire of people to find meaning in their lives by joining others in public settings" (Mitchell 2008, p. 120). Entrepreneurialism is not an individual occurrence; even if its benefits tend to inure to the risk taker, it is a potential available through collective assignment and active organization (Schumpeter 1947). Because it is the potential of the land, the greater substance, which provides opportunity, individuals cannot be entrepreneurial if the society they exist in is not. Without a society an individual can only be an opportunist, as the rewards of an entrepreneur derive from the community. Profit defined in a social context is a matter of sustainable exchange within a value system. Value is a result of discovered and agreed upon community assets. That agreement is communal and exists as a dialogue, not an individual monologue. Therefore, a monologue has little value unless it is in the context of a dialogue.

The BID manager as a New Public Management entrepreneur must master the art of community and the building of dialogues of value that allow each person to act on a value exchange, an opportunity (Grossman 2008; Mitchell 2008). The great role of public administration and management beyond maintaining value is to create it by reinventing a sense of collective action where it is lost or assumed.

In almost every study of Business Improvement Districts, there is a lament that there are no useful comparative studies to determine whether or not BIDs work. "Both the critics and the defenders of BIDs make their assertions without a fig leaf of useful comparative research to cover them" (Houstoun 2003, p. 144). The odd thing about this statement is that Houstoun's entire book is a series of reports offering comparisons. The greatest benefit of a BID, as opposed to a suburban type mall, appears to be that the real community of a BID can be more viable, enjoyable, and functioning. The cause is difficult to measure because an exact sense of community success is difficult to measure. Defining and measuring all the causal factors of a well-managed community is not unlike describing pornography. You know it when you see it, but it's hard to state exactly what it is that is distinct from other activities (Stewart 1964).

A public administrator may be inclined to be bureaucratic or entrepreneurial. Both aspects are two faces of one system that pull public management from centralization to decentralization and back again; from unified benefit to fields of endeavor that need to be tilled; from conservation to risk taking. "Using resources in the most efficient way in order to satisfy citizens demands and take advantage of the opportunities of a competitive and globalised world, for getting societies more in agreement with collective wishes, all this requires changes, imagination and innovation" (Janeiro 2003). This type of public administrator manages the human process of agreement; a process that "brings people together to solve common problems, develop agreements, and manage those agreements with commitment over time" (Grossman 2014). Agreement requires partnership, which implies cooperation, direction, and communication. Collaborative partnership development appears to be the new cornerstone of community development

(Morçöl 2006). The BID manager as public administrator, in its essential form, appears to act as an expert practitioner of economic and social community processes that maximize the potential of the community.

PARTNERSHIP GOVERNANCE AND PARTNERSHIP MANAGEMENT: LESSONS FROM BIDS

The normative conversations about PPPs are generally skewed toward ideas and practices of privatization and the privatizing of public interests (Kettl 1993; Savas 2000). As we have discussed, little is said or observed about the "publicization" (Bozeman 1987; Grossman 2009) of private interests and the expansion of public management capacity, even though these phenomena are the growth areas in government and community development, particularly with the advancement of special districts like Business Improvement Districts. In the literature, examining publicness receives little more than a passing glance. Privatization does have influence on public processes, but publicization also has considerable influence.

One would think upon reading most literature on PPPs that they are created solely as a means of enticing private investors to invest in public projects like hospitals, infrastructure, transportation, and large-scale development. Successes of such PPPs are typically measured by the project investment, the capital raised for that project, and project completion. Success is rarely looked at in terms of the joint management opportunity in the planning, implementation, and maintenance processes. At the end of the project, one is led to assume that the partnership fades, and the two partners return to their respective public or private corners. The partnership is project oriented, task driven, and short-lived.

This is not true of Business Improvement Districts and other subunit public authorities that do projects as an outgrowth of ongoing community development. Another implication is that PPPs leverage efficiency because private sector shareholders are more attentive to financial success than are public stakeholders (Osborne & Gaebler 1992; Ostrom & Ostrom 1977). There is little if any objectively defined evidence to prove this as certain, and it leads to distorted understandings of private and public sector roles.

If we are truthful, we know that private investors in both public and private realms, when permitted, run up the costs of public services and private goods (and the consequences of this production) for some of the same reasons that the government does: lack of foresight, lack of capital, poor management, or simply creative risk (Schumpeter 1947). As in private ventures, often in public processes there is an uncertainty of outcomes tied to the peculiar processes of determining a consensus of the value of an outcome. Often a stated preliminary and planned outcome as it is pursued later sheds light on the full needs and designs of the project, and these adjustments usually mean new and higher costs to achieve the adjustment. Costs that reflect greater quality of life standards like safety, convenience, social connection, and culture and that are not fully understood at the beginning of a project become insistent as the end approaches—sometimes as unforeseen consequences and sometimes as a true evolution in thought and practice.

This is not a private sector or public sector disposition, but a human faculty desirous of growth and development. One aspect of a public–private partnership may be to encourage private investment, but the other is certainly to encourage public participation. The latter institutionalizes the outcomes of commonality and cooperation (Axelrod 1984; Schaeffer & Loveridge 2002), and the former infuses the process of institutionalization with innovation, ideas, performance, and entrepreneurship. Grossman's study of USA BID managers (2008) (see Table 4.1) strongly indicates that an interest in entrepreneurship correlated to social capital and management seems a higher motivator than conditional efficiency. The dependent variable is the Business Improvement District represented as public–private partnership. The independent variables are entrepreneurship, social capital, and management.

Public–private partnerships work to engage the private sector in not only investing in the public welfare, but enhancing public services for niche markets. However, this is and always has been obvious. What is not so obvious is the extent to which private actors not only become public players, but expand our understanding of public authority. The sword, it seems, cuts both ways. Public interests and service may take on private aspects, but private processes not only take on public aspects, but become public (governmental/political) entities and take on "public dimensions" (Bozeman 1987). This observation is operative in Business Improvement Districts. Bozeman states that hybrids like PPPs cause a conceptual ambiguity regarding the nature of publicness, but it could be that the specific hybrid nature of such units of subgovernment break down the public–private dichotomy and open a third door to citizen governance. The following tables reflect results of Grossman's recent study of USA PPP managers.

PPPs represent interdependence in social and economic markets. Managing publicness is managing interdependence. In the study of BID managers (based on a questionnaire

Table 4.1

Survey Question 11: The primary function of the BID is to encourage partnering between government, community, and business to achieve revitalization of the community (Grossman 2008)

Survey Question 11		Frequency	Percent	Valid Percent	Cumulative Percent
Valid	strongly disagree	3	1.1	1.2	1.2
	somewhat disagree	12	4.4	4.7	5.8
	neutral	3	1.1	1.2	7.0
	somewhat agree	90	32.8	35.0	42.0
	strongly agree	149	54.4	58.0	100.0
	Total	257	93.8	100.0	
Missing	System	17	6.2		
Total		274	100.0		

mailed to 600 verified BIDs nationwide in February 2008) over 90% of the respondents indicated that they viewed a BID as a public–private partnership (Table 4.1), and one of the primary jobs of the BID manager was to manage the relationship between the public and private sectors. Sixty-two percent indicated that they viewed their profession as part manager–part entrepreneur rather than strictly a manager. Ninety percent agreed that success is largely due to how well the PPP's public–private partnership works. This straddling of traditional public and private sectors provides insight into the nature of hybrid public processes like BIDs, and substantiates not only the private nature, but the public nature of such endeavors. The BID organization, and specifically its management, represents the same hybrid characteristics as the public entrepreneur and social capitalist. The approach is intended to take nothing away from either sector while adding the best from each to form an alternative that builds local public management capacity. When publicness is a critical determinant, it is a dynamic that recognizes the synergy of public/private balances by trading off weaknesses and strengths as they occur.

MASTERING THE PUBLIC–PRIVATE PUZZLE: LESSONS FROM BIDS—A COMPREHENSIVE COMMUNITY REVITALIZATION STRATEGY

Business Improvement Districts (also known as Special Improvement Districts, Neighborhood/Community Improvement Districts, Business Improvement Areas, and Economic Improvement Districts) are governmental but not government programs. They represent a unique community development strategy determined by the business community. BIDs convey a partnership between the municipal government and a local business community and its citizens and require their desire to work cooperatively, share responsibilities, and work to communicate effectively across private/ public, residential/ business, and government/commerce sectors. At the heart of a BID is management—the management of a public–private partnership that builds on the assets of the community, encourages entrepreneurship, efficiently utilizes resources, and sustains a compelling commitment to public accountability and service. When the business community is truly committed to cooperation and the municipality has the will to provide appropriate authority to the business community, a BID thrives and so does the rest of the town. The challenge before those looking at managing a BID is whether to look forward with commitment or remain looking backward with unresolved complaints. A BID is a structure to manage agreements and commitments about future possibilities legally and effectively. Due to the social processes, success must also be measured by levels of trust/commitment (Cummings 1883), responsibility, and accountability for the community BID planning processes, developmentally, organizationally, and economically, to explore and define the structure and agreements of the public–private partnership.

A BID creates a new form of public management in town, a hybrid form of public administration in which entrepreneurship is supported both publicly and privately, and the BID successfully manages the institutionalized public–private partnership.

To achieve this success the partnership must be well defined, informed, and committed to a positive future understandable to everyone.

BIDs are established politically as subunits of (local) government (Morçöl et al. 2008) but throughout the world, legislation allows it to be, and it usually is, managed by private stakeholders in a local community development process. The private sector stakeholders must accept and understand necessary public processes, and the public sector supports entrepreneurship and the leadership associated with the BID. In this way, the BID is a valued partner of government entrusted to manage its processes, plans, services, and capabilities. Conversely, the BID understands that its legitimization derives from its governmental role, its responsibility to the greater citizenry, and its partnership with the governing body that provides appropriate underwriting, oversight, guidance, and authority. BID management has a specific charge to achieve agreement between the public and private sectors, to remain nonpolitical but politically astute, and to keep all stakeholders motivated and engaged in a process of change that may take many years and requires vigilance. In almost every case, the deterioration of not only physical but social infrastructure requires a BID to plan for and rebuild the infrastructure to sustain future potential. This is a public process that can create private success.

The BID manager, like most public partnership managers, is an entrepreneurial public administrator whose profession arises when "private market solutions are inadequate or infeasible and collective public action is required" (Gargan 1998, p. 1135). In almost every case Business Improvement Districts are created by choice through community-based planning processes. They start at the bottom, the common ground, and work outward. The determining choice of a community is to take collective action (Axelrod 1984), and this inevitably moves toward other established forms of cooperation and collective action: government, so that a private/public partnership is brokered. The desire to sustain this partnership defines the BID management professional. Usually sustained through the provision of business development services, these services reflect the public choice to be "decentralized, participatory, pluralist, and inclusive" (Fry & Nigro 1998, p. 1207), and to manage that choice effectively. BID managers step onto the cutting edge of new public administration as revitalizationalists; facilitators of value-based community identity and the management of the agreements that eventually sustain that identity. This describes a process of transformation from individual, to rational actor, to interdependent transrational activist. The profession of BID management therefore steps beyond and above technical aspects of community development such as clean and safe, promotions, design, and business recruitment and retention, to the practice of governance; a purely public administration task.

"BIDs have become a fundamental way to move cities forward economically and socially, yet in a manner that does not unnecessarily alter the unique characteristics and staying power of vital city places" (Mitchell 2008, p. 120). Nonetheless, the lament for comparative research on BIDs is admirable and necessary, but it must be noted that this is true in virtually every aspect of economic development. Further research would be helpful to determine if an economy improved using basic measurement standards such as: vacancy rates, job creation, sales and property tax collection rates, private sector investment, customer satisfaction surveys, property valuation and tax assessment ratios, business success rates, and market identity.

However, these aspects may be more important in measuring community improvement in a BID: social investment, entrepreneurship, upgraded infrastructure, support from the community, effective public/private partnerships, residential investment, sense of identity and purpose, established functioning community organizations, diversity, political activity, and a sense of being safe and protected; i.e., all the elements of social or community capital. It might be well said that the concern about quality of life, as a community standard that is inclusive and acts as a dialogue of the value of each of us as part of a community, is that which differentiates private administration from public administration. The differentiation is not the desire for quality of life, but the intention directed to the individual or the community. "As BIDs become more a part of local government, the importance of understanding how they work together will increase" (Wolf 2008, p. 286).

BIDs are special districts designed to bring together public, private, and civic actors to achieve comprehensive community revitalization, economic development and quality of life improvements in primary business and mixed use areas. Such partnerships appear to allow the public sector to enjoy more vigorous entrepreneurship while allowing the private sector to utilize public authority and public processes to achieve economic and community revitalization. BIDs are unique because they are authorized by local ordinance, but tend to be managed by private and nonprofit entities that function as publicly oriented public–private partnerships. BIDs dissolve public–private dichotomies to create new hybrid capacities for mutually beneficial community and business development. Performance concerns arise as BID managers employ bridging forms of public management that explores, identifies, and crafts marketplace as well as community values to revitalize a sense of destination and place in traditional and nontraditional business districts. The BID movement may provide new tools for describing public entrepreneurship in public administration necessary to bridge special interests and formulate sustainable social and economic networks.

CONCLUSION

Business Improvement District Management Corporations, and Commissions, are designated in the local enabling ordinances necessary to establish a BID. BID statutes allow the BID to be managed by either a government commission or a nonprofit corporation. Overwhelmingly, BIDs tend to be managed by nonprofit corporations. This may be due to a perceived need to balance perceived public–private roles in achieving a more even partnership. It is not hard to imagine that the private sector is less adept at managing in the public sphere and needs a little encouragement. Nonetheless, this management capacity is established due to a breakthrough in public and private sector behavior. The breakthrough moves past traditional adversarial relationships often experienced between government and business, and institutes the beginning of a true partnership that utilizes the strengths and offsets the weaknesses of each sector.

This allows the public sector to enjoy more vigorous entrepreneurship while allowing the private sector to utilize public authority and public processes to achieve economic revitalization. What occurs is, the public sector takes on private aspects, and the private sector takes on public responsibilities. The increased knowledge of social, political, and economic processes benefits each sector but will confront established systems that have not achieved an institutional understanding of this unique partnership. BID management is unique in that it encompasses a public–private partnership. Functional knowledge of how the partnership effects, changes, and reconstitutes each sector, as well as redefining the roles of each organization stakeholder, is addressed by examining the intention and performance of the BID management organization.

The BID organization, not unlike any business venture, generally must achieve a level of organizational competency based on the cooperation and commitment that established the BID's sense of revitalization. What is also required is a pragmatic evaluation of performance, the thorough knowledge of the nature of the public–private partnership as it is intended to function, and the impetus to move forward built on a professional and detailed long-term "business-style" plan. This formal plan is often addressed after the BID has been established for 3–5 years (Grossman & Ruffin 2007; Houstoun 2003). This plan becomes the road map to true redevelopment, community building, and business development that details the community's assets, markets, potential, and how the BID will utilize them to achieve desired results. The plan establishes promises and activities that unfold a strategic vision of the future. It is a document of change in order to meet an identified future potential. Partnerships require accurate knowledge of each partner's skills and resources, mutual respect for this knowledge, articulated promises of real performance (Dubnick 2005), the understanding that success is built on the willingness to fail, and the sense to lighten up and reflect on successes and failures as well as strengths and weaknesses while being fully committed to the vision and ultimately the promise of the Business Improvement District.

KEY POINTS

- Business Improvement Districts (BIDs) are public–private partnerships.
- The BID partnership represents a movement past a traditional adversarial relationship often experienced between government and business.
- BIDs are created by municipal ordinance, which is the chief reason why BIDs are different from other economic and community development efforts.
- A BID is a unit of government, a special district, with a public–private partnership framework.
- BIDs have evolved from being oriented chiefly to downtowns into wholesale neighborhood improvement districts, tourism improvement districts, industrial improvement districts, and multi-use improvement districts furthering the growth of special district government.

- Business Improvement Districts are properly considered a decentralization practice for downtown revitalization.
- BIDs can properly be labeled as citizen driven. Due to this, what occurs in a BID, as in many PPPs, is not strictly privatization but *publicization*.
- It is a reasonable comparison to describe BIDs as "malls without walls" (Grossman 2014), since the cooperative management and market technologies that malls utilize are the same except that malls have leases and are autocratic, and BIDs have ordinances and are democratic.
- The fundamental capacities managed by BIDs are: PPP Management, Place Management, Comprehensive Community Development, Strategic Design Management, Retail/Commercial Cooperate Management, and Balanced Performance Management.

REFERENCES

Ashoka. (2007). *Summary of Results*. http://www.ashoka.org/files/2006_Summary_of_Results.
Axelrod, R. (1984). *The Evolution of Cooperation*, New York: Basic Books.
Becker, C. (2007). Is Public Administration Dead? *Public Administration Times*, Washington, DC: ASPA.
Becker, Carol, Seth A. Grossman, & Brenda Dos Santos (2011). *Business Improvement Districts: Census and National Survey*, Washington DC: International Downtown Association.
Berk, E. (1976). *Downtown Improvement Manual*, Chicago, IL: The ASPO Press.
Bozeman, B. (1987). *All Organizations Are Public: Comparing Public and Private Organizations*, San Francisco: Jossey-Bass.
Bradley, R. (1995). Downtown Renewal: The Role of Business Improvement Districts: More Important than Ever, *Public Management*. Vol. 77, pp. 9–13.
Briffault, R. (1999). A Government for Our Time? Business Improvement Districts and Urban Governance, *Columbia Law Review*, Vol. 99, No. 2, pp. 365–477.
Brodeur, Mark (2003, April). *Ten Tips for Designing a Consumer Friendly Town*, American Planning Association, EBSCO Publishing.
Cummings, L.L. (1983). Performance Evaluation Systems in Context of Individual Trust and Commitment. In F. J. Landy, S. Zedrick, & J. Cleveland (eds.), *Performance Measurement and Theory*, Hillside, NJ: Erlbaum, pp. 89–93.
Downtown Charlottetown, Prince Edward Island, Canada (2014). Website, www.discovercharlotte town.com/see-do/shopping/, http://www.downtowncharlottetown.com.
Fry, B.R. & L. Nigro (1998). Five Great Issues in the Professionalism of Public Administration. In *Handbook of Public Administration*, 2nd ed., New York: Marcel Dekker, pp. 1163–1208.
Gargan, J.J. (1998). Five Great Issues in the Professionalism of Public Administration. In *Handbook of Public Administration*, 2nd ed., New York: Marcel Dekker, pp. 1089–1163.
Gingrich, Newt (2005). *Entrepreneurial Public Management as a Replacement for Bureaucratic Public Administration: Getting Government to Move at the Speed of the Information Age*, Gingrich Communications.
Gross, Jill Simone (2008). Business Improvement Districts in New York City's Low- and High-Income Neighbourhoods. Chapter 10 in *Business Improvement Districts: Research, Theories, and Controversies*, New York: CRC Press, Taylor & Francis Group.
Grossman, Seth A. (2008). *The Role of Entrepreneurship in Public–Private Partnerships: The Case of Business Improvement Districts*, PhD. dissertation, Rutgers, The State University of New Jersey, School of Public Affairs & Administration, Newark, NJ.

Grossman, Seth A. (2010). Reconceptualizing the Public Management and Performance of Business Improvement Districts, *Public Performance & Management Review*, Vol. 33, No. 3, pp. 361–394.

Grossman, Seth A. (2014). *The Business District Executive Management Certification Program*, Rutgers, The State University of New Jersey, School of Public Affairs & Administration.

Grossman, Seth A. & Fayth A. Ruffin (2007). *Professionalizing the Field of BID Management*, International Downtown Association Conference, September, New York.

Gulick, L. (2003). Notes on the Theory of Organization. In Shafritz & Hyde (eds.), *Classics of Public Administration*, 5th ed., Belmont, CA: Thomson-Wadsworth Publishers, pp. 90–98.

Hernandez, Tony & Ken Jones (2008). The Strategic Foundation of the BID Model in Canada. In *Business Improvement Districts: Research, Theories, and Controversies*, New York: CRC Press, Taylor & Francis Group, pp. 401–422.

Hochleutner, Brian R. (2008). BIDs Farewell: Democratic Accountability of Business Improvement Districts. In *Business Improvement Districts: Research, Theories, and Controversies*, New York: CRC Press, Taylor & Francis Group, pp. 95–110.

Houstoun, L., Jr. (2003). *Business Improvement Districts*, Washington DC: Urban Land Institute.

Hoyt, L. (2001). Business Improvement Districts: Untold Stories and Substantiated Impacts, doctoral dissertation, University of Pennsylvania. *Dissertation Abstracts International*, Vol. 62, pp. 3961–4221.

Hoyt, L. (2006). Importing Ideas: The Transnational Transfer of Urban Revitalization Policy, *International Journal of Public Administration*, Vol. 29, No. 1–3, pp. 221–243.

Ironbound Business Improvement District (IBID), Newark, NJ (2014). Website, www.goironbound.com.

Janeiro, Domingo Bello (2003). *Training of Senior Managers*. Paper presented at the conference Public Administration: Challenges of Inequality and Exclusion. Galician School of Public Administration, International School of Administration, September.

Jeong, M.-G. (2007). Public/Private Joint Service Delivery in American Counties: Institutional Theory of Local Governance and Government Capacity. *World Political Science*, Vol. 3, No. 4, ISSN (Online) 2363–4782, ISSN (Print) 2363–4774.

Justice, Jonathan B. (2003). *Business Improvement Districts, Reasoning, and Results: Collective Action and Downtown Revitalization*, doctoral dissertation, Rutgers University, Newark, NJ.

Justice, Jonathan (2006). Balancing Democracy and Efficiency: Business Improvement Districts in the U.S. and U.K., *Public Administration Times*, Vol. 29, No. 11.

Justice, J., & R. Goldsmith (2006). Private Governments or Public Policy Tools? The Law and Public Policy of New Jersey's Special Improvement Districts, *International Journal of Public Administration*, Vol. 29, No. 1–3, pp. 107–136.

Justice, J. & R. S. Goldsmith (2008). Private Governments or Public Policy Tools? The Law and Public Policy of New Jersey's Special Improvement Districts. In *Business Improvement Districts: Research, Theories, and Controversies*, New York: CRC Press/Taylor & Francis Group, pp. 161–195.

Kennedy v. Montclair Center Corporation Business Improvement District (2014). Superior Court of New Jersey, Appellate Division, Docket No. A-4591–12T2.

Kessler v. Grand Central District Management Association, 1998, 158 F.3d 92, 132 (2nd Circuit).

Kettl, D. (1993). *Sharing Power: Public Governance and Private Markets*, Washington DC: The Brookings Institution Press.

Kettl, D. F. (2002). *The Transformation of Governance*, Baltimore: Johns Hopkins University Press.

Levy, P. R. (2001a). Paying for Public Life, *Economic Development Quarterly*, Vol. 15, pp. 123–131.

Levy, P. R. (2001b). Making Downtowns Competitive, *Journal of American Planning Association*, Vol. 4, pp. 16–19.

Lewis, E. (1984). *Public Entrepreneurship: Toward a Theory of Bureaucratic Political Power*, Bloomington: Indiana University Press.

Lloyd, Greg & Deborah Peel (2008). From Town Center Management to the BID Model in Britain: Toward a New Contractualism? In *Business Improvement Districts: Research, Theories, and Controversies*, New York: CRC Press/Taylor & Francis Group, pp. 71–94.

MacDonald, H. (1996, Spring). BIDs Really Work, *City Journal*, Vol. 6, pp. 29–42.

Mant, J. (2007). *Place Management: Why It Works and How to Do It*. Sydney Vision, UTS Papers in Planning No. 13. Sydney, Australia: Faculty of Design, Architecture and Building, University of Technology.

McClelland, D. C. (1987). Characteristics of Successful Entrepreneurs, *Journal of Creative Behavior*, Vol. 21, pp. 219–233.

McCool, Daniel (1990). Subgovernments as Determinants of Political Viability, *Political Science Quarterly*, Vol. 105, No. 2, pp. 269–293.

Meek, J. & P. Hubler (2006) Business Improvement Districts in Southern California: Implications for Local Governance, *International Journal of Public Administration*, Vol. 29, No. 1–3, pp. 31–52.

Meek, Jack W. & Paul Hubler (2008). Business Improvement Districts in the Los Angeles Metropolitan Area: Implications for Local Governance. In *Business Improvement Districts: Research, Theories, and Controversies*, New York: CRC Press/Taylor & Francis Group, pp. 197–220.

Menzel, D. C. (2000). *Privatization and Managerial Ethics in the Information Age*, abstract, University of South Florida.

Mitchell, J. (2001, June). Business Improvement Districts and Innovative Service Delivery, *American Review of Public Administration*, Vol. 31, No. 2, pp. 201–217.

Mitchell, J. (2008). *Business Improvement Districts and the Shape of American Cities*, Albany: State University of New York Press.

Molotch, H. (1976). The City as Growth Machine, *American Journal of Sociology*, Vol. 82, pp. 309–355.

Morçöl, Göktug (2006). Business Improvement Districts: A New Organizational Form in Metropolitan Governance, *International Journal of Public Administration*, Vol. 29, No. 1–3, pp. 1–4.

Morçöl, Göktug, Lorlene Hoyt, Jack W. Meek, & Ulf Zimmermann (2008). *Business Improvement Districts: Research, Theories, and Controversies*, New York: CRC Press/Taylor & Francis Group, chapter 1.

Morçöl, Göktug & Patricia A. Patrick (2008). Business Improvement Districts in Pennsylvania: Implications for Democratic Metropolitan Governance. In *Business Improvement Districts: Research, Theories, and Controversies*, Boca Raton, FL: Taylor & Francis Group, pp. 289–318.

Morçöl, Göktug & Ulf Zimmermann (2006). Metropolitan Governance and Business Improvement Districts, *International Journal of Public Administration*, Vol. 29, pp. 1–29.

Morçöl, Göktug & Ulf Zimmermann (2008). Metropolitan Governance and Business Improvement Districts. In *Business Improvement Districts: Research, Theories, and Controversies*, Boca Raton, FL: Taylor & Francis Group, pp. 27–50.

Newbert, S. L. (2003). Realizing the Spirit and Impact of Adam Smith's Capitalism Through Entrepreneurship, *Journal of Business Ethics*, Vol. 46, pp. 251–261.

Olson, M. (1971). *The Logic of Collective Action: Public Goods and the Theory of Groups*, Cambridge, MA: Harvard University Press.

Osborne, D. & T. Gaebler (1992). *Reinventing Government*. Reading, MA: Addison-Wesley Publishing Co.

Ostrom, V. & E. Ostrom (1977). Public Goods and Public Choices. In E. S. Savas (ed.), *Alternatives for Delivering Public Services: Toward Improved Performance*, Boulder, CO: Westview Press, pp. 7–49.

Pressman, Jeffrey L. & Aaron Wildavsky (1973). *Implementation*, Berkeley: University of California Press.

Putnam, R. D. (2000). *Bowling alone: The collapse and revival of the American community*. New York, NY: Simon & Schuster.

Ratcliffe, J. & Brenda Ryan (2008). The Adoption of the BID model in Ireland: Context and Considerations. In *Business Improvement Districts: Research, Theories, and Controversies*, New York: CRC Press, pp. 473–498.

Reeves, Alan (2008). British Town Center Management: Setting the stage for the BID model in Europe. In *Business Improvement Districts: Research, Theories, and Controversies*, New York: CRC Press, pp. 423–450.

Ross, B. H. & M. Levine (2001). *Urban Politics: Power in Metropolitan America*, 6th ed., Itasca, IL: F. E. Peacock Publishers.

Ruffin, F. (2008). *Business District Management Certification Program*, Newark, NJ: Rutgers University.

Savas, E. S. (2000). *Privatization and Public–Private Partnerships*, New York: Seven Bridges Press.

Schaeffer, Peter & Scott Loveridge (2002). Toward an Understanding of Public–Private Cooperation, *Public Performance & Management Review*, Vol. 26, No. 2, pp. 169–189.

Schumpeter, J. A. (1934). *The Theory of Economic Development*, Cambridge, MA: Harvard Press.

Scott, W. R. (1995). *Institutions and Organizations*, Thousand Oaks, CA: Sage Publications.

2nd Roc-Jersey Associates, et al. v. Town of Morristown, et al. (1999). 545 NJ, Supreme Court.

Segal, M. B. (1998, April). *A New Generation of Downtown Management Organizations*, Washington, DC: Urban Land Institute.

Stanford University (2005). Stanford Graduate School of Business, Public Management Program: Public Management Initiative, Social Entrepreneurship Conference, Overview.

Stewart, Potter (1964). *Jacobellis v. Ohio*, 378, U.S. 184 United States Supreme Court.

Stokes, R. J., Jr. (2002). *Business Improvement Districts: Their Political, Economic and Quality of Life Impacts*, doctoral dissertation, New Brunswick, NJ: Rutgers University.

Stokes, Robert, Jr. (2008). Business Improvement Districts: Research, Theories, and Controversies. In *Business Improvement Districts and Small Business Advocacy*, New York: CRC Press, pp. 249–267.

Stone, C., & H. Sanders (eds.). (1987). *The Politics of Urban Development*, Lawrence: University Press of Kansas.

Times Square Alliance (2013). Website, http://www.timessquarenyc.org.

Wiklund, D. P., & F. Delmar (2003). What Do They Think and Feel About Growth? An Expectancy-Value Approach to Small Business Managers Attitudes Towards Growth, *Entrepreneurship Theory & Practice*, Vol. 27, No. 3, pp. 247–270.

Wilson, Woodrow (1887). The Study of Administration. *Political Science Quarterly,* reprinted in 1997 in J. Shafritz & A. Hyde (eds.), *Classics of Public Administration*, 2d ed., Chicago: Dorsey Press.

Wolf, James, F. (2008). Business Improvement Districts: Research, Theories, and Controversies. In *Business Improvement Districts' Approaches to Working with Local Governments*, New York: CRC Press, pp. 269–287.

5

Performance Measures in Partnership Governance

Lessons from Public–Private Partnership–Business Improvement Districts

It is axiomatic that government, particularly democratic government applying the ethic of protecting both majority and minority perspectives, is a networking process, but also and consequently partnership driven. Even if the process is less than rational or artful, the desire to bring people together, solve common problems, and develop and manage those agreements with real commitments of resources is the basis of the business of government. The business of democratic government steps beyond governing—as it must—and engages its citizenry, despite its plurality and multisector properties, in the process of community development and management. In the 21st century, public–private partnerships (PPPs) provide a unique perspective on the collaborative and network aspects of public administration. The advancement of PPPs, as a concept and a practice, is a consequence of the New Public Management of the late 20th century, globalization pressures, and the advent of a more strategic rather than bureaucratic state. Today, partnering is the new governance. The term 'public–private partnership' is ubiquitous and applicable to these phenomena but is prey to thinking in parts rather than the whole of the partnership. And this devaluation of context, as it maneuvers across a continuum between both sectors, is hermeneutically abstract, making it difficult to pin down a universally accepted definition of PPPs. If we do not embrace the whole partnership rather than only the parts, as new and complete phenomena, then our assessment of partnering in the evolution of democracies is unsubstantial. And that would be a mistake.

As we have noted, throughout the world, transformational PPPs have emerged at the local level of government as Business Improvement Districts (BIDs). They have received some careful scrutiny in the past twelve years because they provide insights about the challenges of modern government. They also reveal the complexities of PPPs. There is an effective approach to addressing the gap in performance criteria for PPPs by utilizing an Integrated Balanced Scorecard approach developed by Robert Kaplan and David Norton in 1992. This method recognizes the need to integrate various stakeholder perspectives to obtain a correct evaluation of management, investment, and service aspects of an organization. With this comprehensive approach, Kaplan and Norton have anticipated the performance measurement needs of the PPP movement, and the partnering needs of government. This chapter reviews the nature of PPPs and concludes with an integral balanced measurement approach for practitioners of PPPs—an Integrated Balanced Scoring Approach.

FROM PRIVATIZATION TO PARTNERSHIP

As a result of the New Public Management initiatives of the late 20th century, which succeeded in enticing market considerations and strategic thinking into public management, the term 'public–private partnership' has also developed and expanded in conjunction with its increasing application. "It is noteworthy that these partnership approaches reveal how contemporary social democratic and neoliberal policy thinking has evolved beyond nostrums celebrating either state or market . . . experimenting with new government structures that crossed the public–private divide" (Bradford 2003, p. 1028). At first the dichotomous term public—excessive delegation, partnership—seems exotic to management. It speaks of a dangerous liaison, potential treasonous behavior with "the enemy," and political naiveté. "Partnerships are complements not substitutes for existing command and control policies" (Lubell et al. 2002, p. 159). However, when we examine PPPs as complete phenomena, we immediately notice integrating, networking, and collaborating processes, which tells us that alterations, changes, and reformations are occurring and desired. PPPs do have a revolutionary tinge about them. As Stephen Linder points out, "partnerships arise as a derivative reform in areas where privatization seems less tractable" (Linder 1999, p. 37). We can conclude that PPPs by their multisectoral nature, the variety of stakeholders, and the risks associated with change are complex and not easily defined. PPPs are organized along a continuum between public and private nodes and needs as they integrate normative, albeit separate and distinct, functions of society—the market and the commons. The questions that arise are, how do we measure PPPs in a manner that allows for these fluctuations, does not diminish either sector, and in fact reinforces the intended partnership? How do we know PPPs are successful?

There is a difference of purpose between the public and private sectors (Kettl 1993; Moe 1984; Schaeffer & Loveridge 2002; Schumpeter 1947) chiefly due to the accountability for democratic processes, and to most of us it follows that there is a difference between public vs. private sector management. Graham Allison addressed this issue in 1980 paraphrasing Wallace Sayre's comments at a November 1979 Public Management Research Conference in Washington DC, "public and private management are fundamentally alike in all important aspects" (Allison 2004). But there is a fundamental difference. Private management is based on a rationalist perspective, whereas public management must grapple with social and transrational objectives. Management, however, is fundamentally about producing useful results, and both sectors share that objective. At the least, management in both sectors is measured by the results produced.

Virtually worldwide, the interdependencies between the public and private sectors are becoming more apparent, eroding traditional understandings of what is government and what is business and evolving into something quite new—a practice of partnering (Lowndes & Skelcher 1998). Lowndes and Skelcher add that "partnerships are frequently contrasted with competitive markets and bureaucratic hierarchies" (p. 313), which tend to be autocratic. PPPs are in contrast to privatization, as they represent a key aspect of democracy, private sector participation in public life—a definition of citizenship. PPPs serve a policy strategy to support moderation between extreme political views for those either less or more supportive of state action. Consequently, in a democracy, we should expect to find collaborative multisectoral partnerships that aim to resolve economic and social problems, and we should expect them to be evolutionary rather than static. "The idea of 'collaborative advantage' (Huxham 1996) presents an attractive strategic alternative to the market, quasi-market and contractualized command and control relationships that have dominated the public management reform movement internationally in the past decade" (Lowndes & Skelcher 1998, p. 313).

Multisectoral partnering is experienced on a continuum of private to public in varying degrees of implementation according to the need, time restraints, and the issue at hand. Even though these partnerships are now common, it is normal for both private and public sectors to be critical of the other's approach and methods. It is at the merger of these sectors, noticeable in Business Improvement Districts, that we see how a unified partnership has immediate impact in the development of communities and the provision of public services. Carol Becker furthers our understanding of BIDs as public–private partnerships stating, "BIDs . . . are quasi-governmental entities, or organizations that have features of both government and private organizations" (Becker 2010, p. 413) and are not only a forum of debate, but also an arena of action in the interplay of business and culture (Becker 2010; Ewoh & Zimmermann 2010; MacDonald, Stokes, & Blumenthal 2010; Ruffin 2010). Ewoh and Zimmermann add, "Globally business improvement districts have proliferated as the most influential public–private mechanisms for revitalizing business districts and promoting infrastructure improvement projects" (Ewoh & Zimmermann 2010, p. 395). BIDs are more than a public–private interchange. They exist because of a public contract, and like all PPPs begin and end with an intention that private benefit is supported by a clear and present public benefit. This provides us with a definition of public–private partnerships: a contractual agreement between a public agency (federal, state, or local) and a private sector entity (National Council for PPPs 2010). Through this agreement, the skills and assets of each sector (public and private) are shared in delivering a service or facility for the use of the general public. In addition to the sharing of resources, each party shares the potential risks and rewards of the service and organization.

Too often, in the interest of partnership, the public sector will relinquish its oversight role that risks agency loss due to "information asymmetry and diverging preferences," thereby moving delegation to abdication and a shirking of public responsibility by public officials and private developers (Erie, Kogan, & MacKenzie 2010, pp. 649, 655). This alarms public sector advocates (Skelcher 2007). Equally, the public sector, in the interest of partisan politics, may overstate the political nature of BIDs. This can alarm private sector advocates. In either case, when the promise of interchange and teamwork, which sustain the partnership, receives less encouragement and withers, and the public–private partnership is not equitable, it tends to fail (Roelofs 2009). A fundamental objective of PPPs is to enhance public management capacity, and yet this is universally misunderstood and, consequently, poorly measured. Success is achieved when a comprehensive balance of public, private, and partnership interests are managed and measured. As stated above, often overlooked is the primary measure of a BID, like all PPPs, which is not simply the return on investment (ROI) or the quality of life (QOL), but the effectiveness of organization and management capacity (OMC)—how the BID functions as a public–private partnership (Grossman 2010). The result is an overemphasis on privatization, an undervaluing of publicization to describe and evaluate a key strategy of PPPs, and a lag in identifying pertinent evolving management technologies and practices for public administration.

At first glance, PPPs may seem more designed for the realm of economic and infrastructure development than general purpose government. Yet, when we look closer at the growth areas in government, we notice that by sheer numbers, public–private partnerships dominate, typically operating as special districts, and almost always as a form of public contract by expanding public management or services, thereby achieving a key strategic goal: enhanced management capacity. We live in a world of special governing districts (school, water, public safety, redevelopment, business, industry, military) and resultant PPPs and hardly notice it. PPPs and formal public authorities, special districts, are utilized because they resolve difficult and transitioning problems that pose risks for either sector if they act alone. Like all partnerships they are chiefly designed to reduce private sector risk (social predictability) and public sector risk (financial) through appropriate risk delegation and skill alignment of each sector, which supports entrepreneurship. Consequently, as social and economic concerns often have similar and systemic development challenges, PPPs have become a significant part of mainstream political and commercial functions. If we count, the most numerous form of government in the USA is special district PPPs.

In this chapter, a unique model of these districts receiving well deserved recognition and attention are municipally based and established business improvement districts (Briffault 1997; Grossman 2008). BIDs offer a window into the function of PPPs and how they are changing the public management landscape (Grossman 2010; Mitchell 2008; Morçöl et al. 2008). In the literature there is an abundance of information on what BIDs are, what they do, and how they are designed, but little information regarding how PPPs are managed, perform, and what measurements would be most useful in assessing the intended integrative purpose of PPPs. This can be attributed to the lack of performance measurements in the public sector as a whole, but equally to the misunderstanding of the mechanisms of multisectoral partnerships. These mechanisms are well established in BIDs, and are chiefly in three functional areas that apply to the private interests, the public interests, and the partnership as a whole and as complete functioning phenomena. PPPs integrate private sector interests and can be measured as an ROI with public sector concerns measured as QOL. However, a true integration is not simply the merging of sectoral performance areas, just as planning is anemic without implementation but must also include measurements of the OMC of the PPP as a whole. ROI and QOL produce measurable outputs and outcomes. OMC measures empirical and functional processes, communication, identity, the ability to perform as a whole, and the management of the PPP (BDMCP 2010).

PUBLIC–PRIVATE PARTNERSHIPS AND LESSONS FROM BUSINESS IMPROVEMENT DISTRICTS

As we have noted, the predominant literature on PPPs leads us to believe that PPPs are created as a means of enticing private investors to invest in public projects like hospitals, transportation, and large-scale development. The interest in such PPPs is chiefly to raise funds for public transportation and infrastructure without raising taxes. Since most of these projects are already built by private industry through general contracting procedures, it is this financing element that describes the partnership. This is a transactional partnership as there is no long-term shared or hybrid management capacity, and success is primarily measured by return on investment. This joint fund-build approach addresses immediate functional infrastructure problems but is not designed to shepherd social and economic change. It also does not have a well-defined sense of strategic publicization found in most PPPs. Success is rarely looked at in terms of the joint management opportunity and strategic goals. In this scenario, at the end of the project, the partnership fades and the two participants return to their respective public and private corners. The partnership is project oriented and short-lived.

There is an argument that fund-build arrangements are PPPs, only heavily skewed to the private end of the public–private continuum. This is true as an elemental example of PPPs, because it tell us that partnerships in government are fundamental and not new to public administration (Linder 1999). The fund-build type of PPP is not true of most special districts, i.e., water and water treatment districts, many that skew to the public end of the public–private continuum and are subunits of government. Business Improvement Districts fall almost in the middle of the continuum, as they provide services as an outgrowth of ongoing publicly oriented community and economic development.

The implication that PPPs leverage efficiency because private sector shareholders are more attentive to financial success than public stakeholders (Osborne & Gaebler 1992; Ostrom & Ostrom 1977; Savas 2000) has trended research on PPPs toward privatization assessments, as if PPPs solely justified private capability. However, the key interest of PPPs is not efficiency, but innovation to resolve collective action problems and form cooperative ventures. Efficiencies may be obtained due to the private sector's "get it done" sensibilities, but taken as the purpose of establishing PPPs, this is a key reason PPPs encounter political resistance and fail. Although research is just beginning on why PPPs fail, indications are that most PPPs fail because they run into political resistance and, instead of adapting to public needs, resist the requirement to be effective as public actors. This is a prescription for PPP failure.

In a PPP, private sector actors soon find out that in public processes there is an uncertainty, a risk of outcomes tied to the peculiar processes of determining a consensus of the public value of an outcome (Stokes 2002). This is an education, communication, as well as a planning issue, all of which are public rather than private concerns. "Government actors would need to think and behave like entrepreneurs, and business actors would have to embrace public interest considerations and expect greater public accountability" (Linder 1999, p. 37). Often a stated planned outcome as it is pursued has unintended consequences that later shed light on the full needs, implications, and designs of the project. Adjustments are made and usually lead to higher costs to achieve the desired outcome. Costs that reflect greater QOL standards such as safety, convenience, social connection, and historic preservation, not fully understood at the beginning of a project, become insistent as the end approaches. One aspect of a PPP may be to encourage private investment, but the other is certainly to encourage public participation by private actors and assume aspects of governance (strategic publicization). The latter institutionalizes the outcomes of cooperation and interdependency, and the former infuses the process of institutionalization with innovation, ideas, performance, and entrepreneurship (Grossman 2008). Entrepreneurship is understood to be as much a public process as it is a private attribute, and its role in public–private partnerships works to transform private sector ambitions into public accountabilities, and to foster innovation and change in public management. This attests to the strategic nature of PPPs and their role in society to advance social and economic change, provide new solutions, and enhance management aligned with these solutions by drawing "on communal traditions of cooperation" (Linder 1999, p. 36).

Definitions of PPPs tend to stress the contractual relationship between government and the private sector to further "cooperation not competition" (Linder 1999, p. 36) and range between management and political reform problem solving, risk reduction, and innovations in public service. Erie, Kogan, and MacKenzie define PPPs as being "distinguished primarily by the pooling of public and private resources and their ostensive public objective" (Erie, Kogan, & MacKenzie 2010, p. 647). This definition implies the importance of public and private resources, technologies, and capabilities as strategic investments. Jurian Edelenbos and Erik-Hans Klijn (2007), identifying the social capital, trust, and networking properties of PPPs that reduce risk factors, define a PPP "as a cooperation between public and private actors with a durable character in which actors develop mutual products and/or services and in which risk, cost, and benefit are shared" (p. 27). The "durable character" of PPPs implies strategy, management, institutions, and contracts, and cooperation implies usefulness of capacity and social processes. Barbara Gray, in discussing how collaboration works in PPPs, may have most essentially defined PPPs: "as arrangements in which parties who see different aspects of a problem can constructively explore differences and search for solutions that go beyond their own limited vision of what is possible" (Gray 1989, p. 5). This implies that PPPs are not normative approaches to government and collective action. They are transformative, entrepreneurial, and synthesized as new approaches to problem solving.

Hodge and Greve argue that PPPs are a phenomenon of public administration, not just a technique, and define PPPs as "co-operative institutional arrangements between public and private actors" (Hodge & Greve 2009, p. 33). This implies that PPPs are not simply conversational or conceptual, but functioning aspects of society. In the definition process of PPPs, it is helpful to distinguish social definitions of partnering from the managerial aspects of partnering. Institutional arrangements are clearly contractual, not simply procedural or political. The National Council of Public–Private Partnerships defines a PPP as "a contractual agreement between a public agency (federal, state, or local) and a private sector entity. Through this agreement, the skills and assets of each sector (public and private) are shared in delivering a service or facility for the use of the general public. In addition to the sharing of resources, each party shares in the risks and rewards potential in the delivery of the service and/or facility" (2010, www.ncppp.org). The most definitive aspect of a PPP is the requirement that the public side be willing to partner. "Governments pursuing partnerships must assess the "fit" between their preferred paradigm and the prevailing institutional landscape" (Bradford 2003, p. 1029). This implies a rare but realistic sentiment: that formal government may not be the whole solution and neither is the private sector, but if they are willing they can be good partners in creating more holistic and networked approaches to service provision, problem solving, and management. The challenge of partnering is not to diminish, but enhance, each partner. The partnership is based on "dividing outputs equally" (Farrell & Scotchmer 1988, p. 279), even if inputs are unequal. Enhancement occurs within the context of the partnership and is intrinsically connected to the partnership's organization and management functions to produce results and avoid a tragedy of the commons (Elliott 1997).

In the 1970s and leading to the present day, the idea to synthesize various private capabilities, public capabilities, and eventually public and private capabilities appears first as an effort to improve retail by creating professionally managed retail cooperatives (shopping centers and malls) and later traditional downtown business centers. Additionally, from the public sector there was a strong desire to encourage entrepreneurship as well as a desire to eliminate unnecessary redundancy by managing common assets, values, and services. This required organizations built upon interdependence and cooperation. In the private sector, these became privately owned retail cooperatives such as malls; in industry, managed industrial parks; and in traditional downtowns, managed business districts and eventually Business Improvement Districts that function as publicly endowed subunits of government.

Research on BID management and performance, like PPPs in general, is also lacking, and as Jerry Mitchell points out, is often based on "preconceived notions and ideological formulations" (Mitchell 2008, p. 109). There are few agreed upon determinants of such evaluation, and less for public–private partnerships that must factor wholly qualitative needs such as quality of life, learning, and issues of community pride. Much of this lack of research can be attributed to the novel nature of a BID public–private partnership versus the public only or the private only stance many researchers employ. On both sides of the public–private aisle such research would benefit all in understanding the true nature of the system that is an amalgam of private and public infusions. Nonetheless, in May 2007,

Ingrid Gould Ellen, Amy Ellen Schwartz, and Ioan Voicu of the Furman Institute for Real Estate and Urban Policy, New York University, undertook a basic economic evaluation of 55 New York City BIDs and their impact on property values. In asking the question, "Why should BIDs increase property values?" (p. 3) the report answered with this qualitative response, "Fundamentally, the answer lies in their success in improving the level and quality of local public goods provided—either by direct provision or by drawing more of the City's resources" (p. 3). Although they further state that a market or government failure caused this rather than a lack of planning and management, the point is well taken that the effect of a public–private partnership is evident. In conclusion the report also addresses private sector investment concerns, stating that "on average, we find that BIDs generate positive impacts on the value of commercial property, a finding that is robust to alternative in comparison areas" (p. 31). There has been plenty of anecdotal evidence that BIDs have a positive impact, and most of this and the Furman Study indicates that it is the PPP nature of the BID that causes the impact.

As a form of special district government, BIDs are noted for their localized nature at the neighborhood level (Briffault 1997). Special districts range from large to small. A typical large district such as the Tennessee Valley Authority set up by Congress on May 18, 1933, "a corporation clothed with the power of government but possessed of the flexibility and initiative of a private enterprise" (Roosevelt 1933), had a mission to manage power production, navigation, flood control, malaria prevention, reforestation, and erosion control in the Tennessee River Valley throughout the state of Alabama. Another large special district is the Port Authority of New York and New Jersey, established in 1921, which operates the airports, seaports, bridges, tunnels, and other regional transportation services of the New York City/New Jersey area and acts as a developer, most notably of the World Trade Center.

Most special districts are municipal and provide the management of an important resource such as water, public sewer, economic development, or transportation (Caruso & Weber 2008; Houstoun 2003). Some special districts manage development areas such as industrial parks, and in the case of BIDs areas that have special customer service needs or business revitalization concerns such as traditional downtown business centers. All special districts have seven points in common that reinforce aspects of a public–private partnership:

1. Provision of specialized services that address communal needs
2. Financed by special assessments
3. Have government oversight and accountabilities
4. Are part of the government
5. Require government action to be established
6. Are quasi-governmental
7. Encourage the use of or transfer of private sector technology

BID management has a specific job to achieve agreement between the public and private sectors, to remain nonpolitical but politically astute, and to keep all stakeholders motivated and engaged in a process of change that may take many years and requires vigilance.

AN INTEGRAL HYPOTHESIS FOR PRACTITIONERS
OF PPPS—A BALANCED SCORECARD APPROACH

The integral hypothesis for practitioners of PPPs is based on the concept of the Balanced Scorecard. Following prior initiatives, the Balanced Scorecard we know today was developed by Robert Kaplan and David Norton of the Harvard Business School (Kaplan & Norton 1992) as a performance measurement tool. The Balanced Scorecard embraces both strategic planning and a futurist orientation (where are we going?) by integrating this with performance measurement (where are we at?) and arriving at performance management (how are we getting there?). The balance in the scorecard is arrived at by merging economic/private (ROI) and social/public measurements, and scoring the results to get a snapshot of how well the organization is doing in meeting its strategic objectives, promises, and vision of the future. This integral hypothesis creates a balance between three elements: financial and market investment label ROI, nonfinancial and social investments labeled QOL, and a third nonfinancial element, the partnership investment, labeled OMC. As Kaplan and Norton pointed out, a meaningful and true assessment must recognize contextual as well as content-oriented criteria. In the case of PPPs, these criteria must address public, private, and partnership perspectives. For example, a business district may have more customers and a higher ROI score, but the neighborhood may experience increased air pollution due to increased traffic, lack of parking, and noise contributing to a lower QOL score, but the management or management organization communicates well its efforts to address these issues and holds open meetings, which provides a higher OCM score. The truer score is a combination of each element.

The idea of a scorecard is an honest approach to performance measurement. It tells us that measurement is a snapshot of what is happening, not a prediction of what will happen. Of course, if we don't know what is happening, let alone where we are going, any performance passes as accomplishment. The key to the Balanced Scorecard and the Integral Performance Hypothesis for PPPs is an agreement, a promise, on where you are going. Therefore, measurements mean little without the agreement; without a promise of a strategic goal, there is no meaningful measurement. Performance must be measured against a context of a known and purposeful commitment to construct a future reality. Granted the future once arrived at may be different than envisioned, but the premise of this method is that it will be deliberately and consciously managed, not guessed at.

The Kaplan-Norton Balanced Scorecard emphasizes "four perspectives." The four perspectives are:

- Financial: resources, outputs, economy, asset management (ROI)
- Customer: quality of life, safety, cleanliness; livability, destination management, entertainment (QOL)
- Internal Processes: organization, communication, development, skills (OMC)
- Innovation and Learning: entrepreneurship, social capital, adaptation (OMC)

The Balanced Scorecard method is an integrating performance measurement process that aligns with the Agreement-Management-Commitment-Accountability Model (see p. 43) of PPP development, and is well suited for assessing the management of PPPs.

Performance management is as effective as its measurements. Consequently, in most work environments the area in most dire straits is a lack of evaluation and more, the lack of effective evaluation. Correct evaluation allows us to obtain useful information so that we can determine if we are on target with our strategic outlook and project goals (Reenstra-Bryant 2010). Reenstra-Bryant adds, "evaluation is really a set of tools to address the uncertainties associated with program models, develop greater understanding of the results that certain efforts do produce, and identification of needs for revised agendas and strategies" (Reenstra-Bryant 2010, p. 522). Performance measurements provide not only a baseline, but an objective look at "the truth." Managers tend to be consumed with day-to-day operations and seem to have little time to conduct survey and other evaluative research. The success and popularity of the manager and the renewal of the organization's ability to continue are often enough. PPPs feel they are judged every day by business and government providing more than enough scrutiny. This opinion has led to a field that is virtually empty of objective data on its functional aspects, including management, business development and investment, public impact, customer satisfaction, quality of life, and organizational effectiveness.

The context of measurement will largely determine its effectiveness. The context of measurement may be more important than the measurement itself. Our context is a partnership and specifically public–private partnerships. One of the major reasons why performance measurement is seldom able to deliver on its positive potential is because it is almost never properly socialized—that is, built in a positive way into the fabric of the organization. Too much traditional performance measurement has been seen as "the reward for the few, punishment for the many, and a search for the guilty" (Spitzer 2007, pp. 3–4). It is not about doing measurement for the sake of measurement. "It is about creating an optimal environment (context) for its effective use. . . . [N]o organization can be any better than its measurement system" (Spitzer 2007, pp. 14–15).

A UNIVERSAL PUBLIC–PRIVATE PARTNERSHIP SURVEY: ROI, QOL, AND OMC (FULL SURVEY IN APPENDIX 3, P. 227)

In the fall of 2009, responding to this dearth of standardized evaluation criteria for managed business districts, the Business District Management Certification Program at Rutgers University, Newark, NJ (BDMCP 2010) developed a Universal Public Private Partnership & BID Survey based on balancing public, private, and partnership criteria by including but separating three criteria areas: Return on Investment (ROI), Quality of Life (QOL), and Organizational and Management Capability (OMC).

The survey begins by collecting practical and demographic information to determine the type of management, location, size, and the budget of the management organization. The survey is set up in a five-point Likert scale. The scale is numbered from 1 to 5 going left to right. The OMC section has 28 data criteria. The ROI section has 24 data criteria. The QOL section has 22 data criteria. The score is determined by adding up each criterion according to its representative number. Scoring was based on a reasonable proportion of the total score. The total score is determined by adding together the scores of the sections as follows:

The survey is based on the following hypotheses:

- If the management organization's public–private partnership is unsuccessful, then the managed district is less successful.
- If Organization and Management Capability (OMC) are unsuccessful, then the managed district is less successful.
- If Return on Investment (ROI) is unsuccessful, then the managed district is less successful.
- If Quality of Life Improvements (QOL) are unsuccessful, then the managed district is less successful.
- The total of OMC, ROI, and QOL provides a more complete and accurate assessment of success.

The survey serves to assess the general state of the PPP's performance from a broad perspective touching on three key aspects of performance measurement: OMC, ROI and QOL. The overall score relates to the overall condition of performance within the organization; however, it should also be analyzed in three separate sections to determine where improvements that will have the greatest performance impact can be made. Measuring performance personally and organizationally in a systematic manner is necessary to ensure positive progression, effectiveness, and efficiency of programs and management within PPPs. The process of regularly evaluating all the key indicators that lead to the success or failure of a given goal or mission creates an organizational atmosphere that is both proactive and responsive, traits that are paramount to success in an environment of constant social, demographic, and economic change. Further and more refined evaluation of programs and processes related to ROI and QOL are prudent in order to determine necessary actions to improve on those PPP functions. Obviously, more targeted or program-specific evaluations would have to be done in order to determine specific actions to impact improved performance as a whole. By methodically assessing a PPP's organizational and management capability (OMC), return on investment (ROI) related to programs and activities, and the overall quality of life (QOL) as impacted by the management organization, the PPP is able to confidently determine direction, adjust resource allocation, validate actions and engage their constituency (see Appendix 3—Survey, p. 227)

CONCLUSION

It often is a logical assumption that the components of human endeavor, particularly public and private, are compartmentalized and examined as self-fulfilling and functioning. It is as if any part of the performance process is set aside as the entirety of accomplishment all by itself, with little regard for context, interdependency, and partnerships. This has worked to erode trust of performance evaluation. As a whole, balanced performance measures tuned to the frequency of real multisectoral contexts are a more complete measurement of PPPs. Performance measurement creates a history of investment for the record and justification of the expenditure of assets and social capital. It informs us whether we are on target or not. It serves to support all the past efforts of those who have committed to the vision/promise. The data required for the measurement, be they quantitative or qualitative, serve as a road map for future efforts or corrections of the organization and support evidence for continuing success or failure. Evidence-based management allows the assessment of results to determine the effectiveness of strategies and the efficiency of operations to make changes as required and to address shortfalls in delivery of programs. Evaluation allows us to assess how and if promises are being delivered.

When we discuss the public performance of PPPs, we are referring fundamentally to the promise of democracy, as it is constituted in the building of our society. We are describing how this affects the performance of tasks through the balance of competing perspectives and the organization of the PPP as a public institution. PPPs are increasingly significant contributors to the evolution of local governance, including planning processes, the execution of projects, the implementation of policy, and the enhancement of local management capacity. We cannot forget that every performance refers to a promise, or a set of promises, that sets goals and describes an agreed upon future as a strategic objective, both publicly and privately. When we speak about performance in general, we are speaking fundamentally about measuring outputs and outcomes against inputs and implementation in relation to such promises; therefore we are assessing management processes. It follows that performance evaluation is a series of measurements of the inherent promise(s) in every performance along a promise-performance axis, although the chief differences between private and public sector management are the degrees of inclusion and the fulfillment of public outcomes. PPPs promise that there is both value added and risk reduction in collaborating to create something neither sector can do alone very well. If we are on the high end of either of the inclusionary and public outcomes aspects, we can safely presume that we are operating in a more public environment. If we are on the lesser end of these aspects, then we are most likely operating in a private environment. If we are operating contractually at reasonably high levels in both aspects, we are in a public–private partnership like a BID. The importance of this distinction is twofold:

1. Inclusion underwrites democratic functions and tends to diminish autocratic functions, which provides a different perspective on performance.
2. A greater depth and breadth of the promises between people is more imperative in public environments due to:
   a. the extent of partnering needs, which place outputs as parts of outcomes;
   b. the performance process being more nonlinear so that input "A" may not directly impose upon or predict output or outcome "B"; and
   c. the timeline consequently for expected results to occur and retain impact is often expanded.

The PPP organization must achieve a level of organizational competency based on the cooperation and commitment that established the PPP's purpose, and it is arguable that the organization and management capacity (OMC) measurements are most important. As J. Smith and P. Wohlstetter point out, "public–private partnerships are motivated largely by a pursuit of the comparative advantages inherent to organizations in the other sectors" (Smith & Wohlstetter 2006, p. 250). A pragmatic evaluation of performance, the thorough knowledge of the nature of the public–private partnership as it is intended to function, and a balanced scoring of private perspectives regarding return on investment, public perspectives regarding quality of life, and the partnership perspective regarding organization and management capacity to grow and develop the partnership are also required to assess performance effectively.

There are functional performance concerns—the how-to of project management—but there is ultimately the concern about fulfilling the PPP's promises. A commitment does not mean you know how to do something. We are promising that something will be accomplished and, often, we don't know how to do it—not completely. The reality is not entirely mechanical (automatic), it's created (intended)—by us. We wiggle and giggle and play with things to see what works under certain circumstances. When something eventually does work, it does so because we have adequately explained it—put language to it, and manage that explanation, and come to understand it. It becomes the reality we are creating, or intended to create.

KEY POINTS

- PPPs are organized along a continuum between public and private nodes and needs as they integrate normative, albeit separate and distinct, functions of society—the market and the commons.
- If we do not embrace the whole partnership rather than only the parts, as new and complete phenomena, then our assessment of partnering in the evolution of democracies is unsubstantial. The term 'public–private partnership' is prey to thinking in parts rather than the whole of the partnership.
- There is an effective approach to addressing the gap in performance criteria for PPPs by utilizing an Integrated Balanced Scorecard.
- The balance in the scorecard is arrived at by merging economic/private and social/public measurements. This integral hypothesis creates a balance between three elements: financial and market investment label return on investment (ROI), nonfinancial and social investments labeled quality of life (QOL), and a third nonfinancial element, the partnership investment, labeled organization and management capability (OMC).
- A meaningful and true assessment must recognize contextual as well as content-oriented criteria. The context of measurement may be more important than the measurement itself.
- Evaluation addresses uncertainties and allows for appropriate adjustments and changes in strategy.

REFERENCES

Allison, Graham T. (2004). *Public and Private Management: Are They Fundamentally Alike in All Unimportant Respects?* Classics of Public Administration, 5th ed., Belmont, CA: Wadsworth/Thompson Learning.

Becker, Carol (2010). Self-Determination, Accountability Mechanisms, and Quasi-Governmental Status, *Public Performance & Management Review*, Vol. 33, No. 3, pp. 413–435.

Bradford, Neil (2003). Public–Private Partnership? Shifting Paradigms of Economic Governance in Ontario, *Canadian Journal of Political Science*, Vol. 36, No. 5, pp. 1005–1033.

Briffault, R. (1997). The Rise of Sublocal Structures in Urban Governance, *Minnesota Law Review*, Vol. 82, pp. 503–550.

BDMCP [Business District Management Certification Program] (2010). Institute of Business District Management, National Center for Public Performance, School of Public Affairs & Administration, Rutgers University, Newark, NJ.

Caruso, Gina & Rachel Weber (2008). Getting the Max for the Tax: An Examination of BID Performance Measures. In *Business Improvement Districts: Research, Theories, and Controversies*, New York: CRC Press, pp. 319–348.

Edelenbos, Jurian & Erik-Hans Klijn (2007). Trust in Complex Decision-Making Networks: A Theoretical and Empirical Exploration, *Administration and Society*, Vol. 39, No. 1, pp. 25–50.

Ellen, Ingrid G., Amy E. Schwartz, & Ioan Voicu (2007). *The Benefits of Business Improvement Districts: Evidence from New York City*, Furman Institute for Real Estate and Urban Policy, New York University, NY.

Elliott, Herschel (1997). *A General Statement of the Tragedy of the Commons*, Gainesville: University of Florida Press, 1–12.

Erie, Steven P., Vladimir Kogan, & Scott A. MacKenzie (2010). Redevelopment, San Diego: The Limits of Public–Private Partnerships, *Urban Affairs Review*, Vol. 45, No. 5, pp. 644–678.

Ewoh, Andrew & Ulf Zimmermann (2010). The Case of Atlanta Metro Community Improvement District Alliance, *Public Performance & Management Review*, Vol. 33, No. 3, pp. 395–412.

Farrell, Joseph & Suzanne Scotchmer (1988). Partnerships, *The Quarterly Journal of Economics*, Vol. 103, No. 2, pp. 279–297.

Gray, Barbara (1989). *Collaborating: Finding Common Ground for Multiparty Problems*, San Francisco: Jossey-Bass.

Grossman, Seth A. (2008). *The Role of Entrepreneurship in Public–Private Partnerships: The Case of Business Improvement Districts*, doctoral dissertation, Rutgers, The State University of New Jersey, School of Public Affairs & Administration, Newark, NJ.

Grossman, Seth A. (2010). Reconceptualizing the Public Management and Performance of Business Improvement Districts, *Public Performance & Management Review*, Vol. 33, No. 3, pp. 361–394.

Hodge, Graeme & Carsten Greve (2009). PPPs: The Passage of Time Permits a Sober Reflection. In *Institute of Economic Affairs*, Oxford: Blackwell Publishing, pp. 33–38.

Houstoun, L., Jr. (2003), *Business Improvement Districts*, Washington DC: Urban Land Institute.

Huxham, C. (ed.) (1996). *Creating Collaborative Advantage*, London: Sage.

Kaplan R. S. & D. Norton (1992). The Balanced Scorecard—Measures That Drive Performance, *Harvard Business Review*, Vol. 70, Jan–Feb.

Kettl, D. (1993). *Sharing Power: Public Governance and Private Markets*, Washington DC: The Brookings Institution Press.

Linder, Stephen M. (1999). Coming to Terms with the Public–Private Partnership: A Grammar of Multiple Meanings, *American Behavioral Scientist*, Vol. 43, No. 1, pp. 35–51.

Lowndes, Vivien & Chris Skelcher (1998). The Dynamics of Multi-Organizational Partnerships: An Analysis of Changing Modes of Governance. *Public Administration*, Vol. 76 (Summer), pp. 313–333.

Lubell, Mark, Mark Schneider, John T. Scholz, & Mifriye Mete (2002). Watershed Partnerships and the Emergence of Collective Action Institutions, *American Journal of Political Science*, Vol. 46, No. 1, pp. 148–163.

MacDonald, John M., Robert Stokes, & Ricky Blumenthal (2010). The Role of Community Context in Business District Revitalization Strategies, *Public Performance & Management Review*, Vol. 33, No. 3, pp. 439–458.

Mitchell, J. (2008). *Business Improvement Districts and the Shape of American Cities*, Albany: State University of New York Press.

Moe, Terry M. (1984). The New Economics of Organization, *American Journal of Political Science*, Vol. 28, pp. 739–777.

Morçöl, Göktug, Lorlene Hoyt, Jack W. Meek, & Ulf Zimmermann (2008). *Business Improvement Districts: Research, Theories and Controversies*, New York: CRC Press/Taylor & Francis Group, chapter 1.

National Council of Public–Private Partnerships (2010). Webpage, www.ncppp.org.

Osborne, D. & T. Gaebler (1992). *Reinventing Government*, Reading, MA: Addison-Wesley Publishing Co.

Ostrom, V. & E. Ostrom (1977). Public Goods and Public Choices. In E. S. Savas (ed.), *Alternatives for Delivering Public Services: Toward Improved Performance*, Boulder, CO: Westview Press, pp. 7–49.

Reenstra-Bryant, Robin (2010). Evaluations of Business Improvement Districts, *Public Performance & Management Review*, Vol. 33, No. 3, pp. 509–523.

Roelofs, Joan (2009). Networks and Democracy: It Ain't Necessarily So, *American Behavioral Scientist*, Vol. 52, No. 7, pp. 990–1005.

Roosevelt, F. D. (1933). Presidential Address, Tennessee Valley Authority, TN.

Ruffin, Fayth A. (2010). Collaborative Network Management for Urban Revitalization, *Public Performance & Management Review*, Vol. 33, No. 3, pp. 459–487.

Savas, E. S. (2000). *Privatization and Public–Private Partnerships*, New York: Seven Bridges Press.

Schaeffer, Peter & Scott Loveridge (2002). Toward an Understanding of Public–Private Cooperation, *Public Performance & Management Review*, Vol. 26, No. 2, pp. 169–189.

Schumpeter, J. A. (1947). The Creative Response in Economic History, *The Journal of Economic History*, Vol. 7, No. 2, pp. 149–159.

Skelcher, Christopher (2007). Does Democracy matter? A Transatlantic Research Design on Democratic Performance and Special Purpose Governments, *Journal of Public Administration Research and Theory*, Vol. 17, No. 1, pp. 61–76.

Smith, Joanna & Priscilla Wohlstetter (2006). Understanding the Different Faces of Partnering: A Typology of Public–Private Partnerships, *School Leadership and Management*, Vol. 26, No. 3, pp. 249–268.

Spitzer, Dean (2007). *Transforming Performance Measurements: Rethinking the Way We Measure and Drive Organizational Success*, New York: American Management Association.

Stokes, R. J., Jr., (2002). *Business Improvement Districts: Their Political, Economic and Quality of Life Impacts*, doctoral dissertation, New Brunswick, NJ: Rutgers.

Appendix 1

Step-by-Step Guide to Planning and Implementing a Special District/Public–Private Partnership

Creating a Special District/Public–Private Partnership (SD/PPP) requires a consensus-oriented planning process that emphasizes the inherent dignity, values, and assets of the community. People who work on an SD/PPP need to: 1) **Know**: a) the facts about the Special District/Public–Private Partnership legislation and b) what cooperative management is as a technology for social, economic, and business success. 2) **Agree**: a) that working together in a committed and organized manner is appropriate; b) that establishing an SD/PPP provides the remedy for revitalizing, improving, and maintaining community and business standards; and c) that managing the service plan arrived at through this process is to be conducted at the highest professional level possible. A community education/planning process is inclusive and may take time until consensus is reached on the vision, values, purpose, and functions (budget, boundaries, and business) of the district.

- *Consensus*: Consensus is a process that is designed to identify and support agreements rather than an orientation toward resolving disagreements. It is helpful to have a facilitator who understands this process and identifies agreement when it is arrived at. Practicing agreement-management is the basis of asset-based planning strategies, goals and objectives, and ultimately the services rendered by the district.
- *Partnership*: Partnership, in current community development approaches, is a result of providing people with real authority and self-determination. Partnership is built upon: a shared value system that respects the capabilities, time, and energy people in our communities possess; and by acknowledging the inherent assets of the community and its people, the value each point of view and life experience brings to create the community we work, live, and conduct business in.

PHASE ONE—FEASIBILITY

Step One: **Establish a general agreement** to study and plan a Special District/Public–Private Partnership (SD/PPP) by holding community meetings and introductions on what an SD/PPP is, and determining general feasibility: tentative boundaries of potential SD/PPP (if appropriate), budget potential, service needs, and community support.

Step Two: **Establish an official Steering Committee (often by resolution of municipal council.)** Identify well-respected leaders (stakeholders) from the following groups:

> Property owners; business operators; media; residents; financial institutions; consumers; churches, educators; civic leaders; police; public transportation officials; and local governing bodies.

The purpose of the Steering Committee is to guide the SD/PPP education and planning process, conduct meetings and community information forums, present a report and proposal for the SD/PPP to the governing body including a proposed ordinance and budget, and support the preparation and passage of the SD/PPP ordinance.

PHASE TWO—PLANNING

Step Three: **Hire a downtown revitalization and management professional (CPS)** to act as staff to the Steering Committee, conduct necessary research, and educate the community about cooperative management technology and the Special District/Public–Private Partnership legislation (consider visiting other established SD/PPPs).

Step Four: **The Steering Committee conducts an education and training process to learn about: SD/PPPs as an institution; and, Special District/Public–Private Partnership technology** that the community agrees is best for downtown business in light of the potential for an improved business district. Include:

- SD/PPP training, conflict resolution techniques, strategic planning, visioning and team building, analysis of other plans and existing services.

Step Five: **The Steering Committee plans the SD/PPP: There are three required areas of concentration for the Steering Committee:**

1. *Governance*: Boundaries, type of assessment, and style of management
2. *Service*: Budget capability, service priorities and estimated costs, general budget, and planning requirements
3. *Public Relations*: Community notices, press releases, and informal and formal public meetings on the SD/PPP process

Each concentration may be expanded to include additional research as needed, such as: security/cleanliness; public relations/promotions; transportation and infrastructure; and business recruitment and retention.

NOTE: Each plan assesses: 1) The current conditions (Where are we at now?) 2) Where are we going? and 3) How will we get there?

Step Six: **Develop and present an SD/PPP report to include the results of Step Five and include the following:**

1. Description of the district with accurate maps and boundaries
2. A vision and values–based mission statement
3. Explain why the district is beneficial and how this was determined
4. The assessment method and contributors
5. General budget
6. Type of management
7. Structure of the Board of Directors/Commission of the SD/PPP
8. By-laws of management corporation (if appropriate)

Step Seven: **Conduct a community meeting to present committee findings and receive community input.**

Step Eight: **Present revised SD/PPP proposal to governing body and include a proposed Special District/Public–Private Partnership Ordinance and Budget Resolution.**

- **The ordinance** establishes the district and the boundaries, designates the nonprofit management corporation, and may contain guidelines for the minimal makeup of the Board of Directors, and the special assessment method.
- **A resolution** is enacted separately to approve the annual budget and proceed with collection of the SD/PPP assessment.

PHASE THREE—IMPLEMENTATION

Upon the successful acceptance of the proposal and consequent passage of the SD/PPP ordinance and budget, the following initial steps are necessary to establish the management corporation according to the enabling legislation.

Step Nine: **Incorporate management entity** as a nonprofit corporation, conduct first organizational meeting to: accept and approve by-laws, appoint the Board of Directors, elect officers, establish financial accounts, and appoint special committees.

Step Ten: **Organization: implement a working committee structure** as a comprehensive administrative and policy development approach to Board of Director development and a means to keep in touch with your community. With the following committees:

- Executive Committee (Management)
- Quality of Life (Cleanliness, Security, and Transportation/ Parking)
- Marketing, Promotions and Public Relations
- Architecture, Design, and Development
- Business Recruitment and Retention
- Business practices and support services

Step Eleven: **Hire professional management.**

- Downtown revitalization and management is a professional field combining (at minimum) public administration, business administration, and planning. Obtain the best manager you can afford and realize this as the primary aspect of the district's success.
- Look for someone, or a firm specializing in SD/PPPs, that is self-directed, organized, competitive, and likable and has energy. The strengths of your manager should match the needs of your district. Skills to look for are: public relations, knowledge of government and community development, planning, marketing, public administration, design, business advocacy, and economic development.

Step Twelve: **Board Policy and Procedures Manual and Training:** The SD/PPP Board of Directors is accountable both financially administratively. A thorough manual of the duties, roles, and responsibilities of the Board is necessary. Also, this manual should contain work plans, plans of each committee, and legal and fiduciary guides. If the Board has not had strategic Vision and Values training on the role of the SD/PPP Board, this should be conducted. Also, each year as new members arrive, the Board is advised to conduct a retreat to build team skills and review its mission, vision, and standards.

Step Thirteen: **Long-range Strategy: Avoid promising miracles. That is, promise what is needed, but be realistic about how long and the effort required to sustain interest and maintain effective resources.** After the first or second year, organizational operations should be complete and an effective budget should be established based on real experience. Now it is time to consider developing a three- to five-year strategic redevelopment and business plan. The following are included in a plan:

1. **Business and real estate** market research analysis on a local and regional basis and develop a long-range 5–10 year plan to include branding, marketing, and infrastructure development
2. **Comprehensive** inventory/survey of the condition of the district environment, infrastructure, transportation/ parking, and properties in the district
3. **Established** Vendor Regulations and Design Standards
4. **Agreements** with the municipality and other governing agents, other community development entities, and adjoining SD/PPPs
5. **Strategic delivery** of services to enhance business, maintain values, and meet customer needs
6. **Performance** measurement system
7. **Established** accounting and financial system
8. **Determination** of SD/PPP's short and long term borrowing capacity
9. **Public relations** and communications strategy
10. **Community** support, participation, and partnerships
11. **Ongoing** Board of Directors training

Special District/Public–Private Partnership Management succeeds by merging the best aspects of a comprehensive approach to public administration, governance, and community and business development with professional management. The committee structure within the Board of Directors/Commission is a means of coordinating the planning and managing various essential facets of a successful district comprehensively, and assuring necessary community input.

NOTE: Although encompassing all the elements of an SD/PPP, due to the focus on customer and business development, downtown business district revitalization and Business Improvement District (BID) management are specialty areas that focus on:

1. **Professional** business management
2. **Management** and development of social capital by providing a dignified experience to volunteers and fulfilling on declared promises
3. **A comprehensive,** asset-based community development process
4. **Applied,** pragmatic, strategic planning of vision and values
5. **The performance** of services that effectively communicate the community's goals and promises geared to providing enhanced value to the customers' personal, shopping, or business experience
6. **Enhancing** and sustaining a community's historic identity

SD/PPPs provide services that also take advantage of these disciplines, utilizing their unique authority, cooperation, and a citizen-driven planning and management approach.

BUSINESS IMPROVEMENT DISTRICT FUNCTIONS

BIDs are *not* general government agencies, but special agencies of government managed as a public–private partnership (PPP) with primary private sector direction. They do not replace municipal services but may enhance them and provide specifically business-related activities, services, and planning to promote, revitalize, and develop business. The primary focus of a BID is providing competitive services that address customer needs. This is not the specific job of the municipal government, although the government can encourage, support, and partner on these activities. BIDs are separate from government, but operate with significant local government oversight requirements such as: yearly audit; annual approval of their budget; and elected officials on the management board. PPPs are complex and comprehensive and require a unique professional approach when managing business districts.

With this in mind, the purpose of a BID (or SID) is to manage a public–private partnership and to promote business in a businesslike manner, institute physical improvements, and upgrade customer service standards. Business standards are different than local government, which is responsible for the overall standards of living in a community. BIDs are responsible for the standards of the business community, including promotions, cleanup, design, business recruitment, development if appropriate, and maintaining

professional business practices. A BID allows the business community to be professionally managed, determine services it specifically needs to remain competitive, leverage
funds with accountability and integrity, and be a good partner with a variety of different
entities in the community at large.

Businesses know that management is the key to their success, and this is also true of
the business district. It is not the job of government to manage business districts. It is the
appropriate job of business to do this, and BIDs are acknowledged as the best form and
method of accomplishing this. Many business communities are not managed at all. Those
that are thrive. Those that aren't managed well, struggle. This is why BIDs are managed
professionally and at the highest standards possible. Their success relies on the quality of
their management. Management is not a mistake with BIDs; it is a deliberate statement
of their accountability and intention to be successful at meeting customer needs.

A designated nonprofit management corporation manages BIDs or a municipal commission comprising key stakeholders in the BID. That means they are not out to make
a profit for themselves but to support higher profits and a better business environment
for all businesses in the district. BIDs are service oriented, and their orientation is to
their clients and customers. Essentially, BIDs are successful because they consciously
increase the level of customer service in a district by managing common concerns,
issues, and needs of the business community.

BIDs do not replace the work of the local Public Works Department, Redevelopment
Authority, Economic Development Corp. or Commissions, Office on Community, and
Economic Development Offices. BIDs enhance where necessary and appropriate, bring
new ideas where needed, and manage common business concerns, services, and agreements. The BID works with the local government and community to target and enhance
services where needed.

Below are answers to some typical questions regarding BIDs:

1. *HOW IS THE BID CREATED?*—The BID, itself, is usually created by local
   ordinance supported by a community planning process, and does not require approval by the state or county. A community-based planning process establishes
   the extent, purpose, mission, and budget of the BID.
2. *WHO GOVERNS THE BID?*—The BID is governed by a nonprofit management
   corporation or municipal commission designated in the enabling ordinance. It is
   required that the BIDs have a governing body comprising a majority of business
   and property owners.
3. *WHO DETERMINES THE BID BUDGET AND HOW DO BIDS ENHANCE
   THEIR BUDGETS?*—The BID and its governing body determine the budget of
   the BID, and the municipal government must approve it annually by resolution.
4. *WHO COLLECTS THE BID ASSESSMENT?*—One of the chief partnerships of
   a BID is with the local government, which provides oversight and acts as collector of the BID's funds. It is generally the municipality's responsibility to bill
   and collect the funds as a special assessment and ensure that the funds are given
   to the BID.

5. *HOW MUCH IS THE BID ASSESSMENT AND WHO IS ASSESSED?*—BID assessments on average are equivalent to an increase of approximately 5%–9% of the total property tax bill, or an additional $0.19–$0.28 per $100 of the tax rate.

6. *DOES THE BID REPLACE ANY MUNICIPAL SERVICES?*—NO, generally a BID can "only enhance and not replace" municipal services. The BID can provide many services to enhance business and development. (*)

7. *DOES THE BID REPLACE OTHER PROGRAMS OR REDEVELOPMENT AUTHORITIES?*—NO, other Economic Development Corps. and BIDs are designed to complement each other, with the BID acting as a business constituency focused on improvements and customer satisfaction, and the EDC on business recruitment and job creation. Both are intended to revitalize activity of business in commercial, retail, and industrial areas.

8. *IS THERE MUNICIPAL OVERSIGHT OF THE BID?*—YES. There are generally at least four primary oversights: 1) ordinance oversight; 2) most BID statutes require at least one elected person to be a voting member of the BID governing body; 3) the municipal government must approve the annual BID budget and be presented with an annual performance report; and 4) the BID must conduct an annual certified audit, which must be submitted to the municipal government.

A BID is a business-led public–private partnership (PPP), business-oriented organization with real public authority to accomplish agreed upon goals. It unites the business community in an equitable and honest fashion to make a real impact, and promote and advance better business practices and plans. It allows the business community to be a real partner with the larger community and address common needs effectively while working with other businesspeople. It allows businesspeople to do what they do best: solve business problems. It means businesspeople do not have to work alone, but can work together as a team.

Mostly importantly, a BID is usually the first time the business community (as a community) is organized around common goals, operates as a public–private partnership, and is professionally managed and directed.

BUSINESS IMPROVEMENT DISTRICT DATA

Over 1000 municipalities in all 50 states in the USA and numerous other countries, in conjunction with their business communities, have utilized Business Improvement District legislation to revitalize, professionally manage, and market their central business districts, industrial parks, and commercial zones. Business and commercial areas that are facing increased competition, neglect, and deterioration, or simply cannot focus on a community plan for improvement have found remedies provided in Business Improvement District statutes. The statutes allow for the authority, professional management, and committed funding mechanism necessary to effect real results.

Business Improvement Districts are true private/public partnerships and are essentially a public "authority" with the ability to address private business concerns in a cooperative manner. Statutes address three essential parts of this partnership:

1. Creation of a public "authority" public–private partnership with specific service capability, powers, and governance
2. Designation of the form of professional management
3. Funding capability in the form of a special assessment to finance the authority and management of the district

Business Improvement Districts are governed primarily by a private nonprofit organization comprising the members of the district and elected officials. They are designed to be specifically responsive to business and economic revitalization needs by supporting a comprehensive, organized, cooperative, and managed approach to revitalization.

(*) BID—GENERAL ACTIVITIES, SERVICES, AND AUTHORITY

1. Act as an agent of and partner with municipal government—a subunit of local government
2. Adoption of by-laws for the regulation of its affairs and the conduct of BID business
3. Employ such persons as may be required, and fix and pay their compensation from funds available to the BID
4. Apply for, accept, administer, and comply with requirements respecting an appropriation of funds or a gift, grant, or donation of property or money
5. Make and execute agreements which may be necessary or convenient to the exercise of the powers and functions of the BID
6. Administer and manage its own funds and accounts and pay its own obligations
7. Borrow money from private and public lenders
8. Fund the improvement of exterior appearance of properties in the district through grants and loans
9. Fund rehabilitation of properties in the district
10. Accept, purchase, rehabilitate, sell, lease, or manage property in the district
11. Enforce the conditions of any loan, grant, sale, or lease made by the BID
12. Provide security, sanitation, and other services in the district, supplemental to but not to replace those normally supplied by the municipality
13. Undertake improvements designed to increase safety and attractiveness of the district to businesses which may locate there or visitors to the districts
14. Publicize, market, promote, and plan for the district and the businesses included within the district boundaries
15. Recruit new businesses
16. Organize special events in the district

17. rovide special parking arrangements for the district
18. Design and enforce environmental and building design criteria
19. Regulate vending
20. Provide temporary decorative lighting in the district

Appendix 2

Case Study of the Flemington, New Jersey, Business Improvement District Planning Process

This chapter describes the planning process, findings, and proposal for a borough-wide Business Improvement District in Flemington, New Jersey, USA (2011). It includes boundaries, services, management, and a budget that brings together all business and commercial properties in the municipality except industrial and residential properties into one public–private partnership organization to revitalize Flemington's commercial corridors.

PROCESS AND TASKS: OF THE STEERING COMMITTEE

This is the report of the Flemington Business Improvement District Steering Committee. After a year of discussion between the Borough of Flemington, the Hunterdon County Chamber of Commerce, and the Flemington Raritan Business Association, a Business Improvement District Steering Committee was formed by municipal resolution (2011) with $15,000 in funds provided by the Borough of Flemington and $15,000 from the Flemington Business Community. The Flemington Business Improvement District Steering Committee was formed to explore strategies available to the business community specifically and the community of Flemington in general for strengthening the business vitality of the community, including the use and benefit of establishing a Special Improvement District (SID) to be called a Business Improvement District (BID). The Hunterdon County Chamber of Commerce (HCCC) administered the funds, and the Steering Committee conducted a search for a planning consultant to lead them through a BID planning process and act as staff to the Committee. Seth A. Grossman of Cooperative Professional Services (CPS), Frenchtown/Newark, NJ (in association with the Community Advocates of Verona, NJ) was chosen as the consulting planning/staff. The Committee met on Tuesday afternoons at the HCCC offices beginning October 19, 2010, and thereafter to prepare and disseminate this report, support the BID ordinance process, and establish the BID Management Corporation. In this report Special/Business Improvement Districts will be referred to as BIDs. The Committee's tasks were to:

1. Determine the applicability of a BID according to New Jersey statute N.J.S.A. 40:56–80 et seq. for the Borough of Flemington
2. Conduct a discussion and study of business community needs

3. Present a final report of its findings and recommendations to the Mayor and Borough Council

More than fifteen years ago, the Mayor and Council of the Borough of Flemington set as one of its goals the revitalization of the business districts. It was clear that "the era of outlet dominance" was fading as more and larger outlet centers emerged in the region, and discount big box stores such as WalMart, Target, Kohls, TJ Maxx, Lowes, and others also came into the same market. Discounting was no longer a novelty in the area; it was normal. Although Flemington's Business Association as well as the New Jersey Main Street Program and the Partners for Progress produced results, neither was able to sustainably unite the business community, including Liberty Village, Turntable Junction, and the highway shopping centers with the downtown, let alone establish a public–private partnership with the municipal government to accomplish this.

The Flemington Main Street Program existed in 1995–1999. Flemington had several Main Street program failures, which included a lack of leadership and a weak public–private partnership. The "Partnership for Progress Program" had little resources and also ended. The current Flemington Raritan Business Association has been successful with special events but isn't structured to handle much more beyond them.

Competition from regional discounters and highway retailers and the suburbanization of Raritan Township were not well understood. By 2005, deterioration in the downtown area was evident, and after the Union Hotel closed down, it was apparent. Like many New Jersey towns, Flemington is proud of its heritage, architecture, neighborliness, small-town feel, and rural nature, but did not manage these aspects as if they were marketable assets. It was assumed that Flemington would retain its traditional prominence as a central business destination in the region with little attention to competition and marketing. For instance, historic preservation, which should be and is prominent in Flemington, was not fully developed as a marketing asset, but chiefly as a quality of life issue that was in many ways "Flemington's secret." Preservation is understandable and needed, but it must define identity and destination advantages if it is to support economic progress. Borough of Flemington (2014 http://www.city-data.com/city/Flemington-New-Jersey.html, accessed 2/19/15). Borough of Flemington, New Jersey (2014), official website, http://www.historicflemington.com/ (accessed 2/19/15).

Flemington is not alone in this behavior. Many towns in Hunterdon County using the understandable premise of heritage preservation also exhibit exclusionary and insular economic development tactics with the idea that new people and customers are a hindrance rather than an opportunity. Consequently, Flemington did very little to combat a change in the market and has had trouble grasping its gateway status. Instead, it relied on Liberty Village, Pfaltzgraff, Flemington Cut Glass, and Flemington Furs for its advertising, branding, and commercial communications. After

Pfaltzgraff and Flemington Cut Glass closed, two major tourist/shopping draws were gone from the downtown.

Flemington apparently concluded that its destination status was declining and, as a result, approved a variance to allow the Flemington Cut Glass buildings to be demolished and to allow construction of suburban townhouses in their place. This action, leading to the upcoming demise of a key historic building with unique ties to Flemington's history, both as the Beecher Diamond Basket Factory and later as the Cut Glass outlet, demonstrated Flemington's failure to recognize that its historic assets are the key to its revitalization.

When Liberty Village and Flemington Furs were the dwindling remainders from a wider range of attractions, there was no response by the Borough and a sense of market isolation grew, creating a town lost in a sea of opportunity. Consequently, Flemington began to see its greatest assets erode—its name recognition and its historic integrity— and is facing an unprecedented descent into obscurity. The BID action is an honest response to this situation, noting that revitalization will require a united business community, a partnership with the municipal government, and a strong market approach to business development.

Continued efforts by the Borough together with the HCCC and the Flemington Raritan Business Association, business leaders, and the Flemington Business Alliance resulted in a positive action to study and establish an inclusive, professional, and organized business effort utilizing the New Jersey BID/SID laws. The June 7, 2010 Master Plan anticipated the BID action calling for "strategies to encourage community and economic development within the Borough, integrate the residential and commercial segments of Flemington Borough to benefit the entire community, and strengthen and enhance the commercial sector of the Borough, with an emphasis on attracting specialty retail and restaurants and encouraging the redevelopment of underutilized properties, particularly those within the Downtown Business District."

At a meeting in 2009, CPS was invited to talk about the Business Improvement District project similar to BIDs in 85 other New Jersey municipalities, including Washington Borough, Collingswood, Haddon Township, Red Bank, Haddonfield, and Somerville. There was great anticipation to move forward on the work of the Main Street Program, Flemington Raritan Business Association, and Chamber of Commerce. It was recognized that progress was deeply hampered if local government and business could not come together in a viable partnership. The success of the Borough's businesses were threatened by a change in market conditions and suburban development, the current recession, and lack of coordinated management and planning of the Route 31 corridor, which tended to isolate rather than connect the Borough to the region. It also divided the Borough business community among highway businesses, the traditional downtown, and the outlet areas with no coordinated theme or market synergy. Previously, Liberty Village Premium Outlets, Pfaltzgraff, Flemington Cut Glass, Flemington Furs, and Turntable Junction generated this synergy, but, as noted above, competition caught up and surpassed what Flemington could offer under that model. It needed a new model that would include Flemington as a tourist destination. But this moniker—"tourist destination"—sounds too much like the Jersey shore or Disneyland unless Flemington is placed in a regional context and tourism is considered as historic, recreation, artisan, architectural, village, or rural tourism. Then Flemington is a gateway to an exciting historic, dining, and rural village adventure with great shopping and services. This can be accomplished by a synergistic strategy that unites all businesses in a destination-marketing model that manages the community's assets as value-added services and experiences to customers, and builds on excellent customer service capability.

On October 15, 2010, the HCCC contracted with Seth Grossman, Ph.D., President of Cooperative Professional Services, Director of the Rutgers University Institute of Business District Management, former Director of the NJ–DCA Business Improvement District Program, and a recognized expert on Special (Business) Improvement Districts and community development, to work with the Economic Development Committee, conduct a Special Improvement District Planning and Feasibility Study, and assist the Flemington Business Improvement District Steering Committee in reviewing the existing zoned business and commercial districts and current mix of commercial, retail, and residential uses to determine the usefulness and appropriateness of utilizing a business improvement district to strengthen and expand business operations and to improve the economic health and prosperity of the districts to Flemington and its stakeholders within the districts and the community as follows:

OVERVIEW OF PROCESS AND DISTRICT FEASIBILITY

- Review and build upon the efforts of the Business Improvement District Steering Committee as professional staff and planner.
- Provide needed assistance to implement a BID, development of an operating budget and the costs, including the levying and calculation of an assessment of benefiting properties identified.

ORGANIZING COMMUNITY-BASED CONSENSUS

- Assist the Flemington Business Improvement District Steering Committee and the members of the business community in organizing, planning, defining, and implementing a Business Improvement District.
- Using a community-based, 'bottom up' effort which is time and labor intensive, identify the liabilities that the business and property owners of the district wish to see addressed in the work plan which will incorporate strategies to attack and treat those liabilities.
- Assist the business community and Business Improvement District Steering Committee in establishing local priorities and estimating the cost for addressing these concerns.
- Identify how best to maximize the use of a Business Improvement District for meeting the challenges that confront the district.

BID Objectives/Work Program/Budget

Develop a work plan that addresses at least the following five areas: management, business practices and performance, market research and communications, business retention and recruitment, and physical appearance and safety.

- Strengthen the existing partnership with the Hunterdon County Chamber of Commerce and its Business Improvement District Steering Committee and the Borough of Flemington.
- Identify consensus-supported district objectives and boundaries.
- Develop a budget with revenues, staffing, and other expenditures to support those objectives.
- Identify the recommended management strategy and mechanism to operate a District Management Corporation (DMC) and a Business Improvement District.
- Assist the Borough's finance officer and legal counsel in the preparation of all documentation required for the creation of a BID, including a draft ordinance, mechanisms for collecting the assessment, and pass-through mechanisms for the assessment to the DMC.

Organizing the District Management Corporation (DMC)

The organizational options for managing a Business Improvement District using a non-profit District Management Corporation will be outlined as available under existing state legislation.

- Define the roles and responsibilities of board leadership and the organizational structure and format for the proposed DMC.
- Establish the committee structure appropriate to the proposed work plan to ensure the ability of the DMC to implement the work plan and fulfill its obligations to district participants.
- Prepare organizational by-laws and operational budgets and all appropriate documentation needed to activate a DMC.

CONSENSUS BUILDING

- Hold community meetings to which business operators and commercial property owners will be invited.
- Work closely with existing leadership and staff to identify constituencies vital to the success of the effort.
- Identify those members of the community whose direct interest may not be specifically in one of the zoned business and commercial districts but in the overall

economic vitality of the community at large and who have resources to support the Borough and Business Improvement District Steering Committee effort.
• Agree upon list of objectives, priorities, and strategies that will be incorporated into an overall work program.

Enacting a BID, Creating a DMC

Once consensus has been reached on the goals, objectives, budgets, and strategies to be used to improve Flemington's zoned business and commercial districts through the creation of a BID, work closely with prospective DMC members and public officials in:

• Enacting a Business Improvement District ordinance
• Passing an approved budget
• Establishing and designating an appropriate nonprofit District Management Corporation

COMMUNITY OUTREACH

The BID planning process began on October 19, 2010 and concluded on December 23, 2010. Key to the Flemington Borough BID planning process was the agreement to be as comprehensive and inclusive as possible. As discussions became centered on a united Flemington BID, the Steering Committee held a community meeting to introduce the BID planning process on November 10, 2010 and sent out letters to all Flemington businesses, and members contacted people personally. Over 60 businesses attended the meeting and a general consensus to proceed with the BID planning process was achieved. Each regular meeting of the Committee was open to anyone who was interested, and a cross section of the community is represented on the Committee. Also, the Committee conducted a survey in the first week of December, personally handing out the questionnaires and picking up the completed ones. The final community meeting is scheduled for February 1, 2011 at the Flemington Court House on Main Street with invitations, announcements, press releases, reports, and notices. Committee members would continue to meet with people in the proposed BID through January 2011, i.e., after the community meeting.

The Steering Committee met once a week on Tuesday afternoon at 4 pm at the Hunterdon County Chamber of Commerce offices and went through a process of learning about BIDs and the BID statute, the technologies that are used to manage BIDs, and the strategies necessary to create an effective BID. Upon the passage of these recommendations and the final vote on the proposed Flemington Borough BID ordinance, the Steering Committee fulfilled all its tasks and was dissolved. The designated Management Corporation would take over and act as a BID Advisory Board to the Mayor and Borough Council.

BID Steering Committee members were active in discussing with government offi-cials, property owners, business owners, and residents alike about what the BID would mean to the community. They addressed the need to coordinate with the Borough's redevelopment efforts and work with the Borough Administration, which assisted in the research of the BID.

Summary of Recommendations

The committee's recommendations are summarized as follows:

1. One inclusive municipality-wide BID to be created with two sections. Schedule A is the Downtown area including Liberty Village and Turntable Junction, and Schedule B is the Highway area of Route 31, Route 202, and Route 12. The com-mittee recognized four key items: a) the district must be inclusive of all commer-cial interests and represent the variety of people, apartments, and businesses that Flemington Borough is known for; b) the district must have a Board of Directors that represents both districts equitably and works with the greater community; c) the district requires a comprehensive public–private partnership to realize its po-tential and implement its revitalization plans; d) the business community must be synergistic and united in a customer service and destination marketing modality.
2. The boundaries of the Flemington Borough BID include: All commercial busi-nesses, apartments of 5 units or more, and commercial vacant land. Residential properties, 4 units or less will be excluded from the BID assessment. Revitaliza-tion is a town-wide effort and everyone benefits, but its chief beneficiaries are commercial properties and business owners.
3. Addressing the synergy of the Main Street business area, Rts. 31, 202, 12, and Liberty Village and Turntable Junction is paramount to the municipality's eco-nomic success, health, vitality, and welfare.
4. The BID will match up with the Borough's redevelopment plans, housing pro-grams, historic preservation programs, public relations, economic development and revitalization efforts.
5. Addressing business recruitment and retention is fundamental to defining the BID's role.
6. Addressing infrastructure and restoring the architectural integrity of the build-ings is fundamental to defining the BID's role.
7. Addressing marketing, destination management, and tourism and restoring Bor-ough identity and assets are fundamental to defining the BID's role.
8. Township development particularly along highway corridors (as it is currently designed) is a challenge for business in the Borough. A lack of coordinated planning and linkages creating the Borough as a forgotten "hole in the donut" is counterproductive to business development.
9. There will be one coordinating professional Management Corporation for the BID.

10. The BID Management Corporation hires the best professional management possible.
11. The BID uses the property tax formula as the fair method of assessment.
12. Plans and activities of the BID will be comprehensive and include the following service areas: Management and Administration, Marketing, Promotions and Public Relations, Environmental Improvement, Maintenance and Quality of Life, Business Recruitment and Retention, Business Practices, Planning, and Legal.
13. Government and the community work together as a public–private partnership on the tasks and vision of the BID: to honor the community's traditions, maintain community values, and enhance value through excellent service to the Borough's customers exceeding their expectations and needs.

BID PROPOSAL

1. A BID/SID by providing administrative and other business and community development services is beneficial to businesses, employees, residents, and customers.
2. It is in the best interest of the municipality and the public to create a Special Improvement District aka a Business Improvement District, and to designate a nonprofit District Management Corporation that has at minimum one member of the governing body of the municipality on its board of directors as a voting member.
3. A nonprofit Management Corporation will administer the BID, the Flemington Business Improvement District Management Corp., which meets the requirements of the NJ SID statute and represents the various stakeholder groups in the BID/SID.
4. The BID will utilize the property tax assessment method form of assessment financing based on ad valorem property tax values.
5. The following properties in the Borough shall be in the BID. All zoned: 4A 4C, and 1 zoned 4A and 4C. This BID will be municipality-wide in area coverage.
6. A minimum Board of Directors is recommended (as follows) for balanced representation and a public–private partnership to consist of: Highway = Rts. 31, 202, and 12. Downtown is everything else.

    3—Retailers (1 Hwy and 2 Downtown)
    3—Nonretailers (1 Hwy and 2 Downtown)
    3—Downtown commercial
    2—Government (1 Mayor and 1 Borough Council)
    1—Resident at large
    3—Commercial property tenants (2 Hwy and 1 Downtown)
    _____
    TOTAL: 15

The total first-year budget will be $350,000 based on a hybrid budget at approximately 65%—Downtown, and 35%—Hwy 12, 31, 202.

BASIS FOR ACTION: HISTORIC SUMMARY

Brief Historical Perspective of Flemington

The land that comprises Flemington was originally the territory of the Lenni Lenape Native Americans, as was all of Hunterdon County.

In 1712, as part of a land parcel of 9,170 acres (37 km^2), the Flemington area was acquired by William Penn and Daniel Coxe (Borough of Flemington 2014).

The surrounding fertile farmland dictated that the beginnings of Flemington should be essentially agricultural. Early German and English settlers engaged in industries dependent on farm products. As time passed, poultry and dairy farms superseded crops in agricultural importance. Examples of early settlers were Johann David and Anna Maria Ephland, who emigrated in 1709 from Germany through London to New York and settled on their 147.5-acre (0.597 km^2) farm in 1710. They raised their seven children, and two from his previous marriage, on the farm that now makes up the core of Flemington.

In 1785, Flemington was chosen as the County Seat of Hunterdon. Fire destroyed the old courthouse in 1826 and the City of Lambertville made an attempt to have the seat moved, to no avail. Flemington remained the county seat, and the courthouse which stands today at the corner of Main and Court Streets was built in 1828. In July 1996, the new Justice Complex opened its doors.

Flemington Borough

In 1907, the Hunterdon County Court House almost made the record books as the site of the last public hanging in the state. However, as the scaffold, borrowed from Mercer County, was being prepared, the execution of John Schuyler was stayed. The death penalty was later commuted on appeal.

Twenty-eight years later, the century-old courthouse again was in the headlines, but this time the eyes of the entire nation were focused on Flemington. In January of 1935, a German immigrant named Bruno Richard Hauptmann was tried and convicted for the fatal kidnapping of the twenty-month-old son of Charles and Anne Lindbergh, residents of Hopewell. Because of Colonel Lindbergh's fame as an aviator, the trial created a media frenzy. Newsreels of the trial were played in movie houses across the country; radio announcers, among them WOR's Gabriel Heeter, gave the nation a play-by-play account. From his jail cell, the convicted gangster Al Capone offered the FBI his services in solving the kidnapping. The comedian Jack Benny was among the 250 courtroom spectators who, each day, came to witness what became known as "the Trial of the Century."

Across the street from the elegant courthouse, the Union Hotel was jammed with reporters. Many Flemington residents turned into landlords as throngs of newsmen continued to pour into town. In addition to the Lindberghs, other names were in the headlines: David T. Wilentz, attorney general for the State of New Jersey and chief prosecutor (also father of the late New Jersey State Supreme Court Chief Justice Robert Wilentz); and Colonel H. Norman Schwarzkopf, chief investigator for the New Jersey State Police (and father of General Norman Schwarzkopf of Gulf War fame). The presiding judge was the Honorable Thomas W. Trenchard, a seventy-one-year-old jurist known for patience, civility, and fairness, especially to defendants.

In 1856, the Hunterdon County Agricultural society purchased 40 acres (16 ha) of land that would accommodate the people, exhibits, and livestock for the County (Flemington) Fair. The purpose of this Fair was to promote competition among farmers, stock raisers, and machinery manufacturers. The fair was held every year at the Flemington Fairgrounds, which also was the site of Flemington Fair Speedway (later Flemington Raceway). From 1992 through 1995, the speedway hosted the Race of Champions, a prestigious race for Modified racers. The speedway hosted a NASCAR Craftsman Truck Series race from 1995 to 1998. In 2003, the County Fair adopted a new name, the Hunterdon County 4-H and Agricultural Fair, and moved to the South County Park in East Amwell Township (http://www.judiciary.state.nj.us/somerset/hnthist.htm 2010).

Statistics (Borough of Flemington (2014), http://www.city-data.com/city/Flemington-New-Jersey.html)

Flemington is a Borough in Hunterdon County, New Jersey, United States. As of 2009, the population was 4,403 (population change since 2000: +4.8%). It is the county seat of Hunterdon County; 36% of the land in the Borough is commercial. Most of the Borough is in the Amwell Valley (a low-lying area of the Newark Basin, to the east) and north of the Sourland Mountain area, but northwest portions of the Borough sit on the Hunterdon Plateau to the west. It is one of New Jersey's best-preserved ex-urban/rural communities, bordering Pennsylvania as New Jersey's western border along the Delaware River. The area, including Bucks County, Pennsylvania, is a well-established rural getaway for New York City, theater society, and Philadelphia residents due chiefly to easy proximity to major urban areas (a halfway point) and its transportation capability that links east/west traffic to south/north traffic. These linkages become much more difficult north of the Borough. Flemington is located at a strategic gateway to this historic region that extends as far south as Trenton, NJ in Mercer County and as far north as Newton in Sussex County, and east to Somerville, NJ in Somerset County. The Hunterdon County area is well known for its rural character, preserved Victorian villages (Lambertville, Stockton, Frenchtown, Clinton, Lebanon, and Califon; see photos of Inns and manors/B&Bs in Flemington area below), premium shopping outlet center, artisanship, inn culture, theater, music and restaurants, and access to Bucks County, PA. It is paradoxically a long standing, but generally untapped and unmanaged, tourist market for the North Jersey, New York City, and Philadelphia markets with over 20 million people. The region's location, midway on the Boston/Washington corridor, with direct access from Newark Liberty Airport, Philadelphia International Airport, and Lehigh-Allentown Airport, makes it a viable tourist, shopping, and dining alternative to the New Jersey seashore.

What is now Flemington was originally formed as a town by an Act of the New Jersey Legislature on March 14, 1870, within portions of Raritan Township. It became a village as of June 11, 1894, still within Raritan Township. Flemington was finally incorporated as an independent Borough by an Act of the New Jersey Legislature on April 7, 1910, based on the results of a referendum held on April 26, 1910, and was formally separated from Raritan Township. The Borough's incorporation was confirmed on April 27, 1931.

Flemington is an independent municipality located entirely within (and completely surrounded by) Raritan Township with a population of 19,809 people with a median income of $61,524, and is located near the geographic center of the Township. In 1756, Samuel Fleming purchased part of this land, and built his home, which still stands on Bonnell Street, and "Fleming's Town" was born.

As of 2009, there were 4,403 people, 1,804 households, and 997 families residing in the Borough. The population density was 3,927.4 people per square mile (1,515.5/km^2). There were 1,876 housing units at an average density of 1,754.2/sq. mi (676.9/km^2). The racial makeup of the Borough was 89.71% White, 1.19% African American, 0.31% Native American, 3.12% Asian, 0.17% Pacific Islander, 3.14% from other races, and 2.36% from two or more races. People of Hispanic or Latino ethnicity accounted for 10.98% of the population. Flemington is the home of the Mediatech Foundation, a community technology center (http://www.city-data.com/city/Flemington-New-Jersey.html#ixzz19tsiPt1D, accessed 2/19/15).

There were 1,804 households, out of which 26.8% had children under the age of 18 living with them, 38.7% were married couples living together, 11.7% had a female householder with no husband present, and 44.7% were nonfamilies; 37.7% of all households were made up of individuals and 12.1% had someone living alone who was 65 years of age or older. The average household size was 2.26 and the average family size was 3.00.

The median income for a household in the Borough was $39,886, and the median income for a family was $51,582. Males had a median income of $38,594 versus $31,250 for females. The per capita income for the Borough was $23,769. About 5.0% of families and 6.9% of the population were below the poverty line, including 7.5% of those under age 18 and 3.0% of those aged 65 or over.

Flemington Circle is the largest of three traffic circles in the environs of Flemington and sits just to the southeast of Flemington's historic downtown. US Route 202 and Route 31 approach the circle separately from the north and continue south concurrently, and the circle is the eastern terminus of Route 12. It is one of only a handful of New Jersey's once-widespread traffic circles still extant according to its original design. The circle sees significant congestion on weekends because of the new developments and big-box retailers. Unlike most circles, traffic on US 202 does not yield on entry; US 202, being a main four-lane divided highway, gets the right-of-way.

Two other traffic circles exist on Route 12 just west of the Flemington Circle. Both handle a much smaller volume of traffic; the first one, at South Main Street, named the Main Street Circle (old Route 31), is also in Flemington, and the other, at Flemington

Road/Route 523 (old Route 12) and Mine Street, is in Raritan Township. This circle is known informally amongst residents as Dvoor's Circle after the farm that surrounded parts of it. Route 12 traffic has the right-of-way in both of these circles, just as US 202 does in Flemington Circle (http://en.wikipedia.org/wiki/Flemington, New Jersey 2010).

Challenges, Strengths, and Obstacles to be Faced

Development around the Borough of Flemington has proceeded at a remarkable rate in the past 10–15 years with little regard for the Borough. In many ways, the Borough has been lost in such a business development flood, particularly along Rt. 31, that it has been challenged to adjust too successfully. The Flemington market has irrevocably changed and the Borough's business plan must be adjusted. Additionally, Liberty Premium Outlet Village, although continuing to provide excellent shopping, is no longer the novelty it once was, and its need to partner with the Borough and the region is now vital. The strength of Flemington is its vibrant and diverse market and its position as a gateway to one of the region's great destinations—western New Jersey and Bucks County, PA. However, it does not tend to act this way, or manage this key asset well and in a competitive manner. Its current weakness is a lack of management, direction, and cohesion within the business community. The "vision" and primary challenges in this BID process are to recognize Flemington as the center of a new regional market; manage business development along partnering opportunities; and, establish a commitment to professional management and performance (Borough of Flemington 2014).

Tourism and Economic Development

Flemington's reemergence as a quality tourist destination is its single most important challenge. The key aspect of this challenge is that it is not solely a Borough problem, although it must start there, but a regional issue. Though it was evident in the 1980s that the Borough was undergoing a transformation from a retail upscale discount outlet center to a more robust economy revolving around the outlet and the success of Turntable Junction and Flemington Furs, the Flemington area (Raritan Township), because of its central location and ex-urban quality of life, was just beginning to emerge as a successful suburban bedroom community. This dictated that Rt. 31/202 would be developed along big-box and mall-type retail. And this successfully buried this traditional and historic Borough in retail, causing a steady disintegration of Main Street Flemington—a lack of relevance to the market. Flemington's quaintness became just old-fashioned, its charm an inconvenience, its unique shopping just ordinary. Efforts were attempted to address this but never went beyond a localized approach. Feeling threatened, it withdrew from rather than embraced its place as the center of a new regional market.

In the past 10–15 years, development around the Borough of Flemington proceeded at a remarkable rate with little regard for the Borough. The Borough became entangled in a business development flood from the outside, particularly along Rt. 31/202, that it has not adjusted too successfully. The Flemington market changed yet the Borough's business plan did not. Additionally, Liberty Village Premium Outlet, although once unique and continuing to provide excellent shopping, is no longer the novelty it once was, and its need to partner with the Borough and the region is now vital. Liberty Village once defined Flemington as a progressive retail market, but this status is no longer apparent, and its continued success is linked to the Borough as a whole and its complete business culture.

This is good news. The strength of Flemington, both residentially and commercially, is as a vibrant and diverse market and a gateway to one of the region's great value destinations—western New Jersey and Bucks County, PA.

However, it has not acted this way, or managed this key asset well as a competitive advantage. The Borough is challenged to recognize itself as the center of a new regional "tourist" market and in this way to professionally manage business development along partnering opportunities.

Tourism is a two-sided coin. Tourism creates identity and destination ability. It brings in money directly to town and supports a wider range of services and goods than would otherwise be available for the town. Indirectly, tourism supports other people when shop owners in turn employ people and buy goods and services in the area, a phenomenon called an "economic multiplier effect." Tourism supports property values by creating a ready market for stores and homes for the people that own and work in them. Tourism is also behind many efforts to preserve the historic nature of an area.

On the other hand, tourism brings traffic congestion and crowds. The crush of traffic and people may seriously affect the quality of life for the residents. Tourism often adversely affects the ability to provide municipal services like police protection. The structure of taxation in the state does not easily provide a method for capturing a portion of the money spent by tourists to use in providing services necessitated by their presence.

There are mutual interests between business and residents' interests in preserving Flemington's quality of life. A town's culture, values, and history are foundations of the area as a destination. In this way, business owners also have a strong interest in controlling the impacts that come from tourism. If visiting Flemington becomes no longer enjoyable, tourists and residents will go elsewhere. Suitable limits must be established that reflect town values. The management of tourism to sustain these values is essential to the quality of life in the area.

The effects of tourism are not confined to the limits of the Flemington area. Other Hunterdon/Delaware and Raritan River communities such as Lambertville, Stockton, Frenchtown, and Clinton as well as Bucks County, PA are linked together as a rural and village tourist destination exemplified by a unique and strong inn system and 19th and 20th century historic industry and artisanship.

These towns also struggle with many of the same tourism issues as Flemington, such as marketing, circulation, quality of life, and the correct mix of shops in the Central Business District. This argues for these communities to work together to define their niches concentrating on enhanced values, quality, and specialty products instead of insular and chaotic marketing behavior (http://www.city-data.com/city/Flemington-New-Jersey.html).

Outlet centers, malls, and shopping centers have one advantage over a Central Business District. They are managed by a single entity that determines the mix of shops, handles customer complaints, and sees to a host of everyday details that serve customer and organizational interests. Central Business Districts, large and small, have these functions separated between the public and private sectors. No single entity has overall control of these functions. Other towns have solved this problem of managing their downtowns and business areas through a Business Improvement District. Created by local ordinance, a BID provides specific authorities for coordinated planning, organizing, funding, and providing effective services. The Special Improvement District acts as the management structure of the business community's service plans and programs. Its key aspect, in a regional tourism approach, is to be a good partner with business and communities, and chiefly to manage cooperatively effective marketing programs.

Survey Results

The Committee discussed the survey results (47), which support the need for a unified business district that concentrates on marketing, public relations and advertising, services and the infrastructure support that identifies Flemington as a destination. Building a business-friendly recruitment program is also of high value.

If a Business Improvement District was created in Flemington, how important would these activities and services be to you?

PROMOTE FLEMINGTON AS A DESTINATION

Very Important	74%
Important	25%
Not Very Important	1%
Not Important at All	

RECRUIT NEW BUSINESSES

Very Important	78%
Important	17%
Not Very Important	5%
Not Important at All	

COORDINATE SPECIAL EVENTS, PROMOTIONS, ADVERTISEMENT

Very Important	61%
Important	38%
Not Very Important	1%
Not Important at All	

OBTAIN GRANTS FOR PROMOTIONS AND INFRASTRUCTURE
IMPROVEMENT

Very Important	72%
Important	27%
Not Very Important	1%
Not Important at All	

PROVIDE ADDITIONAL GARBAGE CLEANUP

Very Important	21%
Important	38%
Not Very Important	40%
Not Important at All	1%

WORK TO CREATE A TOWN CENTER ATMOSPHERE

Very Important	72%
Important	28%
Not Very Important	
Not Important at All	

WORK TO CREATE A REGIONAL BUSINESS PERSPECTIVE

Very Important	55%
Important	40%
Not Very Important	4%
Not Important at All	1%

PROVIDE ADDITIONAL SECURITY

Very Important	27%
Important	46%
Not Very Important	26%
Not Important at All	1%

If a Business Improvement District were created, how positive would you think these changes would be to you?

HAVE ALL BOROUGH BUSINESSES WORKING TOGETHER

It would help my business   85%
It would not matter   15%
It would hurt my business

REVITALIZATION MAIN STREET

It would help my business   76%
It would not matter   24%
It would hurt my business

INSTALLATION OF BENCHES AND PLANTERS

It would help my business   46%
It would not matter   54%
It would hurt my business

BETTER STREET LIGHTING AND SIGNAGE

It would help my business   61%
It would not matter   39%
It would hurt my business

EXPANSION OF PUBLIC PARKING FACILITIES

It would help my business   63%
It would not matter   37%
It would hurt my business

PUBLIC RESTROOM FACILITIES

It would help my business   29%
It would not matter   71%
It would hurt my business

INSTALLATION OF PAVERS AND NEW SIDEWALKS

It would help my business   40%
It would not matter   60%
It would hurt my business

BETTER CONNECTION BETWEEN LIBERTY VILLAGE AND
RT. 31/2020 AND THE DOWNTOWN

It would help my business	57%
It would not matter	43%
It would hurt my business	

Strategic Planning

At the heart of these plans is a rediscovery of the significant values of the community developed through its history and interpersonal relationships. It is these values that the BID plans intend to build on and manage. The Committee discussed the following assets and values of the community:

ASSETS OF FLEMINGTON

- History
- Architecture
- People
- Liberty Village
- Flemington Furs
- Quaintness
- Charm
- Genuineness
- Comfortable old-time small-town feel
- Walkability
- Alfresco dining
- Artisans and crafts
- Community fireworks
- Salsa night
- Safe and clean
- Economic potential
- Variety of stores

COMMUNITY VALUES

- Honorable
- Communicates well
- Committed to success
- Truthful
- Accountable
- Informative

- Possesses a good relationship with the facts: if you don't know, don't make it up, and if you do make it up, clean it up.
- Fun-loving
- Pragmatic and results oriented
- Creative
- Do our best
- Fair and equitable in action

Summed up, these attributes speak to a great sense of "small town" life. In Flemington Borough this is present in the nature and structure of the town, and is fully recognized as a valuable asset. Flemington Borough is "Main Street America." Little wonder that an eroding of these values, real or perceived, causes anxiety in a traditional town. The challenge to the Borough, and consequently to the proposed BID, is to revitalize and build on its assets (including surrounding communities) and expand and maintain the community's identity and essential value. As proven in other developing areas, much of the current anxiety of the community will prove unnecessary as intrinsic value is enhanced rather than eroded by the challenges of well-planned future growth. Factually, people coming new to the area are attracted for exactly the value that exists and often become staunch supporters of community-based planning. They seek accessible public/community places that build a sense of community and meet real social and economic needs.

Flemington Borough is one of the important gateways to much of the region and the shore communities. Its small-town assets can project a vibrant, well-maintained, upscale, safe, clean, and attractive downtown and adjacent business corridor. Revitalization should be pedestrian friendly and provide facilities to accommodate vehicles and bicycles . . . a vibrant business environment with mercantile and service type businesses . . . (the community) . . . would provide shopping, dining, socializing, entertainment, and commercial activities for daytime and evening hours. The Borough recognizes that to maximize its potential, a legal and capable community partnership must be present. One that brings together free enterprise participants, government, and the community. Perhaps one of the most important findings of the Steering Committee was the lack of a comprehensive organization actively promoting the interest of the local merchants . . . and commercial property owners. Fundamental to the success of the Borough is its ability to bring the community together as "one community," and elevate the management of services that significantly enhance community assets. Revitalization plans are "daunting" if left to one aspect of the community, such as local government. Its success relies on an integrated community approach and the maintenance of focused community partnerships.

THE FLEMINGTON BID PLANNING PROCESS

The Committee discussed the inclusion of more people that would accurately represent the stakeholders in the business community. After the November 10, 2010 Community Meeting, the Committee added three participants.

The beginning of the Steering Committee process is to train the Committee regarding the legal status of the BID as a private-public partnership with the Borough, obtain an understanding of cooperative retail/commercial management technologies, and apply these to determining the boundaries, services, and budget, and training about public–private partnership management that applies to BIDs.

Below are summaries of the planning and training process to date.

PURPOSE OF THE STEERING COMMITTEE

The BID Steering Committee led the community-based planning process necessary to determine if a BID was applicable and, if so, how it would be organized and what it would do to enhance business. The planning process consists of three essential stages. (A BID is a Business Improvement District, and a SID is a Special Improvement District. They are virtually the same thing, and the terms are used interchangeably.)

1. *Getting Started*—which consists of getting organized and understanding what a BID is and how a BID works
2. *Analysis, Planning, and Product*—which consists of research, discussion, and reaching out to the public
3. *Presentation to Governing Body*—which consists of the necessary public hearings and reports to the Mayor and Council

STEERING COMMITTEE RESPONSIBILITIES

The Steering Committee meets weekly over the 3–5 month planning period and is responsible for administering an inclusive and comprehensive analysis and discussion of how a BID will benefit the community. The Steering Committee will present its conclusions as a proposal for or against the establishment of a BID to the community and Municipal Council. Upon submission of this proposal, the Steering Committee will have concluded its tasks. If a BID is established (by ordinance), a Board of Directors will be convened and this Board will replace all BID Steering Committee functions and be legally responsible for managing the BID.

STAGE ONE—GETTING STARTED

First Step: Communication/Organization

This includes the initial convening of the BID Steering Committee, the establishment of leadership, and establishing the purpose and process.

Second Step: Education

What are we doing and why, and who are we? What is a Business/Special Improvement District? What must we do to become one?

Third Step: Strategy and Accountability

Management and Vision: how will we do it and who will do what?

STAGE TWO—ANALYSIS, PLANNING, AND PRODUCT

Fourth Step: Concept and Direction

This includes research, discussion, planning, and product.

Fifth Step: Inclusion and Consensus

Present preliminary proposal for a BID to the community affected. This will include public meetings, communication to the public, explanation of planning process, and conclusions. Ensure broad community input. Prepare final formal proposal.

STAGE THREE—SUBMISSION OF REPORT TO GOVERNING BODY

Sixth Step: Commitment

Submit proposal and, if appropriate, the BID ordinance and budget to municipal governing body for approval.

Seventh Step: Completion

Conclude all BID Steering Committee business.

STAGE FOUR—SUBMISSION OF REPORT TO GOVERNING BODY

Eighth Step—Implementation

Assess process, create nonprofit corporation to manage the BID, welcome new BID Board of Directors, and hire management.

THREE ESSENTIAL ELEMENTS TO SUSTAINING AN EFFECTIVE BID

1. AGREEMENTS. BIDs manage agreements, not disagreements. These agreements become the strategy and the services the BID provides.
2. MANAGEMENT. Professional management is the key to success. Volunteers generally do not manage BIDs.
3. COMMITMENT. BIDs are committed to accomplishing their agreements, everyone in the BID contributes equitably, and BIDs have a guaranteed source of basic funds from a mandatory public assessment. This enables the BID to be fully accountable and no-nonsense about fulfilling its promises.

—Agreements, Management, and Commitment—

The Business Improvement District (BID) (aka Special Improvement District [SID]) enables local property owners, merchants, and residents to plan for, manage, and finance supplemental services and improvements beyond those already provided by the municipality. The BID is funded by a "special assessment" levied against properties within the district designated in the BID ordinance. The level of assessment is determined by the BID. Although the municipal government collects the special assessment, it is not commingled with other general government funds. BIDs concentrate on improving customer service—adding value to the customer's experience of the business district and the community.

The local government, by statute, collects the BID assessment. BID funds are held in a special account and returned to the BID management entity in its entirety to be used for BID purposes. A nonprofit corporation, usually called a District Management Corporation (or DMC), or a municipal Committee comprising property owners, tenants, residents, other nonprofits, and public officials, is responsible for administering the BID. The establishment of the BID is the decision of the local property owners, merchants, and tenants who feel that additional services, improvements, and professional management of the business environment are needed.

The Committee began discussions about the preliminary discussion of boundaries. Upon establishing preliminary boundaries, CPS will conduct a budget probability analysis.

FOCUS OF A BID: *The customer*: By managing community assets, BIDs provide services to add value to their customers' experience of the community.

RETAIL/COMMERCIAL COOPERATIVE MANAGEMENT

The BID Concept

Special (Business) Improvement Districts (SIDs/BIDs) utilize the same "technology of management" that cooperative apartments, malls, and commercial parks use. This technology is "Cooperative Professional Management" and it is designed to manage communities in a comprehensive manner. The technology does not address individual property directly, but rather the community as a whole accomplishing a community purpose. For instance, a sole proprietor may own malls, and many proprietors may own town centers and co-ops. This may affect the management process, but it does not affect the goal of management, which is to address common concerns. In each one of these places, there are multiple users renting or owning, and the users are tied to a specific environment with a specific purpose. Being clear about that purpose is fundamental to this cooperative professional management technology.

Town centers and the BIDs that manage them are not unlike malls, which have overall business growth and development as their primary and common purpose. All business areas are communities. A common purpose in itself defines a community. A clear vision of what is possible for the community and shared by all causes the purpose to grow and develop. Communities (of all kinds) thrive when a shared vision is achieved and well managed as the underlying means of addressing common concerns. The chief concern of a business district is the customers' satisfaction with the value they receive. Value is accessed by the customer in four ways:

1. The environment
2. Media
3. The type of shop and products offered
4. The professional level of management provided

Cooperative Professional Management is comprehensive in addressing each of the four ways the customer accesses value in the community, and is grounded in partnership building. Success is directly attributed to the clear expression and availability of the community's vision. Cooperative Professional Management is a management technology that fundamentally ensures the successful delivery of a community's vision and values.

A COMPREHENSIVE APPROACH

Business Improvement Districts are service districts, public agencies, and public–private partnerships between the business community and the local government. Both need to be managed well. Their interest is in serving their customers so that the customer has an efficient and enjoyable experience—an experience of receiving value. Customer service is a key technology for BIDs.

It goes without saying that customers need to be generated and, once generated, they need to be taken care of, attended to, and adjusted to. As we pointed out in the previous section, there are four ways customers get their perspective of your district and access value. For this reason, BIDs are not single project oriented, or in fact "project-oriented." BIDs are service-oriented with each project expanding or establishing a service that articulates the community's values inherent in a shared vision. The four ways the customer accesses your community and its values are by specific types of managed services that fit into general "service domains." These domains are required by the BID to be successful and able to manage each aspect of "The Conversation." It is essential to be balanced and comprehensive with each domain. Each service domain manages an aspect of the conversation your customers have about your district. Most BIDs have the following service domains: Management, Environmental Maintenance and Design, Communications—Promotions and Public Relations, Business Recruitment and Retention, Business Practices and Performance, Planning and Development, and Volunteerism and Leadership.

COMMITTEE DISCUSSIONS

At the October 19, 2010 meeting, the Committee reviewed the purpose and tasks of the committee for newly arrived members. The BID Committee met, introduced Seth A. Grossman of Cooperative Professional Services, staff and planner of the BID process, and reviewed the overall purpose and procedures of the BID Steering Committee, emphasizing the public–private partnership intention of the BID statues. It is noted that Mayor Hauck, three Borough Council people: Erica Edwards, Sandy Borucki, and Michele Oberst, and 11 businesspeople were in attendance. It was agreed that the meeting date of the Steering Committee would be every Tuesday (unless rescheduled) at 4 pm at the Hunterdon County Chamber of Commerce offices, Liberty Village, Flemington, NJ except the week of November 1, when the committee would meet on Thursday, Nov. 4 at 4 pm. The meetings would last approximately 1.5 hours and would go longer only if the Committee agreed. The Committee discussed the inclusion of people in the BID planning process that would accurately represent the stakeholders in the business community. Of chief concern was the timeline of the planning process. An initial idea was to work to a December 27, 2010 conclusion, but upon reflection and discussion, the Committee unanimously agreed that, in order to be inclusive, the process could be longer and should be organized to optimize appropriate community input. The first such event would be an Introduction to the BID Planning Process–Community. The Committee also discussed the following:

- The "Goal of a BID": to create a sustainable public–private partnership that provides and improves the community by enhancing value to the customer.—Customer Service—BIDs are customer service districts.
- The importance of teamwork and integrity were addressed.
- *Teamwork*: a managed conversation about partnership ("we" rather than "me")
- *Integrity*: being our word as ourselves; managing our commitments; being on time
- *Introduction to the BID Process*—Community Meeting; to be rescheduled for November 9, 2010, 6 pm at the Flemington Court House.

The Committee had previously elected Mark Mulligan (Developer) and Robert Shore (businessman) as Co-Chairpersons and Frank Banisch (Professional Planner) and Chris Phelan (CEO of the Hunterdon Chamber of Commerce) as Co-Vice Chairpersons.

At the November 4, 2010 meeting, a review of the purpose and tasks of the committee was conducted. Again, the committee was asked if other people or areas of the proposed BID should be asked to join the committee, as well as the time and date of the committee meetings—4 pm, Tuesday (unless otherwise announced). A Community Meeting-Intro to the BID was scheduled for November 10 at 6 pm at the Court House. Don Smartt, who will be the Phase Two consultant, was present and discussed aspects of a BID and potential BID management.

Numerous questions were asked regarding the authority of the BID and the autonomy of the BID management group noting that the BID is a partnership with the local government, which enhances but does not replace municipal services. The management organization, which can be a nonprofit or a public commission, determines the budget. CPS will conduct the initial budget analysis, and members can discern an approximate cost based on industry averages of 7% of the total property tax bill although the committee must determine the actual amount. The budget is reviewed and approved by the Municipal Council each year and this is a key oversight. The enabling BID ordinance is the contract between the municipality and the BID, which can be altered, amended, or terminated through a normal ordinance process. Plus every year the Municipal Council, which acts as a review of the BID, must approve the budget. Technically the BID can be terminated at any time by the Municipal Council but is usually done upon request of the business community. The BID may be suspended by not approving a budget, thereby restricting funds.

Although all BIDs use similar technologies to suburban malls and other retail-commercial cooperatives, they operate not as a private-private partnership, but as a public–private partnership and can provide services that the state statute allows to improve the district and promote customer service. Each BID is uniquely and specifically designed for the community it is in. As stated above, the first budget is estimated using industry averages, and the district can support what is felt. BIDs are chiefly concerned with adding value to customer experiences of the district and do this with a high level of customer service not unlike a suburban mall. BIDs are similar in management technology to suburban malls and can be considered to be "malls without walls."

The strongest similarities between malls and BIDs are in customer service, management of common areas and concerns, and the district's destination capacity. The difference is that suburban malls are singularly owned and use tenant/lease arrangements in a private-private partnership, whereas BIDs have multiple owners and public right-of-ways in a public–private partnership.

PRELIMINARY BOUNDARIES were not discussed and committee members were asked to consider their ideas. It has been put forth that, at first, the BID will look at a municipal-wide BID in three sections: Downtown-Main Street including Liberty Village, Route 31/202, and Route 12. When boundaries are put forth, they can be reduced or altered. Also, different parts of the district can have different levels of assessment such as: a high impact central area with lower impact surrounding areas. When the boundaries are sufficiently determined, tax and property information will be obtained from the Borough of Flemington on these commercial properties to estimate budget potential.

It was suggested that property valuation is the preferred assessment method. Purely residential properties are usually excluded from the budget, but state statute does allow them to be included. The argument for a municipality-wide BID was put forth to unite and focus the business community, looking for synergies that can build the community, not differences that erode the community, cause confusion, and place the Borough at a competitive disadvantage.

NOTE: A BID may include or exclude any properties in the municipality with the exception of government properties, which are categorically excluded. Boundaries of a BID do not need to be contiguous (one whole). BIDs may have an area-wide reach, but are set up in the local ordinance by lot and block; therefore a BID may have a "Swiss cheese" look to it if we only look at assessed properties. Also, municipalities may have as many BIDs as they need, or combine all businesses and commercial areas into one BID. In fact, the inclusion of an entire town, both commercial and residential in its BID, is possible. Each town must determine what works for it. BIDs are created by local ordinance at the municipal level of government and are not required to ask permission or receive authorization by county, state, or federal agencies. BIDs need only meet the criteria established in the state statute.

November 10, 2010: The Committee continued with a discussion about the legal status of BIDs, and the asset-based planning. Flemington's assets that were pointed out: Flemington is a "gateway" to western New Jersey and Pennsylvania; it is convenient and has a great regional location; the river; it has a positive small-town feel where everyone knows your name and you feel welcome. It has great potential based on its many assets.

This meeting focused on how asset-based planning helps us arrive at a strategic vision and what blocks that process. We will conduct an exercise on Complaints vs. Commitments, which highlighted our access to developing a community vision, and what blocks it. In this exercise, we looked at the dividends and liabilities of managing disagreements that lead to failure, confusion, and mismanagement. These root causes point to the limiting nature of complaints and assumptions. Yet these complaints can show us a more positive and powerful way of addressing our needs, goals, and aspirations. This is because, behind a complaint is a thwarted commitment. If we pay attention, a complaint will show us the path to success because what sets up the complaint is, again, a commitment to make things work, but the inability to know how. Complaints generally are a way to cover that we don't know something, or better said, it covers up the problem that what we know isn't solving a perceived problem. Complaints occur because we do not know how to express or implement a particular commitment to have something occur. This inability thwarts the commitment from becoming accomplished. Instead we resort to the control and power (albeit limited) a complaint offers. Consequently, we tend to know our complaints very well while losing sight of what we are truly committed to.

It is our sense of individualism—that we must somehow be able to solve problems by ourselves—that keeps a complaint in place. Until we learn how to work together, we ineffectively try to resolve the "thwarted commitment." Rather than facing that we do not know how to resolve the problem alone, we keep a personal complaint in a place that has us feel "correct" about the issue, and allows us to avoid the domination of the unknown.

The cost/liability of this method is that we cannot fulfill our commitment and reduce our ability to be in powerful relationships with others. It is through dialogue and partnership rather than personal action that a commitment becomes an accomplishment. A commitment must have a partner and by "its" nature is *inter*dependent, and cannot be "owned" by one person. In this way we can see that a commitment is "owned" by the community, and then can be expressed both individually, and communally. CPS training is directed toward finding our commitments, not succumbing to compromise, and establishing agreements on a community (team) level.

The Committee discussed the management approach of BIDs: The first agreement of the Steering Committee is the Vision Statement (this is: what the BID/Community is at its best and what future it is committed to). Following this, we will attempt to articulate the Vision as a set of Standards or Values. These values are at the root of how the BID works to accomplish its primary goal: *Adding value to the customer's experience.* Having a clear *community vision* and values is the basis for developing plans and services. This is because an individual business's success—the sense of gaining maximum potential and accomplishment—is directly linked to the effectiveness of a community to maintain and communicate its vision and values. The foundation of a community's assets is summed up in its vision and values. And these are built on agreed upon and well-articulated community commitments. In this way the district's vision is also its promise to the greater community.

BIDs utilize the same concept of management that is used by cooperative apartments, malls, and commercial parks. they identify common areas of interest, usage, and challenges that are required to maintain a competitive, successful, and effective environment and then employ professional management to address those common issues. Management is always an additional fee above regular rent or taxes. In itself, management is a special or enhanced service. This technology is based on seven key standards:

1. Commonalties/inclusion rather than personalities/exclusion
2. Interdependence rather than independence
3. Comprehensive rather than one-track
4. Management rather than no management
5. Professional rather than amateur
6. The district's customers as the focus rather than just "my customers"
7. *Integrity*—being who you say you are

A paramount concern of the cooperative management approach (BID) is customer service. Attention is placed on the customer's experience and perception of the district. In a comprehensive manner, the BID works to manage its customers 'experience of their district so that customers feel welcome, comfortable, and enthusiastic about shopping in the district. Cooperative Professional Services defines this process as "Managing The Conversation" (the internal perceptions of your customers about your district or business).

COMPREHENSIVE COMMUNITY DEVELOPMENT

Cooperative Community Development addresses quality of life standards that your customers experience as added value. This is achieved by clearly identifying and managing the community's assets. The District's Vision Statement must be a profound expression of these assets.

To reach the key objectives of downtown revitalization and management, there are various descriptions of the areas that must be worked on and evolve simultaneously. For instance: The Main Street Program identifies four comprehensive aspects: Organization, Promotions; Design; and Economic Restructuring. CPS identified seven:

1. Management and Resources
2. Quality of Life
3. Communications (Promotions/Public Relations)
4. Business Recruitment and Retention
5. Business Practices and Performance
6. Design and Development
7. Partnership and Leadership

November 16, 2010: The meeting centered on reviewing the BID Steering Committee–Community Meeting of November 10, 2010. The purpose of the meeting was to invite the business community, include their input, and explain and obtain support for the BID planning process. The Community Meeting—Introduction to the BID Planning Process was held at the Flemington Court House, Flemington NJ. Mayor-Elect—Erica Edwards, Bob Benjamin, Mark Mulligan, Frank Banisch, and Seth A. Grossman were the speakers. Mark Mulligan acted as the MC. Steering Committee members manned the doors, handed out pamphlets, and made sure people signed in, and there was a refreshments committee. The evening accomplished the purpose; substantially over 64 people came, including most of the Steering Committee. It was successful because the BID process was inclusive and explained well, as indicated by the participants' responses. The participants embraced the BID concept, expressed satisfaction and trust of the Steering Committee, and encouraged us to move forward. This was not magic. It was a result of hard work. A special thank you to Frank Banisch who also edited and improved the Power Point Presentation, and Chris Phelan who manned the computers, made copies, brought the projection screen, and was instrumental in organizing everything.

November 23, 2010: the Steering Committee discussed looking at a municipality wide BID in three parts: 1) the Downtown area, 2) Rts. 31/202–Rt.12, and Liberty Village, and 3) all 4C–apartments three units or under. CPS will provide a budget analysis of this BID and will request property and tax data for the identified zones. In order to obtain a realistic perspective of potential BID capability, based on the tax data, an analysis of the budget potential will be conducted based on 3%–7% industry averages. These averages are a 3%–7% additional assessment based on the total property tax of the most recent year provided by the Borough's tax assessor. The Committee has agreed that only commercial properties and commercial vacant lots will be analyzed at this time (coded as: 4A, 4B, 4C); residential properties (coded: 2) will not be considered as assessed members of the district even if they are in the district.

The Committee began a strategic planning process by distinguishing between strategic (future/goals oriented) and tactical (methods and fix-it oriented) planning. We discussed and did an exercise on how to create a team approach to strategic planning by looking at: 1) the limiting aspects of complaints; and 2) the expanding aspects of assets by an exploration of the question, "What do you love about Flemington?" It is often a question not asked . . . enough. It should be the chief item of importance on a citizen or customer survey because it tells us what is most important about our community. It is a question that is answered on many levels: physical, emotional, perceptual, visceral, social, economic, and conversational. It opens up the comprehensive nature of the community, its assets developed and undeveloped, its social connectivity, and its message.

The budget and programs—what we do in a BID—should be organizational structures to manage, improve, and sustain our community assets. These assets are what are valuable about the community, and it generates all business interests. The district's destination capability and potential are its greatest assets. We need to understand this well and create a Vision Statement that describes it. Business districts must be good at understanding these assets and how they can be communicated through advertisement and every service the organization pursues.

Boundaries and Budgets: This basis of analysis may be altered, and an adjusted analysis may be needed after our meeting and our full Steering Committee meeting.

One of the essential parts of the BID study is an analysis of proposed properties in the BID—the BID boundaries. State law specifies that BIDs must be made by properties listed by lot and block. In order to analyze boundaries and budgets of the BID we need tax assessment and property information for properties in the following areas. It is noted that we have not yet confirmed actual boundaries or membership of the BID by the full Steering Committee, and that the analysis reflects general concepts of the BID to date with CPS guidance. The BID analyzed is a municipality-wide BID in three parts: 1) Downtown—Liberty Village, 2) Rts. 31/202, Rt. 12, and, 3) 4C–apartments five units or more.

November 30, 2010: BID assessment analysis boundaries were discussed. It was agreed that there will be three categories of a municipality-wide BID: 1) downtown, 2) Rts. 31/202 and Rt. 12, and 3) 4C–apartments of five units or more. The BID assessment analysis looked at all the commercial properties in the three categories and the total property taxes provided by the municipality. The property taxes were analyzed from 10% to 3% to provide guidance on the amount Committee members felt was a functional amount. The median amount Committee members agreed to was 7%. However, this amount is not the final amount as the Committee is still researching what the BID will do. Some members felt that members can only pay so much and too much might create a backlash indicating public concerns. Others felt that too little a budget would jeopardize the chances of the BID being successful indicating private concerns. Also, the Committee discussed a hybrid budget scenario where the downtown would pay a different amount than the other categories. Additionally, there were supporters of a strong marketing budget where others felt a stronger business recruitment effort was warranted. The Committee agreed to add all vacant commercial land. The Committee also was presented with 6 Service Domains of a BID that will define the budget.

In designing a retail/commercial cooperative such as a BID, addressing only one improvement aspect prolongs the revitalization process and may even be detrimental. Moving on four or six "fronts," also known as "Domains" or service-areas, at the same time is required to create a solid foundation and a full service district. Moving in less than four or six domains can cause a distortion of services sometimes to the point of completely missing what is required to serve the customers appropriately. Grounded in a good community survey, a comprehensive approach will allow for sustainable improvements and revitalization. Four to six key service-area Domains operate simultaneously to build a solid foundation and strategy. Each Domain has a front: a line of action and a budget. Six key service-area Domains are:

1. Management/Organization
2. Public Relations/Promotions/ Marketing/Advertising
3. Environmental Improvements/Quality of Life
4. Business Recruitment and Retention
5. Planning and Legal
6. Business Development, Practices, and Support

The Committee continued its strategic planning. Strategic Planning builds upon a vision and develops an implementation strategy to work toward fulfilling that vision. Strategic Planning builds from the bottom, or community, upward and the community builds a consensus for a common vision. Strategic Planning works toward cooperation, coordination, and collaboration across the board to create sustainable communities. This process demands that each individual think and act more as a "community," and outside of the ordinary limits of what is possible and known. For BIDs, the "vision" is about creating "Places of Confidence and Inclusion." A Vision Statement is best understood as a promise to the community—a community promise, because it states clearly what is expected by the organization that will manage the expectations. There are two essential stages to Strategic Planning: a) Vision and b) Implementation.

Strategy. Fundamentally, all planning has three elements or steps illustrated by these three questions: 1) Where are we now? 2) Where are we going? 3) How will we get there? Strategic Planning adds an initial extra step: *Visioning*: Designing a vision of a possible future from a future standpoint not from a standpoint of "fixing" the past. Planning can be defined as "an anticipated set of actions designed to achieve a desired set of objectives." Therefore, a strategic plan will have a *Vision Statement* which states who you say you are as if you were already there.

The Committee discussed the survey noting that it had two purposes: 1) to have Committee members engage with proposed BID members, and 2) to get proposed BID members input into the general interests of a BID, and explain what a BID is. The survey is not a true research survey and was designed to help Committee members engage the public in a discussion about the proposed BID. The Committee approved the survey, members chose areas of the proposed BID, and surveys were to be conducted before Tuesday, December 7, 2010, to be handed in at the Dec. 7 meeting.

The Committee discussed the idea that 1) an agreement to manage town values and provide a "quality" experience is the basis of community-agreement; and 2) that "selling out" or diminishing our values is the cause of divisiveness, disagreement, stagnation, and deterioration. The Committee identified the following values, which are what the BID is committed to:

COMMITMENTS (COMMUNITY VALUES):

- Be honorable
- Communicate
- Be committed to success
- Be truthful
- Be accountable
- Be informative
- Have a good relationship with the facts: if you don't know, don't make it up, and if you do make it up, clean it up.
- Know the importance of fun
- Be pragmatic and results oriented
- Be creative
- Do our best
- Be fair and equitable
- Be in action

BIDs manage assets as the method of conducting community development. Assets are what the BID is accountable for and are directly linked to values and can be derived by asking people what they love and feel is great about a town.

ACCOUNTABILITIES (ASSETS):

- History
- Architecture
- The people
- Liberty Village
- Flemington Furs
- Quaintness
- Charm
- Genuineness
- Comfortable old-time small-town feel
- Walkability
- Alfresco dining

- Artisans and crafts
- Community fireworks
- Salsa night
- Safe and clean
- Economic potential
- Variety of stores

A community's success is directly linked to the maintenance and delivery of its values. This emphasis provides the arena of an asset-based rather than a "fix-it" based planning approach capable of accomplishing a community-vision. With this approach, each service, project, and expression of the BID enhances specific identifiable community-values rather than disagreement based on problem identification or misidentification. A community "adds value" by enhancing what is authentically valuable about the community.

A Vision Statement is a promise to create and maintain a community's future based on its assets and values. It is a not a goal, or a desire, it is a statement of what the BID stands for and how it will organize its investments. The Committee began a Visioning process based on the following structure:

The Vision Statement will follow this structure: The Flemington Business Improvement District is a community of _____ (accountabilities) _____ committed to _____. This is who we are. This is what you can count on.

December 14, 2010: The Committee completed the survey and CPS will compile results.

The Committee worked on the Vision Statement. This "vision" sets the direction of the BID, the future it intends to achieve, and the BID's essential agreement of purpose. It combines an understanding of the town's assets to the level of accountabilities and resources to the level of commitments having weighed assets and liabilities in a strengths/weaknesses/opportunities/threats (SWOT) analysis. During the week, the committee will review this and make corrections. The values/accountabilities are a set of Standards of Excellence that guide the BID's mission. The "Mission Statement" is to maintain these standards. Adhering to these standards and measuring the BID's success against them provides an honest indicator that value is being added to the customer's experience of the BID.

MISSION STATEMENT

The mission of the Flemington Business Improvement District is to professionally manage the organization so that our community values, listed below, are delivered effectively to our customers, exceed their expectations, and provide an experience of enhanced value.

COMMUNITY VALUES:

- Be honorable
- Communicate
- Be committed to success

- Be truthful
- Be accountable
- Be informative
- Have a good relationship to the facts
- If you don't know, don't make it up, and if you do make it up, clean it up.
- Fun is important
- Be pragmatic and results oriented
- Be creative
- Do our best
- Be fair and equitable
- Be in action

The Committee reviewed the Vision Statement and approved the version (below). The survey was also reviewed and, although not statistically valid due to the number of responses (47), it was an exercise that put the committee into action and in dialogue with those affected by a proposed BID and this increased the level of knowledge about the BID in the community. Most importantly, the survey substantiated that the Committee was going in the correct direction (85%), agreed that having businesses working together is good for business, and the key topics of interest such as promoting Flemington as a destination (74% very important), business recruitment (78% important), work to create a town center atmosphere (72% very important), revitalizing Main Street (76% would help business), and better signage and parking (63% would help business). The Committee discussed briefly an informal final Community Meeting that will present the Committee's findings and request community input into the BID plan. This will occur on February 1, 2011 after the Committee approves all necessary parts of the plan including but not limited to: boundaries, budget, governance, and services. In regard to governance, the Committee discussed the possibility of the business and professional association becoming the BID Management Corporation.

SWOT ANALYSIS:

Strengths	Weaknesses
Inventory of businesses	Government to business communication
Industrial diversity	Business retention
Great people	Loss of artisan heritage
Opportunity in town	**Loss of destination** (branding)
Proximity to markets	**Disjointed business community**
Good government	Disinterested businesses
Local small business niches	Not competitive
Great demographics	**No management** of the business
Name of town	
History	
Architecture	

Active civic engagement
A safe and clean town
Transportation hub
Charm
Good schools
Community events

Opportunities	**Threats**
Vibrant business district	High vacancy rate
Be a destination	**Competition**
Increase tourism	Difficult to get to
Increase property values	**Lack of communication**
Be welcoming to business	High cost of doing business
Environment	Low-end discounters
Utilize vacancies	Stalled economy
Changing demographics	Changing demographics
	Loss of brand identity
	Loss of interest

The Committee wanted more time to discuss the proposed BID budget. Additionally, around the issue of the budget, serious concerns were expressed about oversight to make sure that the budget was not arbitrarily increased or decreased. Grossman stated that the oversight requirements already in place are quite substantial—the budget must be approved by Municipal Council and not just the BID Management Corporation; an annual report is due with the budget request; a certified public audit must be conducted, and the enabling ordinance and oversight by the Borough controls the BID. An arbitrary cap on the budget circumvents this process and does not allow the BID or the Borough to adjust to real situations, or have the authority to be responsible to the community.

DECEMBER 23, 2010: The Committee discussed Management.

The management entity of a BID is specifically designated in the enabling ordinance. The Committee discussed various management forms for the BID and agreed upon the private nonprofit form of management. Although guidance on the positions of the management Board will be discussed, enacting the management capacity will be primarily in phase 2 implementation after the BID ordinance is enacted.

There are two types of management that BIDs can consider reflecting the form of public–private partnership of the BID. The chief role of the BID management is to manage the public–private partnership. This partnership sets a new tone for government and business relations in the municipality, and leverages the assets and capabilities of each sector to provide services, improvements, and ongoing management. Some BIDs are more public than private, some more private than public.

The first type of management, and the preferred type in New Jersey, over 97%, is the private nonprofit Corporation. It establishes a more private form of public–private partnership. The nonprofit Corporation manages the BID and although a separate and distinct corporation under NJ Law, it is designated in the enabling BID ordinance to manage the BID and is subject to all the requirements of a BID. Although an agent of the municipal government, it is not a government office and operates as a private nonprofit Corporation. The nonprofit has a Board, which elects its members, although the first Board of Directors is appointed by the Trustees of the Corporation according to its by-laws. All BIDs have a few selected positions such as one elected official from the municipality. The Corporation hires the manager and has no public requirements in this contract, and the municipal government has less direct influence. The Corporation would be the Flemington Business Improvement District Management Corporation (FBID).

The second type of management, of which approximately 3% of New Jersey BIDs utilize, is a Municipal Commission. This type of management establishes a more public form of public–private partnership. In this case, a Commission is designated in the enabling ordinance to manage the BID as an office of the municipal government. It also hires the manager, but it may purchase the services of the municipality by utilizing and subsidizing a designated staff member and then it may be subject to public regulations, or it may hire someone outside of government not unlike the nonprofit Corporation. The Commission is usually appointed by the Municipal Council, but would also have by-laws articulating how it is organized, its purpose, and functions. In the case of the Commission, the local government has more direct influence.

BUDGET

The following budget was revised and approved as follows:

TOTAL BUDGET: $350,000
Based on a hybrid budget at approx. 6%—Downtown *and* 4%—Hwy 12, 31, 202
PROGRAMS (Total: $212,000)
Business Recruitment and Development: ($90,000)—services, research, plan and package, legal-attorney
Marketing and Public Relations ($85,000): Public relations/marketing specialist. One of the primary goals of the BID is to promote and market the district as a destination to shop and conduct business, newsletters, banners, and advertisement and support festivals and other promotional events.
Design, Quality of Life, and Improvements: ($37,000)—Infrastructure planning, signage, pedestrian safety, workability, and parking.
A focus on pedestrian crossing upgrades, signage, and lighting upgrades, and planning.

MANAGEMENT AND ADMINISTRATION ($138,000)

This amount serves to cover the costs of management, an accountant, office supplies and equipment, insurance, and other administrative costs. The management entity of a BID is specifically designated in the enabling ordinance. The Committee discussed various management forms for the BID and agreed upon the private non-profit form of management.

The preferred type in New Jersey, over 97%, is the private nonprofit Corporation. It establishes a more private form of public–private partnership. The nonprofit Corporation manages the BID and, although a separate and distinct corporation under NJ Law, it is designated in the enabling BID ordinance to manage the BID and is subject to all the requirements of a BID. Although an agent of the municipal government, it is not a government office and operates as a private nonprofit Corporation. The nonprofit has a Board, which elects its members, although the first Board of Directors is appointed by the Trustees of the Corporation according to its by-laws. All BIDs have a few selected positions such as one elected official from the municipality. The Corporation hires the manager and has no public requirements in this contract, and the municipal government has less direct influence. The Corporation would be the Flemington Business Improvement District Management Corporation (FBID).

THE COMMITTEE APPROVED THE FOLLOWING ITEMS:

1. *A BID/SID* by providing administrative and other business and community development services is beneficial to businesses, employees, residents, and customers.
2. **It is in the best interest of the municipality and the public to create a Special Improvement District aka a Business Improvement District, and to designate a nonprofit District Management Corporation that has, at minimum, one member of the governing body of the municipality on its Board of Directors as a voting member.**
3. A nonprofit Management Corporation will administer the BID: the Flemington Business Improvement District Management Corp., which meets the requirements of the NJ SID statute and represents the various stakeholder groups in the BID/SID.
4. **The BID will utilize the property tax assessment method form of assessment financing based on ad valorem property tax values.**
5. The Board of Directors will consist as follows: (Example for discussion: Highway = Rts. 31, 202, and 12. Downtown is everything else.)

   3—Retailers (1-Hwy and 2-Downtown)
   3—Non-retailers (1-Hwy and 2-Downtown)
   3—Downtown commercial
   2—Government (1-Mayor and 1-Borough Council)
   1—Resident at large
   3—Commercial property tenants (2-Hwy and 1-Downtown)
   TOTAL: 15

6. **The total first-year budget** will be $350,000 based on a hybrid budget at approximately 6%—Downtown and 4%—Hwy 12, 31, 202 as agreed above.

BID COMMITTEE FINDINGS

The BID Steering Committee found that:

1. There is currently no management of the Flemington Borough business, commercial, and industrial districts as a whole. We tend to react rather than plan and manage. Volunteers are good and achieve some results; however, they can only do so much without professional management. There is no one coordinating authority managing the business of businesses in Flemington Borough specifically.
2. There is no locally coordinated effort or organization to address customer and business needs.
3. The business communities, local government, and residents can be in a better partnership.
4. The business zones require enhanced services beyond what the municipality can provide.
5. Working in a professional and organized manner leverages better results and builds partnerships necessary to keep the municipality competitive and growing correctly.
6. Businesses in Flemington Borough need to be included at the level of real partners with government in the revitalization effort.
7. In order for customers to feel welcomed and cared for, a business community must be well managed and customer-conscious.
8. A coordinated and effective business community is the key partner in the entire Borough's success.
9. Maintaining and building upon community assets is an effective strategy that provides enhanced value to our community and guests.
10. A professional organizational structure is necessary to build a community-based effort that has real authority, works on the basis of managed agreements, honors its commitments, and respects the skills and knowledge of its contributors.

STRATEGIC PLAN AND BUDGET

The Steering Committee engaged in a strategic vision process to address these concerns. The process started with agreeing to a "Vision Statement" and the Values (Standards of Excellence) of the Flemington Borough Special Improvement District:

VISION STATEMENT

The Flemington Business Improvement District is a united community dedicated to service and creating memorable and rewarding experiences for our customers and visitors while improving the quality of life for the entire community.

We are an exceptional historic town rich in Victorian architecture and artisan heritage.

Flemington is a gateway to a unique and beautiful area and a destination for adventure, shopping, dining, and entertainment in a traditional American town—quaint yet sophisticated, friendly, vibrant, and committed to excellent service.

We are a safe, fun, family-oriented, creative, and sustainable community, which exemplifies the best in tourism. Flemington's excellent business environment delivers the best hospitality, shopping, and dining experiences.

MISSION STATEMENT

The mission of the Flemington Business Improvement District is to professionally manage the organization so that our core values, listed below, are delivered effectively to our customers, exceed their expectations, and provide an experience of enhanced value and excellence.

CORE VALUES

- Be honorable
- Communicate
- Be committed to success
- Be truthful
- Be accountable
- Be informative
- Have a good relationship to the facts
- If you don't know, don't make it up, and if you do make it up, clean it up.
- Fun is important
- Be pragmatic and results oriented
- Be creative
- Do our best
- Be fair and equitable
- Be in action

COMPREHENSIVE STRATEGY

The Steering Committee discussed how to include the community survey input, achieve the vision, and provide comprehensive services that could be built on over the years. Six general service areas were identified and a budget, which allows for furnishing those services.

1. Management and Administration
2. Promotions, Advertising, Public Relations, and Special Events

3. Environmental Improvements, Quality of Life, and Maintenance
4. Business Recruitment and Retention
5. Planning and Legal
6. Business Development, Practices, and Support

FIVE KEY COORDINATED SERVICE AREAS

Cooperative Business Management starts by understanding that every aspect of the business environment contributes to a successful experience by the customer. Cooperative Business Management is a comprehensive and coordinated approach. It requires the attention of an active professional management effort. Successful business districts (including malls, shopping centers, and shopping strips) manage the business environment in a comprehensive manner as a service to the customer. Service is the competitive edge. Management is the key to success. Services are grouped into the following six categories:

Management and Administration: the Flemington Borough Business Improvement District Management Corporation, a nonprofit corporation, will manage the BID. The Management Corporation will hire a professional manager or consulting service and maintain a professional office.

Marketing and Public Relations: The BID will develop destination-marketing strategy, a corporation design theme; provide joint advertising; conduct appropriate market surveys; support and design special events; support retail promotions; coordinate public relations; and have a customer information center.

Design, Quality of Life, and Improvements: The BID will support the Downtown Revitalization Plan, the connection of Rt. 31, Rt. 202 and Rt. 12 to the Main Street–Central Business District, and provide for better managed and enhanced parking sites; improved safety and cleanup efforts; enhanced street lighting, signage, and more pedestrian friendly designs. The BID will also provide for more user-friendly outdoor design for streets and sidewalks, including benches, trees, lighting, facades, etc. It will also address pedestrian access, wayfinding and signage improvements as well as traffic problems in general.

Business Recruitment and Development: The BID will develop business investment guides and financing programs; business development, support and training programs; develop cultural, retail and dining theme plans; develop long-range strategies; and pursue public and private funding.

Planning and Legal: The BID will develop Board training, an annual BID budget and work plan, as well as short- and long-term business plans. The management will work on redevelopment strategies and coordinate with the city's economic and redevelopment plans and projects. It will work as a team player with local banks, community organizations, and cultural organizations. The BID management will also address upgrades to local regulations and codes.

Business Practices and Performance: The BID will operate as a business community in a cooperative and planned manner necessary for effectively responding to customer demands. Common business standards and operating procedures, such as standardized times when all businesses are open, address the organizational capacity of the district and communicate a higher level of business sense and service.

FLEMINGTON BOROUGH BUSINESS IMPROVEMENT DISTRICT PROPOSED FIRST YEAR BUDGET

The BID assessment preliminary budget: $350,000. This budget does not include any grants, gifts, contributions, or other public funds such as private grants or city funds. The 2011 budget is summarized as follows:

Budget Analysis

AREA	AMOUNT
Schedule A (Downtown Business Area)	$230,000
Schedule B (Rts. 31, 202, and 12)	120,000
TOTAL:	**$350,000**

The committee recognized that the BID would be capable of leveraging additional funds. It can also seek and receive funds from the Borough and other public sources, from fundraisers, from receiving fees for services, and the BID may also obtain grants and loans that will augment the budget provided by the assessments and build appropriate partnerships.

It is important to emphasize that only commercial property owners will be assessed; homeowners will not be impacted directly by the assessment, but rather will reap the benefits that the Special Improvement District will bring to the community.

SECOND COMMUNITY MEETING

Citizen participation is an essential part of any BID planning process. The BID has impact and relies on its members to move forward. Receiving input from the BID members and establishing an open process will help the BID succeed. Not unlike the November 9, 2010 meeting, the Committee will hold a meeting on February 1, 2011 with the proposed BID Community and discuss the Committee's findings, recommendations, and draft proposal, and answer questions while recording input.

After the final Community Meeting, the Committee must decide whether the input received changes to their proposal. After changes are made, the Committee may decide to send a report and proposal to the Municipal Mayor and Council. The report may be accepted as is or sent back to the Committee for adjustments. If it is accepted as is, the Municipal Council will schedule two (2) hearings: the first to place the BID ordinance and budget on the docket, and the second as a public hearing and vote on the establishment of the BID and its first year budget. This process takes at least two months.

It is not until the BID ordinance is passed or fails that the Committee's work is complete. If the BID is established, the BID Corporation or Committee takes over. The Corporation can be established immediately. But the budget will not begin until January 1, 2011.

Recommended Minimum Board of Directors for the Flemington Business Improvement District Management Corporation

3—Retailers (1-Hwy and 2-Downtown)
3—Nonretailers (1-Hwy and 2-Downtown)
3—Downtown commercial
1—Liberty Village Representative
2—Government (1-Mayor and 1-Borough Council)
1—Resident at large
3—Commercial property tenants (2-Hwy and 1-Downtown)

TOTAL: 16

FLEMINGTON BID ORDINANCE

BOROUGH OF FLEMINGTON
COUNTY OF HUNTERDON, NJ
ORDINANCE CREATING A SPECIAL IMPROVEMENT DISTRICT FOR FLEMINGTON BOROUGH BUSINESS COMMUNITY

WHEREAS, business and property owners in Flemington Borough have petitioned the Governing Body to create a Special Improvement District also known as a Business improvement District with a non-profit Management Corporation pursuant to N.J.S.A. 40:56–65 et seq.; and

WHEREAS, the Governing Body finds that all business, industrial, and commercial properties in Flemington Borough are integral, vital, economic, and social; and

WHEREAS, the anticipated services to be provided to this Special Improvement District will serve to enhance the safety, welfare, and economic growth of Flemington Borough, its inhabitants, and the Borough of Flemington as a whole; and

WHEREAS, based upon these findings and the desires of business owners, merchants, and property owners in Flemington Borough, the Governing Body hereby desires to establish the Flemington Borough Special Improvement District designated in Schedules A & B as the Flemington Borough Business Improvement District.

NOW, THEREFORE, BE IT ORDAINED BY THE GOVERNING BODY OF THE BOROUGH OF FLEMINGTON as follows:

SECTION 1: Definitions.

a. "Special Improvement District & Business Improvement District" (sometimes also referred to as the "District") means areas within the Flemington Borough designated by this Ordinance as areas in which a special assessment on property within the District shall be imposed for the purposes of promoting the economic and general welfare of the District and the Municipality.

b. "District Management Corporation" means the "FLEMINGTON BOROUGH BUSINESS IMPROVEMENT DISTRICT MANAGEMENT CORPORATION" (also referred to as "Management Corporation"), an entity to be incorporated pursuant to Title 15A of the New Jersey Statutes and designated by Municipal Ordinance to receive funds collected by a special assessment within the Special Improvement District as authorized by this Ordinance and any amendatory supplemental ordinances.

SECTION 2: *Findings*—pursuant to N.J.S.A. 40–56–65 et seq. ("The Act") the Governing Body of the Borough of Flemington hereby determines the following:

a. That the areas within Flemington Borough that are described by block and lot and by street address as set forth in *Schedules A (Downtown) and B (Highway)* of this ordinance, and the property owners, tenants, and inhabitants therein benefit from being designated as a Special Improvement District uniting the business community and will benefit the whole of Flemington Borough with the exception of the following properties that will not be assessed members of the Special Improvement District:

i) Any property owned and operated by the municipal, county and state governments

ii) 100% of residential structures 4 units or under

b. That a District Management Corporation would provide administrative and other services to benefit the businesses, employees, residents, and consumers in Flemington Borough, the Flemington Borough Special Improvement District also known as the Flemington Business improvement District, and will also assist the Borough of Flemington in promoting economic growth and employment;

c. That a special assessment may be imposed and collected by the Borough of Flemington either with the regular property tax payment (or payment in lieu of taxes) or otherwise on properties located within the Borough's limits and that these payments shall be transferred to the district management corporation to effectuate the purpose of this ordinance and to exercise the powers given to it pursuant to this ordinance;

d. That it is in the best interests of the Borough of Flemington and its inhabitants to create a Special Improvement District and to designate a nonprofit District Management Corporation to manage the Special Improvement District; and

e. That the business community should be encouraged to provide self-help and self-financing programs to meet local needs, goals, and objectives and should be encouraged to supplement any of the authorized services and improvements through formation of an independent District Management Corporation formed under Title 15A of the New Jersey statutes.

Section 3—Creation of the District

a. There is hereby created and designated within the Borough of Flemington a Special Improvement District authorized pursuant to N.J.S.A. Title 40:56–65 et seq. to be known as the Flemington Borough Special Improvement District ("District") and is hereby established consisting of the properties designated and listed on Schedules A (Downtown) and B (Highway), annexed hereto by tax block and lot numbers and street addresses. A District Management Corporation will govern the Special Improvement District.

b. Schedules A and B of this ordinance may be amended by ordinance to add and delete particular properties which have a change in use affecting the appropriateness of including them as part of the Special Improvement District. Any change in the schedules of properties to be considered part of the Special Improvement District will require an ordinance amendment.

c. The District is comprised of all zoned commercial and industrial properties and applicable commercial vacant land as described by lot and block in Schedules A & B as follows: All commercial properties (zoned 4A, 4B, 4C, and commercial 1) as a municipality-wide special improvement district including shopping centers, Liberty Village and Turntable Junction, the Main Street business area and its connectors and extensions, Reaville Avenue, Rt. 31, Rt. 202, and Rt. 12. Nonconforming properties, which are not used as commercial properties, and vacant land that is noncommercial may be excluded. Residential properties of 4 units or less are considered residential, and strictly residential areas are not in the District. Residential properties in the commercial areas are in the District, but are excluded from the District assessment.

Section 4—Assessments

a. All costs of improvements and maintenance, other than the costs of improvements and maintenance ordinarily incurred by the Borough of Flemington out of general funds, shall be determined and approved pursuant to N.J.S.A. 40:56–80 or N.J.S.A. 40:56–85 as determined by the District Management Corporation. The formula for the assessment is as follows: each property's current assessed value, as determined by the Borough of Flemington Tax Assessor for real estate tax purposes, will be multiplied by the appropriate factored amount to sustain the approved annual budget to determine the amount of the special improvement district assessment based on ad valorem property tax values. The foregoing assessment shall be collected as a special assessment against the properties that are within the district as defined in Schedules "A and B."

Section 5—Designated District Management Corporation

a. The Governing Body of the Borough of Flemington hereby designates THE FLEMINGTON BOROUGH BUSINESS IMPROVEMENT DISTRICT MANAGEMENT CORPORATION ("district management corporation"), a nonprofit corporation of the State of New Jersey, as the District Management Corporation for the District.

b. That the District Management Corporation, in addition to acting as an advisory board to the governing body, shall also have all powers necessary and requisite to effectuate the purposes of this ordinance, as specified in N.J.S.A. 40–56–65 et seq. including but not limited to:

  1. Adoption of by-laws for the regulation of its affairs and the conduct of its business and prescribe rules, regulations, and policies for the performance of its functions and duties;

  2. Employ such persons as may be required, and fix and pay their compensation from funds available to the Corporation;

  3. Apply for, accept, administer, and comply with requirements respecting an appropriation of funds or a gift, grant or donation of property or money;

  4. Make and execute agreements which may be necessary or convenient to the exercise of the powers and functions of the Corporation including contract with any person, firm, corporation, government agency, or entity;

  5. Administer and manage its own funds and accounts and pay its own obligations;

6. Borrow money from private lenders;
7. Fund the improvement of exterior appearance of properties in the district through grants and loans;
8. Fund rehabilitation of properties in the district;
9. Accept, purchase, rehabilitate, sell, lease, or manage property in the district;
10. Enforce the conditions of any loan, grant, sale, or lease made by the corporation;
11. Provide security, sanitation, and other services in the district, supplemental to those normally supplied by the Borough of Flemington;
12. Undertake improvements designed to increase safety and attractiveness of the district to businesses which may locate there or visitors to the districts, including but not limited to parking, litter cleanup and control, landscaping, signage, and those improvements generally permitted for pedestrian malls under N.J.S.A. 40:56–66 pursuant to pertinent regulations of the governing body;
13. Publicize, promote, and plan for the district and the businesses included within the district boundaries;
14. Recruit new businesses to fill vacancies in, and to balance the business mix of, the district;
15. Organize special events in the district;
16. Provide special parking arrangements for the district;
17. Design and enforce environmental and building design criteria under N.J.S.A. 4:50–66 as amended;
18. Regulate vending;
19. Provide temporary decorative lighting in the district; and,
20. Effectuate the purposes and intents of N.J.S.A. 40:56–66 as amended.

a. That the District Management Corporation shall utilize affirmative action goals and guidelines in its hiring and expenditures whenever possible. Pursuant to N.J.A.C. 17:27–5.2, the District Management Corporation will not discriminate against any employee or applicant for employment because of age, race, creed, color, national origin, ancestry, marital status, or sex. The District Management Corporation will take affirmative action to ensure that such applicants are recruited and employed, and that employees are treated during employment without regard to their age, race, creed, national origin, ancestry, marital status, or sex.

b. Upon further written agreement, the Borough of Flemington may delegate to the District Management Corporation the contracting of work to be done on any street, or on other municipal property, included in the Special Improvement District. In that event, the Corporation shall be a "contracting unit" within the "Local Public Contracts law" P.L. 1971, c.198 (N.J.S.A. 40A: 11–1 et seq.).

The plans and specifications shall be approved by the municipal engineer prior to initiation of any action for the award of a contract under the act.

Section 6—Annual Report and Budgets

a. The District Management Corporation shall submit a detailed business plan and budget for the upcoming year, no later than November 1 of the current fiscal year starting the year after this ordinance is adopted, for the approval by resolution of the governing body, pursuant to the provisions of N.J.S.A. 40:56–84. The budget shall be submitted with a report, which explains how the budget contributes to the goals and objectives for the Special Improvement District.

b. The fiscal year of the District Management Corporation shall be January 1 to December 31.

Section 7—Annual Audit of the District Management Corporation

The District Management Corporation shall also cause an audit of its books, accounts, and financial transactions to be made and filed with the governing body. This audit shall be completed and filed with the Governing Body within four (4) months after the close of the fiscal year of the corporation. A certified duplicate copy of the audit shall be filed with the County of Hunterdon Tax Assessor, Director of the Division of Local Government Services in the State of New Jersey Department of Community Affairs within five (5) days of the filing of the audit with the governing body.

Section 8—Annual Report to Municipality

The District Management Corporation shall submit an annual report to the governing body pursuant to N.J.S.A. 40:56–80 within 90 days of the close of the fiscal year. This report shall consist of a narrative covering the previous year's operation and detailed financial statements.

Section 9—Municipal Powers Retained

Notwithstanding the creation of the Special Improvement District, the Borough of Flemington expressly retains all its powers and authority over the area designated as the Flemington Borough Special Improvement District.

Section 10—Severability

If any section, subsection, sentence, clause, phrase, or portion of this ordinance is for any reason held to be invalid or unconstitutional by a court of competent jurisdiction, such portion shall be deemed a separate and distinct and independent provision, and such holding shall not affect the validity of the remaining portions hereof.

Section 11—Effective date

This ordinance shall take effect upon passage, approval, and publication as required by law.

SCHEDULES "A and B"

The attached list of properties makes up this Special Improvement District as well as an area-wide impact area of both districts as a whole.

BUDGET RESOLUTION

Flemington Bid Year 2011 Budget Resolution

WHEREAS, at its meeting of February 15, 2011, the governing body of the Borough of Flemington introduced the Flemington Borough Special Improvement District budget for the period January 1, 2011—December 31, 2011, which budget is annexed hereto; and

WHEREAS, after individual notice to the owners, and notice of advertisement in a newspaper of general circulation, the governing body of Flemington Borough conducted a public hearing on February 28, 2011; and

WHEREAS, the governing body of Flemington Borough has determined that at least one (1) week prior to the hearing a complete copy of the proposed budgets were (a) advertised; (b) posted in the Borough Clerk's office; and (c) made available to each person requesting the same before and during the public hearing; and

WHEREAS, all persons having interest in the budget were given the opportunity to present objections; and

WHEREAS, the governing body of the Borough of Flemington having considered the comments at the public hearing is of the opinion that it is appropriate and desirable to ratify and adopt the budget without amendment as advertised; and

WHEREAS, pursuant to N.J.S.A. 40:56–80 and N.J.S.A. 40:56–84, the governing body of the Borough of Flemington is required to adopt the budget by resolution after closing the hearing;

NOW, THEREFORE, BE IT RESOLVED the governing body of the Borough of Flemington that:

(1) The Flemington Borough Special Improvement District 2011 budget is approved by the governing body of the Borough of Flemington and it is approved for the period of January 1, 2011—December 31, 2011 in the amount of $350,000 to the Flemington Borough Business Improvement District Management Corporation

(2) This special assessment is hereby imposed and shall be collected with either the regular tax payment (or payment in lieu of taxes), or otherwise, on properties located within the Borough of Flemington as set forth within the ordinance and the assessment as follows:
Schedule A shall be assessed at $230,000; and, Schedule B shall be assessed at $120,000;

(3) Payments the District received by the Borough of Flemington shall be transferred to the Flemington Borough Business Improvement District Management Corporation to be expended in accordance with the approved budget; and

(4) The Borough Clerk is hereby authorized to forward a certified copy of this resolution to the Flemington Borough Business Improvement District Management Corporation, the Burlington County Board of Taxation, and the Director of the Division of Local Government Services in the State of New Jersey Department of Community Affairs

2011 BUDGET

Flemington Business Improvement District Management Corporation

Management and Administration ($138,000): This amount serves to cover the costs of a management, accountant, office supplies and equipment, insurance, and other administrative costs. The management entity of a BID is specifically designated in the enabling ordinance. The Committee discussed various management forms for the BID and agreed upon the private nonprofit form of management.

Business Recruitment and Development: ($90,000)—services, research, plan and package, legal-attorney

Marketing and Public Relations ($85,000): Public relations/marketing specialist. One of the primary goals of the BID is to promote and market the district as a destination to shop and conduct business, newsletters, banners, and advertisement and support festivals and other promotional events.

Design, Quality of Life, and Improvements: ($37,000)—infrastructure planning, signage, pedestrian safety, and workability. Parking—a focus on pedestrian crossing upgrades, signage, and lighting, upgrades, and planning.

BY-LAWS OF THE FLEMINGTON BUSINESS IMPROVEMENT DISTRICT MANAGEMENT CORPORATION, INC
Adopted as of April 5, 2011
Affirmed by the Board of Trustees on April 5, 2011

ARTICLE I

Name; Offices; Corporate Seal

1.01 *Name.* The name of the corporation is the Flemington Business Improvement District Management Corporation, Inc. (the "Corporation") and shall also be known as the Flemington Business Improvement District, or Flemington BID, or FBID and such other assumed names as the Board of Trustees shall determine from time to time. (The term Special Improvement District is synonymous with Business Improvement District. Generally, Special Improvement District [SID] refers to the New Jersey state statute N.J.S.A. 40:56-65 et seq, and Business Improvement District [BID] refers to local application).

1.02 *Offices.* The principal office of the Corporation shall be located at such location or locations in Flemington, New Jersey, as the Board of Trustees ("Trustees" is used herein to refer to "Trustees" as such term is defined under the New Jersey Non-profit Corporation Act) may hereafter designate from time to time.

1.03 *Corporate Seal.* The Board shall procure a corporate seal, which shall be circular in form and shall bear, on its outer edge, the name "Flemington Business Improvement District"; and, in the center, the words and figures "Incorporated March 22, 2011, New Jersey." The Board may amend the form of the seal or the inscription thereon at its discretion.

ARTICLE II

Purposes

2.01 *Purposes*. The Corporation is organized and shall be operated exclusively for charitable and educational purposes, within the meaning of Section 501(c) (3) of the Internal Revenue Code of 1986, as amended (the "Code"), and the Regulations thereunder as they may hereafter be amended. The purposes and powers of the Corporation are more particularly set forth as follows:

(a) To serve as the professional and business association and district management corporation for the Flemington Business Improvement District and other Special Improvement Districts pursuant to N.J.S.A. 40:56-65 et seq. (the "Act") and as approved in the enabling Flemington Business Improvement District Ordinance as amended and other subsequent Special Improvement District ordinances. As such, the Corporation shall have the powers and comply with all requirements as set forth in the Act and in the approved Flemington Special Improvement District Ordinance.

(b) Serve the special improvement district, the business community, and the municipal government to formulate, promote, and implement the economic revitalization and general welfare of the special improvement district and the Borough of Flemington, New Jersey

(c) Promote and preserve the cultural, historic, tourist, and civic interests of the Flemington special improvement district and the Borough of Flemington

(d) Mobilize available public and private resources for the purposes set forth herein

(e) Provide a mechanism by which service and professional firms, retail establishments, property owners, employers, citizens, and others can cooperate to promote business opportunities, employment, consumer choices, shopper's facilities, and the general civil interest

(f) Form affiliated corporations, nonprofit or for profit, to help carry out its purposes; and

(g) To do any other act incidental to or connected with the foregoing purposes or any advancement thereof, either directly or indirectly, either alone or in conjunction or cooperation with others; to do any and all lawful acts and things and to engage in any and all lawful activities which may be necessary, useful, suitable, desirable, or proper for the furtherance, accomplishment, fostering, or attainment of any or all of the purposes for which the Corporation is organized; and to aid or assist other organizations whose activities are such as to further accomplish, foster, or attain any such purposes.

(h) Notwithstanding any other provision of these By-laws, the Corporation shall not conduct any activities not permitted to be performed by (i) a corporation exempt from Federal income tax under section 501(c) (3) of the Code (or the corresponding provision of any future United States Internal Revenue Law) or (ii) a corporation permitted to deduct its contributions under Section 170(c)(2) of the Code (or the corresponding provision of any future United States Internal Revenue Law).

(i) The Corporation shall not carry on propaganda or otherwise attempt to influence legislation. The Corporation shall not engage in any transaction or permit any act or omission that shall operate to deprive it of its tax-exempt status under Section 501(c) (3) of the Code. The Corporation shall not in any manner, including, but not limited to the publishing or distribution of statements, or to any extent participate in or intervene in any political campaign on behalf of any candidate for public office nor shall it engage in any "prohibitive transaction" as defined in Section 503(b) of the Code.

(j) The Corporation shall not have capital stock, and no stock or shares shall be issued. No incorporator, Trustee, or officer shall at any time be considered to be an owner of any of the assets, property, or income of the Corporation, nor shall he or she, by distribution, liquidation, dissolution, or in any manner, be entitled to or receive any said assets, property, or income, all of which shall be devoted exclusively and forever to the purposes of the Corporation or disposed of herein provided. The Corporation is organized and shall operate not for profit, and no part of its net earnings shall inure or may lawfully inure to the benefit of any private shareholder, incorporator, Trustee, officer, or individual. The above provisions, however, shall not prevent the payment of reasonable compensation to any person, organization, firm, or corporation for services rendered to the Corporation.

(k) The Corporation also has such powers as are or may hereafter be granted under laws of New Jersey that are in furtherance of the Corporation's exempt purposes within the meaning of Section 501(c)(3) of the Code or the corresponding section of any future Federal tax code.

ARTICLE III

Members

3.01 *Membership.* The members of the Corporation (the "Members") shall be as follows:

(a) The incorporators of the corporation until Articles 4.01 through 4.03 are enacted hereof upon which the elected Board of Trustees are the members of the Corporation.

(b) Elected and appointed members of the Board of Trustees. Selected Trustees are not members of the corporation, but have full voting privileges.

(c) Membership is assigned to a single person, and no person shall hold more than one (1) membership interest, either as an individual or as part of a business entity.

3.02 *Rights of Members.* The rights of each Member and Selected Trustees shall be oversight of the corporation operations and activities and voting for the Trustees and Officers of the Corporation as set forth in Article IV hereof. There shall be no proxy voting, however, voting electronically or by telephone shall be permitted if the Trustees present by majority vote agree.

3.03 *No Transfers of Membership Interests.* No Member, directly or indirectly, shall assign, transfer, hypothecate, pledge, encumber, give, or otherwise voluntarily or involuntarily dispose of any or all of his or her Membership Interest in the Corporation.

ARTICLE IV

Board of Trustees

4.01 *Board of Trustees.* The original Board of Trustees will consist of the three incorporators of the corporation, but no later than immediately following designation by the local enabling special improvement district establishing the Flemington Special Improvement District (SID, also known as a business improvement district or BID) or as deemed necessary by the incorporators for any reason, an organization meeting will be held to expand the Board in accordance with the special improvement district planning documents and/or enabling ordinance. Upon the SID designation there shall be added immediately the positions of the Board of Trustees of the Corporation in Article 4.03 who will assume all the powers and authority of the Trustees.

Each Trustee must be at least eighteen (18) years of age, be up to date in SID assessment payments, and in good standing, and may not be running or bidding for elected office in the County of Hunterdon and Borough of Flemington, NJ unless in a current elected position. The policies, activities, and affairs of the Corporation shall be determined and managed by the Board of Trustees who shall exercise all the powers of the Corporation and shall keep full and fair accounts of all its transactions, and formulate and approve the yearly budget of the Corporation. For designation purposes the Board of Trustees is referred to, in these By- laws, as the "Board," and each person serving on the Board is referred to individually as "Trustee and/or Trustee," and, if more than one (1) Trustee is referred to, as "Trustees" (as set forth in Article 1.02, "Trustees" is used herein to refer to "Trustees" as such term is defined under the New Jersey Nonprofit Corporation Act 15A: 9–1 et seq.). The Board may be amended to properly represent an expanded or diminished Flemington Special Improvement District or other Special Improvement Districts as they may be established by local ordinance.

4.02 *Term of Office.* After the organizational meeting, the Elected Trustees shall be divided into three (3) classes, with one-third Trustees in the first class (the "Class A"), one-third Trustees in the second class (the "Class B"), and the balance of Trustees in the third class (the "Class C"). All original Trustees will serve until the first election meeting of the Corporation in September 2012 in which Class A will be up for election and the staggered annual election process will commence, and there will not be an election for

Trustees until that meeting. The term of office of Class A shall expire at the first election meeting of the Corporation in September 2012; the term of office of Class B shall expire at the election meeting of the Corporation in September 2013 of the Corporation, and the term of office of Class C shall expire at the election meeting of the Corporation in September 2014. Except as otherwise provided in Article 4.03(b), once the initial terms of the three (3) classes of Trustees have expired the successor Trustees shall be elected for a *term of three (3) years in a staggered manner*, such that one class of Trustees shall expire annually and that new Trustees for the expired class will be elected every three years.

4.03 *Composition of the Board of Trustees.* The Board shall be comprised of the following:

(a) There shall be at minimum sixteen (**16**) Trustees elected by the voting Members at the Annual Meeting (the "Elected Trustees") of the Corporation and two (2) selected Trustees who shall be the Mayor and one elected official of the Borough of Flemington's Common Council and is appointed by the Borough's Common Council, as such term is defined in Articles 4.02 and 5.01. The Elected and Selected Trustees shall be voting Trustees, and shall consist of property owners, business and or residents located in the Flemington Business Improvement District as follows:

3—Retailers (1-Hwy and 2-Downtown)
3—Nonretailers (1-Hwy and 2-Downtown)
4—Downtown commercial
1—Liberty Village Representative
1—Resident at large
4—Commercial property tenants (2-Hwy and 2-Downtown)
TOTAL: 16

(b) There shall be three (3) selected Trustee as follows: an elected member of Borough of Flemington Common Council appointed by Common Council of Flemington, the Mayor of the Borough of Flemington, NJ, and the Executive Trustee/CEO of the Hunterdon County Chamber of Commerce. The Selected Trustees shall be full voting Trustees. If the Corporation employs or contracts for a professional manager, the manager shall not be a voting member of the Board of Trustees.

(c) There will be four non-voting Trustees that are appointed by the Board of Trustees at their discretion and are not required to be filled.

TOTAL: Nineteen (19) Voting Trustees and up to Four (4) Non-Voting Trustees

4.04 ELECTION OF TRUSTEES

(a) Except as set forth in Articles 4.02 & 4.03 hereof, Trustees shall be elected by plurality vote of a full Board quorum.

(b) The election of Trustees shall be held annually in the month of September or October ("Election Meeting"). The President will appoint a nomination committee no later than June 1 of the same year prior to the election date. The date and time to receive nominations shall be determined by the Nomination Committee and shall be published once (1) time in a newspaper of general circulation in the Borough of Flemington to receive nominations from the members of the Flemington Business Improvement District identified in the enabling ordinance. Such publication requirement shall be completed no later than thirty (30) calendar days prior to the scheduled annual election of Trustees. The nomination requests will be mailed via regular mail to each BID members, property owners, and business owner in the BID forty-five (45) calendar days prior to the scheduled Election Meeting and must be returned, postmarked, and received within 30 calendar days prior of the Election Meeting. Nominations must include name, address, business affiliation, position for which nominated, telephone numbers, and email addresses, and a signed agreement by the nominee to serve if elected. Members nominating others shall personally verify and vouch that the nominee accepts their name submitted for nomination. BID members, property owners, and business owners shall submit nominations in the following manner: (i) via regular mail return receipt requested, which must be received by the Nominations Committee; (ii) via hand delivery to the Nominations Committee; or (iii) by email or in person to Executive Committee Meeting or manager. All nominations must be received prior to the expiration of the thirty (30) calendar deadline. The Nominations Committee may, in accordance with the by-laws, move a Trustee from one classification to the other, but in order to maintain a balance in the classes, the class (A, B, or C) must remain the same. The Elected Trustees will be determined by a majority vote of the Members present at the election meeting. Trustees elected at the Election Meeting shall take office effective immediately upon determination of the results of the election.

(c) The Board shall vote as follows:

    (i) Each Trustee may only have one (1) vote regardless of how many properties or businesses he or she owns.

    (ii) *There shall be no proxy voting*; however, voting electronically or by telephone shall be permitted if the Trustees present by majority vote agree.

(d) There shall be an appointment of all the Trustees at the organizational meeting by the incorporators. Thereafter, the number of Trustees to be elected in each election shall be staggered in accordance with Section 4.02. and a copy thereof will be permanently inserted in the minutes book.

4.05 REMOVAL OF TRUSTEES

(a) At any meeting of the Trustees, duly called and at which a quorum is present, may, by a majority vote of the quorum, remove for cause any Trustee from office and may appoint a successor to serve for the balance of the term of such removed Trustee;

(b) A Trustee shall be deemed to have been automatically removed from office for cause without further action being necessary on the part of such Trustee or on the part of the Board, in the event that such Trustee fails to attend two (2) consecutive full meetings of the full Board. Attendance at an Executive Committee meeting will be considered attendance at a full Board meeting. However, all removals must be confirmed by the Executive and/or Full Board. Following the removal of a Trustee in the manner provided in this Article 4.05(b), the Secretary of the Corporation shall report such fact to the Board at the meeting of the Board next following the second absence; or

(c) A Trustee shall be deemed to have been automatically removed from office for cause without further action being necessary on the part of such Trustee or on the part of the Board, in the event that such Trustee fails to attend at least three (3) out of four (4) of the regular meetings of the Board in any calendar year. Following the removal of a Trustee in the manner provided in this Article 4.05(c), the Secretary of the Corporation shall report such fact to the Board at the meeting of the Board next following the absence causing the removal; or

(d) Vacancies occurring in the Board for any reason may be filled by a vote of majority of the Trustees present at the Full Board meeting. A Trustee appointed to fill a vacancy shall be appointed to hold office for the unexpired term of his or her predecessor.

(e) Notwithstanding the provisions of Articles 4.05(b) and (c) hereof, upon the removal of a Trustee pursuant to either such provision, the removed Trustee may petition the Board in writing for reinstatement as a Trustee of the Corporation. Any such petition for reinstatement must (i) set forth in detail an explanation for each absence which explanation must demonstrate just cause for the reinstatement and (ii) must be received by the Secretary of the Corporation not later than ten (10) days prior to a regularly scheduled Board meeting in order for such petition to be considered at such meeting. Upon the receipt of any such petition for reinstatement by the Corporation, the Board at its next regularly scheduled meeting following receipt of any such petition in accordance with this Article 4.05(e) shall consider each such petition and only upon the affirmative vote of a majority of the Trustees present shall such removed Trustee be reinstated. A reinstated Trustee shall be deemed to have no absences upon such reinstatement. (f) This Article 4.05 shall not apply to the Selected Trustees.

ARTICLE V

Meetings of the Trustees

5.01 *Annual Meeting.* The annual meeting of the Board of Trustees shall be held in December of the preceding year (the "Annual Meeting of the Board") for the election of officers and to conduct such other business as may come before the Board. The Secretary shall cause to be mailed to each Trustee at his or her address a notice stating the time and place of the Annual Meeting of the Board. All voting shall take place at said meeting. Officers shall be elected by a quorum majority of those full voting members of the Board in attendance, excluding vacancies. Officers elected at the Annual Meeting of the Board shall take office effective immediately upon election.

5.02 *Regular Meetings.* Regular meetings of the Board of Trustees shall be held at least four (4) times per year, which shall include the Annual Meeting of the Board. The Annual Election Meeting may be considered one of these meetings. The Board of Trustees first at its Organizational Meeting and thereafter at its Annual Meeting shall establish the other meeting dates. Meetings shall be held at locations and at times chosen by the Trustees at the Annual Meeting of the Board, and no additional notice of place, day and hour of regularly scheduled meetings need be given to any Trustee.

5.03 *Organizational Meeting.*

(a) At the organizational meeting of the Corporation, the Board shall be appointed by the existing Trustees/Incorporators to serve until the first election meeting of the Corporation in September 2012 with adherence to the minimal standards in the Flemington Special Improvement District Steering Committee final report and recommendations, and the enacted Flemington SID Ordinance. Thereafter, the Board shall be elected at the Annual Election Meeting of the Corporation as provided in Articles 4.02 and 4.04 hereof. Upon appointment the Board of Trustees shall assume all duties and authority of Trustees of the Corporation as stated in these by-laws.

5.04 *Special Meetings.* The President may call special meetings of the Board. Notice of the place, day, and hour of such special meeting shall be given to each Trustee at least twenty-four (24) hours before the meeting, by delivering notice to him or her personally, or by delivering the same at his or her residence or usual place of business, or by contacting him or her by telephone, or by Internet/electronic email. Any notice of a special meeting shall state the business to be transacted. Special meetings may be conducted by telephone, or by Internet electronic email.

5.05 *Quorum.* A quorum at the meetings of the full Board of Trustees shall consist of seven Trustees of the Board and of those seven, two Trustees must be elected officers of the Board. A quorum must be present in order to vote on any measure. Quorums of all other committees, including the Executive Committee, must consist of at minimum three business people or property owners of the Flemington Business Improvement District of which one must be a Trustee. Except as otherwise provided in the Certificate of Incorporation, these By-Laws or the laws of the State of New Jersey, three members of those voting Trustees present at such regular meetings such as an Executive Committee meeting, shall be sufficient to pass any measure as long as one Trustee is an officer of the Board. In the absence of a quorum, the Trustees present by a majority vote and without notice other than by announcement may adjourn the meeting, from time to time, until a quorum shall attend. At any such meeting after an adjourned meeting at which a quorum shall be present, any business may be transacted which might have been transacted at the adjourned meeting as originally notified. There shall be no proxy voting; however, voting electronically or by telephone shall be permitted if the Trustees present by majority vote agree.

5.06 *Compensation.* No compensation shall be paid to any officer or Trustee of the Board. Nothing herein shall prevent any officer or Trustee from being reimbursed for out-of-pocket expenses or compensated for services rendered in any other capacity to or for the Corporation, provided, however, that any such expenses incurred or services rendered shall have been authorized in advance by resolution of the Board.

5.07 *Contracts and Service.* The members, Trustees, and officers of the Corporation may be interested directly or indirectly in any contract relating to or incidental to the operations conducted by the Corporation, and may freely make contracts, enter transactions, or otherwise act for and on behalf of the Corporation, notwithstanding that they also may be acting as individuals, or a trustee of trusts, or as agents for other persons or corporations, or may be interested in the same matters as stockholders, members, trustees, or otherwise. Notwithstanding the foregoing, any contract, transaction, or act on behalf of the Corporation in a matter in which any member, Trustee, or officer is personally interested as a stockholder, Trustee, or otherwise must be disclosed to the Trustees, conducted at arm's length, shall not violate any prohibition against the Corporation's use or application of its funds for private benefit and shall be approved in accordance with N.J.S.A. 15A: 6-8 as the same may be amended or modified and any successor statute thereto. Common or interested Trustees may be counted in determining the presence of a quorum at a board meeting at which such a contract or transaction is authorized, approved or ratified; however, such authorization, approval, or ratification shall only be effective by affirmative vote of a majority of the disinterested Trustees present and voting.

ARTICLE VI

Committees of the Board of Trustees

6.01 *Committees Generally.* By resolution adopted by a quorum of the Board, the Board may provide for such standing or special committees with such powers and duties, as it deems desirable and may discontinue the same at its pleasure. The members of all such committees shall be appointed and the committee chairman named by the President. At least one member of each standing or special committee shall be a member of the Board; the remaining members of such committees may, but need not be, members of the Board and preference shall be given to assessed members of the special improvement district. Each committee shall keep full and fair accounts of its transactions and accurate minutes of its meetings. The President shall fill vacancies on any committee.

6.02 *Executive Committee*—An Executive Committee consisting of the elected officers of the Board of Trustees may be established to conduct the day-to-day business of the Corporation as outlined in the approved budget. The Executive Committee consists of the officers of the corporation and may include the chairs of appointed standing committees as voting members of the Executive Committee if those chairs are Trustees. All Board members are encouraged to attend the Executive Committee meetings and will be permitted to vote at that meeting. An Executive Committee will be official if at minimum three Trustees are present as follows: one elected officer is in attendance and two other elected Trustees are present. A quorum of the Executive Committee will consist of three (3) people, one of which must be a duly elected officer. The President may call special and emergency meetings of the Executive Committee.

6.03 *Committee Reports.* All recommendations by a committee shall be reported orally and recommendations requiring policy or budget support shall be put in writing to the Executive Committee of the Board if requested by the President.

6.04 *Meetings of Committees.* Each committee shall meet at the call of the chairman of the committee or any two (2) members of the committee. The President is the chairperson of the Executive Committee as established in Article VII, and if absent the chairmanship will follow succession as described in Article VII.

6.05 *Participation in Committees.* In selecting members of committees, the Board and the President shall encourage widespread participation among non-members of the corporation, assessed members of the Flemington Special Improvement District, and others concerned with the purposes of the Corporation and/or the Flemington Business Improvement District Management Corporation. From time to time, special committees may be named to advise the Board on issues on which additional perspective may be required and public meetings may be held to solicit advice from those concerned about the economic and social well-being of the district.

ARTICLE VII

Officers

7.01 *Executive Officers.* By a quorum of the full membership of the Board, excluding vacancies, at the Annual Meeting, the Board shall elect a President, a Vice President, a Treasurer, a Secretary from among the Elected Trustees, and an Assistant Secretary from the staff or Elected Trustees whose sole function is to act as the corporate notary. The Assistant Secretary will have no special voting rights and must be a duly elected Trustee to vote. All officers shall serve for a one (1) year term originally at the Organizational Meeting of the Corporation and henceforth at the Annual Meeting of the Board. By a quorum of the full membership of the Board, excluding vacancies, the Board shall appoint other subordinate officers as it may desire either from within or without its membership, also to serve for one (1) year terms. No person may hold more than one (1) office; and no officer shall execute, acknowledge, or verify any instrument in more than one capacity.

7.02 *Vacancies.* Except as provided in Article 7.03 herein below, in the event any office becomes vacant by death, resignation, retirement, removal, disqualification, or any other cause, the Board may elect, by a majority vote of the full membership of the Board, excluding vacancies, an officer to fill such vacancy, and such officer shall hold office and serve until the next Annual Trustees Meeting. In the event that any officer cannot conduct the duties of his or her office for a period exceeding sixty (60) days, the Board may deem such office vacant.

7.03 *President and Vice Presidents of the Board of Trustees.*

(a) President.

(i) The President shall preside at all meetings of the Corporation and of its Board.

(ii) The President shall have general charge and supervision of the activities and affairs of the Corporation.

(iii) The President may call special meetings of the Board.

(iv) The President shall have and may exercise such powers as are, from time to time, assigned to him or her by the Board.

(v) With the approval of the Board and in conjunction with the Secretary, the President may enter into and execute in the name of the Corporation, contracts and other instruments in the regular course of business, except where the execution of such instruments is expressly delegated by resolution of the Board to another officer or agent of the Corporation such as the Manager.

(b) First Vice President.

(i) In the event the President is absent or unable to act, or at the request of the President, the Vice President shall perform the duties and exercise the functions of the President, and when so acting shall have the powers of the President.

(ii) The Vice President shall have such other duties as may be assigned to him or her by the President.

(c) Second Vice President.

(i) In the event the President and First Vice-President are absent or unable to act, or at the request of the President in the absence of the First Vice President, the Second Vice President shall perform the duties and exercise the functions of the President, and when so acting shall have the powers of the President.

(ii) The Second Vice President shall have such other duties as may be assigned to him or her by the President.

7.04 Secretary

(a) The Secretary shall keep or cause to be kept corporate records in which shall be entered all information required by these by-laws or by-law to be kept by the Corporation, which shall include, but is not limited to, the minutes of the meetings of the Board in books provided for such purpose.

(b) The Secretary shall perform any and all legal duties under the Certificate of Incorporation and incident to the corporate office of Secretary.

(c) The Secretary shall be responsible for providing notice of meetings and other actions to Trustees whenever required by these by-laws or by-law.

(d) The Secretary shall be the custodian of the Corporation's seal and shall affix same to all documents which require said seal and which he or she has been authorized to execute on behalf of the Corporation and when so affixing may attest to the same.

(e) The Secretary shall perform all other duties as, from time to time, may be assigned to the Secretary by the Board or the President.

(f) The Board of Trustees may elect an Assistant Secretary to act solely as Corporate Notary.

(g) In the event the President and Vice President are either absent or unable to act, or at the request of the President, the Secretary shall perform the duties and exercise the functions of the President, and when so acting shall have the powers of the President.

7.05 Treasurer.

(a) The Treasurer shall be the custodian of all funds, securities, and receipts of the Corporation, and shall cause to be deposited in the name of the Corporation all monies and other valuable effects in such depositories as may be designated by the Board.

(b) The Treasurer shall disburse the funds of the Corporation as authorized by the Board and through the corporation's agent/manager. The Treasurer shall keep or cause to be kept proper vouchers of all sums disbursed, and maintain complete and regular accounts in accordance with a system satisfactory to the Board and the Manager.

(c) Upon the request of the Board, and at least annually, the Treasurer shall submit to the Board an account of the financial condition of the Corporation.

(d) The Treasurer shall perform any and all legal duties under the Certificate of Incorporation and incident to the office of a treasurer of a Corporation and such other duties as may be assigned to him or to her by the Board or the President.

(e) In the event the President, Vice President, and Secretary are all absent or unable to act, or at the request of the President, the Treasurer shall perform the duties and exercise the functions of the President, and when so acting shall have the powers of the President.

7.06 *Subordinate Officers.* The Board may from time to time appoint such subordinate officers as it may deem desirable in the manner provided herein. Each such officer shall perform such duties as the Board or the President may prescribe.

7.07 *Personnel.* The Board may hire and/or retain an administrator, Chief Executive officer, manager, staff, and/or consultants as necessary to achieve the purposes of the Corporation.

7.08 *Removal.* Any officer of the Corporation may be removed from office with or without cause by the affirmative vote of a quorum of the Board.

ARTICLE VIII

Conduct of Business

8.01 *Checks, Drafts, Etc.* Except as otherwise provided in these By-Laws, all checks, drafts, or other orders for payment of money, and all notes, bonds or other evidences of indebtedness issued in the name of the Corporation shall be signed by such officers and/or Trustees in such manner as shall, from time to time, be determined by resolution of the Board. In no event shall the signatures of fewer than two (2) such officers and/or Trustees be necessary to bind the Corporation on any such checks, drafts or other order for payment of money, note or other evidence of indebtedness.

8.02 *Annual Reports.* There shall be prepared annually a full and correct statement of the affairs of the Corporation, including a balance sheet and statement of operations for the preceding fiscal year, audited and certified by an independent Certified Public Accountant, which shall be submitted to and reviewed by the Board at a regular meeting of the Trustees and filed immediately thereafter at the principal office of the Corporation. The Treasurer shall prepare such statement, or the Board, in conjunction with the independent Certified Public Accountant, may designate such other executive officer of the Corporation as. The public upon request made to the Corporation shall make a copy of the report available at the principal office of the Corporation for inspection.

Within ninety (90) days after the close of each fiscal year, there shall be filed with the Clerk of the Borough of Flemington an annual written report for the preceding fiscal year.

8.03 *Fiscal Year.* The fiscal year of the Corporation shall be the year beginning January 1st and ending December 31st, unless otherwise provided by the Board by resolution.

8.04 *Bonds.* The Board may require any officer, agent, or employee of the Corporation to give a bond to the Corporation conditioned upon the faithful discharge of his or her duties with one or more sureties and in such amount as may be satisfactory to the Board.

8.05 *Contracts.* Except as otherwise provided in these By-Laws, the Board, by resolution, may authorize any officer or officers, agent or agents, to enter into any contract or execute and deliver any instrument in the name and on behalf of the Corporation, and such authority may be general or confined to specific instances.

8.06 *Deposits.* All funds of the Corporation not otherwise employed shall be deposited from time to time to the credit of the Corporation in such banks, trust companies, or other depositories as the Board by resolution may select or as may be designated by any officer or officers, agent or agents of the Corporation to whom such power is delegated by resolution of the Board.

8.07 *Acceptance of Gifts.* The Board or any officer or officers, agent or agents of the Corporation to whom such authority is delegated by resolution of the Board may accept on behalf of the Corporation any contribution, gift, grant, bequest, or devise for the general purposes or for any special purpose of the Corporation followed by proper acknowledgment.

ARTICLE XIV

Amendments

9.01 *Amendments.* A motion to amend, alter, repeal, or enact a new By-law may be introduced, considered, discussed, and voted on at any meeting of the Board, provided at least ten (10) days prior to such meeting a full written statement of the exact language of the motion and the time, place, and date of the meeting when the motion(s) will be introduced has been forwarded to every member of the Board by certified mail. An affirmative vote of a quorum of the entire Board shall be required to carry said motion. The procedures and notice of requirements of this section shall apply irrespective of any contrary provisions, which may be contained in these By-laws.

ARTICLE X

Indemnification; Exculpation

10.01 INDEMNIFICATION

(a) For the purposes of this Article X, all definitions set forth in N.J.S.A. 15A: 3-4, as amended from time to time, shall apply.

(b) Indemnification of any person who is a Trustee, officer, employee, or corporate agent of the Corporation shall be provided to the fullest extent permitted by N.J.S.A. 15A: 3-4 as same may be amended or modified and any successor statute thereto or any other applicable provision of law. Such indemnification shall include, without limitation, indemnification against the actual amount of net loss including counsel fees, reasonably incurred by or imposed upon him or her in connection with such action, except as to matters for which he or she shall be ultimately found in such action to be liable for gross negligence or willful misconduct. In the event of any settlement of such a case, indemnification shall be provided only in connection with such matters covered by the settlement as to which the Corporation is advised by counsel that the person to be indemnified had not been guilty of gross negligence or willful misconduct.

(c) Any corporate agent may be insured by insurance purchased and maintained by the Corporation against any expenses incurred in any such proceeding and any liabilities asserted against the corporate agent in the capacity as corporate agent, whether or not the Corporation would have the power to indemnify such corporate agent under N.J.S.A. 15A: 9-1 et seq. as same may be amended or modified and any successor statute thereto.

10.02 *Exculpation.* Unless acting in bad faith, neither the Board as a body nor any Trustee, officer, or corporate agent shall be personally liable to any Member of the Corporation in any respect for any action or lack of action arising out of the execution of his or her office. Each Member of the Corporation shall be bound by the good faith actions of the Board, officers, and corporate agents of the Corporation, in the execution of the duties and powers of said Trustees, officers, and corporate agents. However, nothing contained herein shall be construed so as to exculpate Trustees, or any of them, from discharging their fiduciary responsibilities.

10.03 *Interpretation.* This Article X is subject to N.J.S.A. 15A: 9-1 et seq. as the same may be amended or modified and any successor statute thereto. Nothing in this Article X shall be construed so as to conflict with or violate the terms of N.J.S.A. 15A: 9-1 et seq. Any and all requests for indemnification under this Article X shall be made, and shall be heard and decided by the Board, in accordance with the applicable terms of N.J.S.A. 15A: 9-1 et seq.

ARTICLE XI

Dissolution

11.01 *Dissolution.* Upon the dissolution of the Corporation, assets shall be distributed for one or more exempt purposes within the meaning of section 501(c)(3) of the Code (or the corresponding section of any future Federal tax code) or shall be distributed to the Federal government, or to a state or local government, for a public purpose. Any such assets not so disposed of shall be disposed of by a court of competent jurisdiction of the county in which the principal office of the Corporation is then located, exclusively for such purposes or to such organization or organizations, as said Court shall determine which are organized and operated exclusively for such purposes.

REFERENCE

Flemington, Borough of, Flemington, NJ (2011). Business Improvement District Planning Process, Report. Submitted by Seth A. Grossman, Cooperative Professional Services, Newark & Frenchtown, NJ.

Appendix 3

A Universal Public–Private Partnership/ Managed Business District Survey (Grossman 2014)

SECTION ONE: BASIC INFORMATION

1.a. Official name of the Public–Private Partnership (PPP)/Managed Business District (in the enabling ordinance).

_____

1.b. Ordinance Identification Number: _____

2. Registered Name and Address of the PPP's/ Managed Business District's Management Organization:

_____

Name

_____

Address

    2.a. Is the Management Organization of the PPP legally a: (Circle one):

        Government Office   Private Non-Profit Corp.
        For Profit Corp.   Municipal Commission

    2.b. If a Corporation: Federal tax status identification number {Ex. 501 (c) (6)}:

_____

    2.c. Is the management corporation or commission designated in the enabling BID ordinance? Circle one: YES   NO

3. Management Corp. Telephone and Email Address:

_____   _____

Telephone   **Email Address**

4. Name of the designated Chief Executive Officer/Manager:

_____

4.a. The CEO/Manager is (Circle one): (Ft=Full Time. PT=Part Time)

FT Employee   PT Employee
Independent Contractor   Government
Employee Volunteer

4.b. The CEO/ Manager is/has (Circle all that apply):

Business District Management Certification
Degree in Public Administration
Main Street Certified Manager
Degree in Business Administration
Certified Business Administrator
Certified Public Manager
Certified Economic Development Director
OTHER: _____

5. Person completing this Questionnaire (Print Clearly)

_____

Name   **Title**   **Affiliation**

6. CEO/Manager (circle one):   Male   Female

7.a The Organization's current publicly funded-*only* budget is: Circle one.

a. $99,000 or below   d. $1,000,001 to $2,000,000
b. $100,000 to $250,000   e. over $2,000,000
c. $251,000 to $1,000,000

7.b The Organization's current privately funded-*only* budget is: Circle one.

a. $99,000 or below   d. $1,000,001 to $2,000,000
b. $100,000 to $250,000   e. over $2,000,000
c. $251,000 to $1,000,000

8.a The Organization's *total* budget is: Circle one.

a. $99,000 or below   d. $1,000,001 to $2,000,000
b. $100,000 to $250,000   e. $2,000,000–$3,000,000
c. $251,000 to $1,000,000   f. over $3,000,000

8.b Last fiscal year total budget: $ _____

9. Does government levy a mandatory tax, assessment, or fee on your behalf? Circle one.

Yes, government levies and collects it on our behalf.
No, we bill it and collect ourselves.
Not applicable, no mandatory public assessment

10. Are you *required* by ordinance and/or statute to have an elected official on your Board of Directors or Commission? (Circle one):   Yes   No

11. Are you required by ordinance and/statute or by laws to have an elected official on your Board of Directors or Commission *as a voting member*? (Circle one): Yes   No

SECTION TWO—ORGANIZATION AND MANAGEMENT CAPABILITY

1. Determine the percent increase from the previous year's *publicly funded only* budget in relation to the current year's budget (divide previous year's budget by the current budget)—Circle one.

   a. More than 10%   c. 1%–4%   e. Decrease
   b. 5%–10%   d. No Change

2. Determine the percent increase from the previous year's *total* budget (assessment and other funds) in relation to the current year's total budget (divide previous year's budget by current budget)—Circle one.

   a. More than 10%   c. 1%–4%   e. Don't know
   b. 5%–10%   d. No Change/Decrease

3.a. The average CEO/Manager has been in the job position: Circle one.

   a. Over 10 years   c. 5–7 years   e. 1–2 years
   b. 7–10 years   d. 3–4 years   f. Less than 1 year

3.b. The Organization has had how many CEO/Managers to date?

_____

4. The number of members of the Board of Directors, or Commission, of the Management Organization is equal to the following percentage of businesses in the district: Circle one.

   a 5% or more   c. 3%–3.9%   e. 1%–1.9%
   b. 4%–4.9%   d. 2%–2.9%

5. The District's Management Organization meetings are open to the public:

   a. Always   c. Sometimes   e. Don't know
   b. Almost always   d. Rarely

6. The Management Organization encourages partnering between government, community, and business to achieve revitalization of the community:

   a. A great deal   c. Somewhat   e. Not at all
   b. A fair amount   d. Only a little

7. How involved, on average, are the people on the BID Board of Directors in other social, community, or professional organizations? Circle one.

a. A great deal   c. Somewhat   e. Don't know
b. A fair amount   d. Only a little

8. The Management Organization is trusted by:

8.a. The Local Government: Circle one.

a. A great deal   c. Somewhat   e. Not at all
b. A fair amount   d. Only a little

8.b. The Business Community: Circle one.

a. A great deal   c. Somewhat   e. Not at all
b. A fair amount   d. Only a little

8.c. Other local Community and Economic Development Organizations: Circle one.

a. A great deal   c. Somewhat   e. Not at all
b. A fair amount   d. Only a little

8.d. The Local Chamber of Commerce: Circle one.

a. A great deal   c. Somewhat   e. Not at all
b. A fair amount   d. Only a little

8.e. The Community at large: Circle one.

a. A great deal   c. Somewhat   e. Not at all
b. A fair amount   d. Only a little

9. The BID's public–private partnership between government and the business community works productively: Circle one.

a. A great deal   c. Somewhat   e. Not at all
b. A fair amount   d. Only a little

10. People help each other learn in this organization. Circle one.

a. A great deal   c. Somewhat   e. Not at all
b. A fair amount   d. Only a little

11. There is consistency between words and behavior in this organization. Circle one.

a. A great deal   c. Somewhat   e. Not at all
b. A fair amount   d. Only a little

12. There are clear expectations established in this organization. Circle one.

a. A great deal   c. Somewhat   e. Not at all
b. A fair amount   d. Only a little

13. The Management Organization can implement changes in its services quickly. Circle one.

a. A great deal	c. Somewhat	e. Not at all
b. A fair amount	d. Only a little	

14.a. There is a high degree of collaboration in this organization with other organizations. Circle one.

a. A great deal	c. Somewhat	e. Not at all
b. A fair amount	d. Only a little	

14.b There is a high degree of collaboration in this organization within the organization. Circle one.

a. A great deal	c. Somewhat	e. Not at all
b. A fair amount	d. Only a little	

15. In this organization, scenarios and guidelines are used more often than rules. Circle one.

a. A great deal	c. Somewhat	e. Not at all
b. A fair amount	d. Only a little	

16. This organization is designed around collaboration rather than compromise. Circle one.

a. A great deal	c. Somewhat	e. Not at all
b. A fair amount	d. Only a little	

17. Government has determined a different level of funding than the one originally requested by the District Management Organization. Circle one.

a. Not at all	c. Somewhat	e. A great deal
b. Only a little	d. A fair amount	

18. Report performance information to a governmental organization. Circle one.

a. Monthly	c. Biannually	e. Not at all
b. Quarterly	d. Annually	

19. At minimum, report performance information to the public. Circle one.

a. Monthly	c. Biannually	e. Not at all
b. Quarterly	d. Annually	

20. Publish an annual financial and performance report (paper or electronically). Circle one.

a. Monthly	c. Biannually	e. Not at all
b. Quarterly	d. Annually	

21. Time of passage of annual budget by local government (or appropriate authority) after the Management Organization has approved a budget: Circle one.

a. 1–3 months   c. 5–6 months   e. 9 months or more
b. 4–5 months   d. 6–8 months

22. Board of Director's attendance at Board Meetings, averaged annually. Circle one.

a. more than 80%   c. 40%–59%   e. less than 20%
b. 60%–79%   d. 25%–39%

SECTION THREE—RETURN ON INVESTMENT

1. The District's Management Organization is considered an innovative organization. Circle one.

a. A great deal   c. Somewhat   e. Don't know
b. A fair amount   d. Only a little

2. The Management Organization is an agent for change in the community. Circle one.

a. A great deal   c. Somewhat   e. Don't know
b. A fair amount   d. Only a little

3.a. The Management Organization takes risks to improve the community. Circle one.

a. A great deal   c. Somewhat   e. Don't know
b. A fair amount   d. Only a little

3.b. The Management Organization is a public–private partnership. Circle one.

a. A great deal   c. Somewhat   e. Don't know
b. A fair amount   d. Only a little

3.c. The Management Organization enters into partnerships with the public and private organizations. Circle one.

a. A great deal   c. Somewhat   e. Don't know
b. A fair amount   d. Only a little

4. The Management Organization identifies resources and leverages assets: Circle one.

a. A great deal   c. Somewhat   e. Don't know
b. A fair amount   d. Only a little

5. In this organization, work is designed to permit experimentation. Circle one.

a. A great deal   c. Somewhat   e. Don't know
b. A fair amount   d. Only a little

6. **The organization is quick to respond to market opportunities and threats. Circle one.**

   a. A great deal   c. Somewhat   e. Don't know
   b. A fair amount   d. Only a little

7. **The current vacancy rate in the service district is: Circle one.**

   a. Less than 3%   c. 6.1%–10%   e. Don't know
   b. 3.1%–6%   d. 10%–15%

8. **The vacancy rate in the service district compared with last year is: Circle one.**

   a. Less than 3%   c. 6.1%–10%   e. Don't know
   b. 3.1%–6%   d. 10%–15%

9. **The value of commercial property in the district has risen in three years by:**

   a. 15%–25%   c. 0%–4.9%   e. Don't know
   b. 5%–14.9%   d. Lost value

10. **The total failure rate for commercial businesses is: Circle one.**

    a. 3% or less   c. 8%–10%   e. Don't know
    b. 4%–7   d. 10% or more

11. **Number of new restaurants in the district in the last complete calendar year. Circle one.**

    a. 6 or more   c. 3–4   e. Don't know
    b. 4–5   d. 2–0

12. **Number of new retail establishments in the district in the last complete calendar year. Circle one.**

    a. 6 or more   c. 3–4   e. Don't know
    b. 4–5   d. 2–0

13. **Since its inception, *compared with the total public funds budgeted received so far (total years)*, the Management Organization has caused what dollar ratio of hard, physical, capital improvements to the District?—*Round off*. Circle one.**

    a. 1: 5 or more   c. 1:3 times   e. Don't know
    b. 1:4   d. 1: 2 or less

14. **Amount of the total current budget directed to advertising and marketing is:. Circle one.**

    a. 25% or more   c. 10%–14%   e. Don't know
    b. 15%–24%   d. 9% or less

15. **Visits to the Management Organization's website increased in the past complete calendar year by: Circle one.**

    a. 35% or more   c. 15%–24%   e. Don't know
    b. 25%–34%   d. 1%–14%

16. Number of documented overall complaints in the last calendar year as compared with the previous calendar year about the Management Organization decreased by: Circle one.

a. 50% or more   c. 10%–24%   e. Increased
b. 25%–49%   d. $10% or less

17. How many outdoor billboard-type advertisements were placed in the last calendar year? Circle one.

a. 20 or more   c. 6–14   e. None
b. 15–19   d. 1–5

18. Number of documented formal tours of the service district in the last calendar year: Circle one.

a. 50 or more   c. 6–24   e. Don't know
b. 25–49   d. 1–5

19. Data: Total square footage of commercial property in the service district is collected: Circle one.

a. Annually   c. Every three years   e. Don't know
b. Every two years   d. Every four years

20. Cost per square foot of commercial space in the most recent complete calendar year increased from the previous year by: Circle one.

a. 10% or more   c. 2%–4%   e. Don't know
b. 5%–9%   d. 1% or below

21.a. Website is updated: Circle one.

a. Daily   c. More than Monthly   e. Don't know, or don't have
b. Weekly   d. Monthly   a website

21.b. Facebook, etc. (or social media site) is updated: Circle one.

a. Daily   c. More than Monthly   e. Don't know, or don't have
b. Weekly   d. Monthly   a social media site

SECTION FOUR—QUALITY OF LIFE

1. The District's Management Organization is guided by an agreed upon Vision Statement as a promise to the community. Circle one.

a. A great deal   c. Somewhat   e. Don't know
b. A fair amount   d. Only a little

2. **The District's Management Organization has improved the quality of life in the community. Circle one.**

   a. A great deal
   b. A fair amount
   c. Somewhat
   d. Only a little
   e. Don't know

3. **What best describes your perception of the cleanliness of the service district compared with last year? Circle one.**

   a. Much cleaner
   b. Somewhat cleaner
   c. The same
   d. Somewhat dirtier
   e. Dirtier

4. **What best describes your perception of safety in the service district? Circle one.**

   a. Much safer
   b. Somewhat safer
   c. The same
   d. Somewhat less safe
   e. Unsafe

5. **Generally speaking, how professional is the Management Organization? Circle one.**

   a. Excellent
   b. Very good
   c. Good
   d. Fair
   e. Poor

6. **Attendance at Board meetings is: Circle one.**

   a. Excellent
   b. Very good
   c. Good
   d. Fair
   e. Poor

7. **The Management Organization conducts customer satisfaction surveys: Circle one.**

   a. Monthly
   b. Quarterly
   c. Biannually
   d. Annually
   e. Not at all

8. **The Management Organization's collaborations with the local government increased by: Circle one.**

   a. 26% or more
   b. 16%–25%
   c. 6%–15%
   d. 5% or less
   e. Decreased

9. **Collaborations with other Community Development Corporations increased by: Circle one.**

   a. 26% or more
   b. 16%–25%
   c. 6%–15%
   e. Decreased
   d. 5% or less

10. **Number of community festivals/promotions held in the current year. Circle one.**

   a. More than 20
   b. 11 to 20
   c. 3 to 10
   d. 1 to 2
   e. Don't know

11. Number of bank robberies decreased/increased in the last complete calendar year compared with the previous calendar year by: Circle one.

a. decreased more than 50%   c. stayed the same   e. Don't know
b. decreased 1% to 49%   d. increased

12. Number of assaults decreased/increased in the last complete calendar year compared with the previous calendar year by: Circle one.

a. decreased more than 50%   c. stayed the same   e. Don't know
b. decreased 1% to 49%   d. increased

13. Number of commercial robberies decreased/increased in the last complete calendar year compared with the previous calendar year by: Circle one.

a. decreased more than 50%   c. stayed the same   e. Don't know
b. decreased 1% to 49%   d. increased

14. The percentage of money in the Management Organization's total budget spent on cleanliness and safety: Circle one.

a. less than 10%   c. 26% to 35%   e. more than 40%
b. 11% to 25%   d. 35% to 40%

15. Number of documented compliments about the BID organization's performance increased by: Circle one.

a. 50% or more   c. 10%–24%   e. Decreased
b. 25%–49%   d. $10% or less

16. Number of years since a comprehensive streetscape improvement project was conducted on the major thoroughfare: Circle one:

a. less than 5 years   c. 11–20 years   e. Don't know
b. 6–10 years   d. 21–30 years

17. Collection of District-wide customer email contact data: Circle one.

a. Annually   c. Quarterly   e. Not at all
b. Bi-annually   d. Monthly

18. Number of public meeting places, parks, plazas, etc. created or rebuilt since the District was formed: Circle one.

a. 20 or more   c. 10–14   e. None
b. 15–19   d. 1–10

19. Upkeep and maintenance of private property buildings and business signage has improved: Circle one.

a. A great deal   c. Somewhat   e. Not at all
b. A fair amount   d. Only a little

20. Rate the service district's advertising branding: Circle one.

    a. Excellent   c. Good   e. Poor

    b. Very good   d. Fair

21. The service district boundaries have expanded: Circle one.

    a. Three times   c. One time   e. Decreased in size

    b. Two times   d. Never

22. The Management Organization assists in and/or sponsors the creation of other PPPs or managed business districts: Circle one.

    a. A great deal   c. Somewhat   e. Don't know

    b. A fair amount   d. Only a little

SCORING

ONLY SECTIONS 2–4 are scored.

    EACH STATEMENT HAS FIVE ANSWERS: Choose *only one* for each statement.

    METHOD OF SCORING: Use five-point scale from left to right: a = 5; b = 4; c = 3; d = 2; and e = 1.

    ADD CHOICE IN EACH STATEMENT FOR A TOTAL SCORE.

    INTERPRETATION KEY: Highest score is 370—Very Successful—High performing well-established public–private partnership; regional to multi-regional impact player. High score range is 300–370: Successful—Consistently good to excellent performance; good to excellent public–private partnership; could be better in key areas; local to regional impact player. Be wary of stagnation. Moderate score range is 222–300: Fair to good performance, struggles at times particularly with public–private partnership; -needs improvement in key areas; stagnant in key areas; local impact player. Low score range is below 221: Poor to fair performance—ineffective public–private partnership; struggles, is not innovative; verging on failure; confused regarding district to municipal impact. Danger zone is below 150: in various states of failure—confused to negative impact player.

REFERENCE

Grossman, Seth A. (2014). *A Universal Public–Private Partnership/Managed Business District Survey*, Newark and Frenchtown, NJ.

Index

Note: Page numbers with *f* indicate figures; those with *t* indicate tables.